Proficiency Testbuilder

4th Edition with Key

Mark Harrison

MACMILLAN

Macmillan Education
4 Crinan Street
London N1 9XW
A division of Macmillan Publishers Limited
Companies and representatives throughout the world

ISBN 978-0-230-43691-6 (with key)
ISBN 978-0-230-43694-7 (without key)

The author would like to thank Dominika Gajek for providing
sample answers.

The author and publishers would like to thank the University of
Cambridge Local Examinations Syndicate for the assessment criteria
and sample answer sheets.

The author and publishers are grateful for permission to include
the following copyright material: Material from 'Trouble Man,
Marvin Gaye in Meaty Beaty Big & Bouncy' by David Ritz. Published
by Hodder & Stoughton. Used by permission of Ritz Writes, Inc;
Adapted material from article 'Laughing is good for you – seriously'
by Verity Owen, first appeared in The Daily Telegraph 16.06.00,
reprinted by permission of Telegraph Media Group; Material from
'Tube inspired a book' was taken from The Hendon & Finchley
Press, 2001. Used by permission of Barnet Press series, North
London & Herts Newspapers; Material from 'Over the Limit' by Bob
Monkhouse. © Bob Monkhouse, 1998. Published by Random House
Books. Used by permission of Random House Books and the Estate
of Bob Monkhouse c/o Laurie Mansfield Associates; Material from
'Six Feet Under' by Dorothy Simpson. Reproduced with permission
of Curtis Brown Group Ltd, London on behalf of the Estate of
Dorothy Simpson. Copyright © Dorothy Simpson, 1982; Adapted
material from article 'Kents Cavern: inside the cave of stone-age
secrets' by Karolyn Shindler, first appeared in The Daily Telegraph
20.12.11, reprinted by permission of Telegraph Media Group;
Adapted material from article 'Are you a maven or a connector?'
by Damian Thompson, first appeared in The Daily Telegraph Arts
& Books 06.05.00, reprinted by permission of Telegraph Media
Group; Material from 'C'mon man – get a grip' by Geoffrey Wall
taken from the Daily Telegraph Weekend, 26/09/1998. Used by
permission of David Higham Associates Limited; Material from 'A
Literature Festival for Every Occasion' by Melvin Bragg – appearing
in The Times, 30/06/1997. Copyright © Melvin Bragg. Used by
permission of Melvin Bragg c/o Sheil Land Associates; Material
from 'Careers in Catering' by Russell Joseph. Published by Kogan
Page, 1997; Adapted material from article 'How to get a new life' by
Brigid McConville, first appeared in The Daily Telegraph 22.03.99,
reprinted by permission of Telegraph Media Group;
Material from 'Peerless Flats' by Esther Freud. Published by
Bloomsbury Publishing Ltd. 1993 © Esther Freud. Reproduced
by permission of Bloomsbury Ltd. and the author c/o Rogers,
Coleridge & White Ltd., 20 Powis Mews, London W11 1JN; Material
from article 'Why advertising matters' by Stephen Armstrong, first
appeared in The Sunday Times Supplement 30.04.00, reprinted by
permission of News International Group Ltd.; Material from article
'Why advertising matters' by Stephen Armstrong, first appeared in
The Sunday Times Supplement 30.04.00, reprinted by permission of
News International Group Ltd.; Material from MICHAEL RIDPATH:
'FREE TO TRADE' first published in Great Britain by Heinemann,
Copyright © Michael Ridpath. Used by permission of Blake
Friedmann; Material from article 'The perils of pizza making' by
Chandos Elletson, first appeared in The Times Weekend 16.10.99,
reprinted by permission of News International Group Ltd.; Adapted
material from article 'Clive Anderson's favourite autumn walks'
by Clive Anderson, first appeared in The Daily Telegraph 27.10.11,
reprinted by permission of Telegraph Media Group; Material from
'GETTING TO YES' 2/e by Roger Fisher, William Ury and Bruce
Patton. Copyright © 1981, 1991 by Roger Fisher and William Ury.
Reprinted by permission of Houghton Mifflin Harcourt Publishing
Company and Random House Books UK. All rights reserved;
Adapted material from article 'It's a dirty job, but if he didn't do it...'
by Jonny Beardsall, first appeared in The Daily Telegraph Weekend
05.06.99, reprinted by permission of Telegraph Media Group;
Adapted material from article 'Happy hero of the silent era' by
Mark Monahan, first appeared in the The Daily Telegraph 29.03.99,
reprinted by permission of Telegraph Media Group; Extracts from
'How Household Names Began' by Maurice Baren by permission
of the publishers, Michael O'Mara Books Limited. Copyright
© Maurice Baren 1997; all rights reserved; Adapted material from
article 'We lived without TV for a year and loved every minute of
it' by Miranda Ingram, first appeared in The Daily Mail 17.08.00,
reprinted by permission of Solo Syndication; Material from article
'The Horse's Tale' by Rachel Campbell-Johnson, first appeared in
The Times Magazine 21.06.97, reprinted by permission of News
International Group Ltd.; Adapted material from article 'Celebrity
crossover' by Tim Dowling, first appeared in The Daily Telegraph
Magazine 26.02.00, reprinted by permission of Telegraph Media
Group; Material from 'King of the Watchmakers' by Mark Forster,
from the Coventry Evening Telegraph. Used by permission of BMP
Media; Material from 'More Than a Game' by Dominic Lawson,
ed. Philip Watson © Dominic Lawson is used by permission of
The Orion Publishing Group, London and Condé Nast Publications
Limited; Material from 'All the Rage' by Ian McLagan, published by
Macmillan UK, 1998. Copyright © Ian McLagan; Adapted material
from article 'John McCarthy Obituary' copyright © Telegraph Media
Group Limited 2012, reprinted by permission of Telegraph Media
Group; Adapted material from article 'Cheer Up, life can only get
worse!' by Quentin Letts, first appeared in The Daily Mail 21.06.00,
reprinted by permission of Solo Syndication; Adapted material from
article 'Seeing is believing – any moment now....' by Anna Fox and
Roger Highfield, first appeared in The Daily Telegraph 26.04.00,
reprinted by permission of Telegraph Media Group; Adapted
material from article 'Why we need a new patent law', copyright
© James Dyson 2000, first appeared in The Daily Telegraph 2000,
reprinted by permission of Telegraph Media Group; Material from
article 'The past comes to life' by Clive Lewins, first appeared in
The Times 15.10.94, reprinted by permission of News International
Group Ltd.; Material from 'I Wouldn't Give Paddy Burt the Mumps'
by Paddy Burt, published in the Daily Telegraph 20/05/2000. Used
by permission of Paddy Burt; Excerpt from 'SWING HAMMER
SWING!' By Jeff Torrington. Copyright © 1992 by Jeff Torrington.
Reprinted by permission of Houghton Mifflin Harcourt Publishing
Company and Random House Books UK. All right reserved;
Adapted material from article 'The slow arrival of the wheel' by
James Dyson, copyright © James Dyson 2000, first appeared in The
Daily Telegraph 2000, reprinted by permission of Telegraph Media
Group; Adapted material from article 'Frantic Semantics: Bogus'
by John Morrish, first appeared in The Daily Telegraph Magazine
26.02.00, reprinted by permission of Telegraph Media Group; Extract
from 'The Longman History of the United States of America' by
Hugh Brogan. © Hugh Brogan. Published by Longman and used
by permission of Pearson Education Limited; Material from article
'Rainmaker with his head in the clouds' by Anjana Ahujam first
appeared in The Times 16.02.98, reprinted by permission of News
International Group Ltd.; Adapted material from article 'Why all
parents have a favourite child' by Jemima Lewis, first appeared in
The Daily Telegraph 11.12.11, reprinted by permission of Telegraph
Media Group; Material from 'How to Improve Your Confidence' by
Kenneth Hambly © Kenneth Hambly, 1987. Published by Sheldon
Press. Used by permission of SPCK; Adapted material from article
'I think I have a way with pain' by Will Cohu, first appeared in The
Daily Telegraph Arts & Books 06.05.00, reprinted by permission of
Telegraph Media Group; Adapted material from article 'Rhythm 'n'
roads' by Mick Brown, first appeared in The Daily Telegraph Travel
20.11.99, reprinted by permission of Telegraph Media Group.

The authors and publishers would like to thank the
following for permission to reproduce their photographs:

Alamy/Caro p132(D), Alamy/Jeff Gilbert p135(A), Alamy/Juice
Images p132(A), Alamy/Peter Titmuss p135(B), Alamy/Westend61
GmbH p132(C); **Bridgeman Art Library**/Angus McBride, People
of the Great Thaw/Private Collection /© Look and Learn p137;
Corbis/Tony Metaxas/Asia Images p136(D), Corbis/Ocean p134(C);
Getty Images/Bryan Bedder p132(B), Getty Images/Paul Bradbury
p134(D), Getty Images/Brand X Pictures p136(E), Getty Images/
Digital Vision p133(B), Getty Images/Nick Dolding p134(E), Getty
Images/David Freund p133(A), Getty Images/Ariel Skelley p136(C)

Printed and bound in Thailand
2018 2017 2016 2015 2014
12 11 10 9 8 7 6 5 4 3

CONTENTS

INTRODUCTION 4

INTRODUCTION

Proficiency Testbuilder 4th edition is much more than a book of practice tests. A completely new version for the revised **Cambridge English Proficiency** examination in operation from 2013, it is designed not only to enable students to do tests of exactly the kind they will encounter in the exam itself, but also to provide them with valuable further practice, guidance and explanation. This will enable them to prepare thoroughly for the exam and increase their ability to perform well in it.

Proficiency Testbuilder 4th edition contains:

Four complete practice tests

These tests reflect exactly the level and types of question to be found in the exam.

Further Practice and Guidance pages

These are included for each part of each paper and they come immediately after the part of the exam they relate to (see Contents, page 3).

For each part of each paper, they include **What's Tested** sections, which provide detailed explanations of the precise focus of each part of the exam; **Tips** sections, which provide advice on the best approaches to answering the questions, and **Exercises**, which take a step-by-step approach to answering the questions in the test, encouraging students to draw their own conclusions as to what the correct answers are and enabling them to develop and apply the right processes when answering the questions in the exam.

For PAPER 1 READING AND USE OF ENGLISH the Further Practice and Guidance pages contain exercises and questions directly related to the questions in the test.

For PAPER 2 WRITING the Further Practice and Guidance pages provide outlines enabling students to plan their answers. They also contain **authentic sample answers** for each kind of writing that may be included in the exam (article, report, etc.) for students to assess.

For PAPER 3 LISTENING the Further Practice and Guidance pages contain exercises directly related to the questions in the test.

For PAPER 4 SPEAKING the Further Practice and Guidance pages provide exercises on vocabulary likely to be useful in general terms, exercises on vocabulary relating to the themes for discussion in the tests and practice in talking about pictures.

Key and Explanation

This contains full explanations of every answer to every question in the tests.

For PAPER 1 READING AND USE OF ENGLISH this section contains detailed explanations not only of the correct choices, but also of why other options are incorrect. Within these explanations, important grammatical and lexical information is provided, and key vocabulary in the texts is explained.

For PAPER 2 WRITING this section contains mark schemes for each question and assessments of the sample answers.

For PAPER 3 LISTENING this section contains detailed explanations not only of the correct choices, but also of why the other options are incorrect. Within these explanations, key vocabulary in the pieces is explained.

For PAPER 4 SPEAKING definitions are given of the vocabulary in the Further Practice and Guidance pages.

How to use the *Proficiency Testbuilder 4th edition*

Teachers and students who have the edition with key can use the book in a number of ways:

1 Simply follow the instructions page by page. Clear directions are given as to the order in which to do things. If you follow this order, you:

- complete one part of a paper, perhaps under exam conditions and then

either

- do the Further Practice and Guidance pages relating to that part and check the answers to the questions in those pages. Then review the answers given to the questions in the test in the light of what has been learnt from doing the Further Practice and Guidance pages. Finally, check the answers to the questions in the test and go through them.

or

- check the answers to the questions in the test and go through the explanations of them if there are no Further Practice and Guidance pages and then

- move on to the next part of the test.

2 Vary the order.

You may wish to do some of the Further Practice and Guidance pages before answering the questions in the test that they relate to. Alternatively, teachers may wish to do the Further Practice and Guidance pages as discussion or pairwork, or ask students to prepare them before class.

The Certificate of Proficiency in English

The following is a summary of what the exam consists of and the marks for each task. Full details of what is tested in each part of each paper are given in the Further Practice and Guidance pages.

PAPER 1 READING AND USE OF ENGLISH (1 hour 30 minutes)

Part	Task	Marks
1	short text with eight gaps: eight multiple-choice questions (four options per question), choose the correct word(s) to fill each gap 1 mark per question	8
2	short text with eight gaps: fill each gap with one word 1 mark per question *Open cloze*	8
3	short text with eight gaps: fill each gap by forming the correct word from words given next to the text 1 mark per question *Word formation*	8
4	six single sentences: use a word given to complete a gapped sentence so that it means the same as the given sentence up to 2 marks per question *Key word formation.*	12
5	long text: six multiple-choice questions (four options per question) 2 marks per question	12
6	gapped text, seven missing paragraphs: fill the seven gaps from a choice of eight paragraphs 2 marks per question	14
7	text in sections or series of short texts: ten matching questions (match information/point with section of text or short text in which it appears) 1 mark per question	10
	TOTAL: 53 questions	**72**

PAPER 2 WRITING (1 hour 30 minutes)

Part	Task	Marks
1	essay, summarising the key points in two short texts and giving opinions on what is stated in the two texts (candidates must do this task)	20
2	questions 2–4: choose one from article, report, review, letter OR questions 5a and 5b: write about one of the set books	20
	TOTAL	**40**

Marks for each answer are based on the mark scheme for each question, which results in a score out of 20 (see Key) and the General Assessment Criteria, which give a Band Score from 0–5 (see page 138).

PAPER 3 LISTENING (approximately 40 minutes)

Part	Task	Marks
1	three short recordings: two multiple-choice questions (three options per question) for each recording (six questions) 1 mark per question	6
2	monologue or conversation: complete nine gapped sentences with information from the recording 1 mark per question	9
3	interview or discussion: five multiple-choice questions (three options per question) 1 mark per question	5
4	five short monologues on a common theme: two matching tasks (match options to speakers, choose from eight options for each speaker in each of the two tasks) 5 questions per task = 10 questions 1 mark per question	10
	TOTAL: 30 questions	**30**

PAPER 4 SPEAKING (16 minutes)

Part	Task	Marks
1	social and personal conversation (candidate and examiner) (two minutes)	
2	talking about pictures: candidates discuss together one or more pictures and do a decision-making task (four minutes)	
3	each candidate speaks alone for two minutes based on a prompt card; each candidate is also asked a question about what the other candidate has said (three minutes per card = six minutes) discussion between candidates and examiner on the same topics (four minutes)	
	TOTAL	**20**

A mark out of 40 is given, based on various categories of assessment (see page 139).

NOTE: If there are two candidates and an examiner, Part 1 = three minutes and Part 2 = six minutes, meaning that the total time is 19 minutes.

MARKING

Marks are calculated out of a total of 200 as follows:

Reading & Use of English:
80 marks
Candidate score ÷ 8 x 10
Example: 56 marks out of 72 =
70 marks out of 80

Writing: 40 marks
Candidate score out of 40

Listening: 40 marks
Candidate score ÷ 6 x 8
Example: 24 marks out of 30 =
40 marks out of 50

Speaking: 40 marks
Candidate score x 2

This gives a total of 200 marks.
Divide by 2 to get a percentage.

Approximate percentages for
each grade:

Pass

A	80% and above
B	75-79%
C	60-74%

TEST ONE

PAPER 1 READING AND USE OF ENGLISH 1 hour 30 minutes

PART 1

For questions 1–8, read the text below and decide which answer (A, B, C or D) best fits each gap.
In the exam you will mark your answers on a separate answer sheet.

There is an example at the beginning (0).

0   **A**   accomplished   **B**   completed   **C**   ended   **D**   achieved

0	A	B	C	D
	▭	▬	▭	▭

Meeting Marvin Gaye

When I first met Marvin Gaye in his Sunset Strip studio, I had just **(0)** .... a two-year project
co-writing the autobiography of Ray Charles, an inspiring collaborator, but an authoritative and often
(1) .... figure. Marvin came on like a brother. He was warm, witty and **(2)** .... to laugh.
He spoke like he sang, in whisper-quiet melodies and soft falsettos. His conversation had a lyricism all of
its **(3)** .... His affectations – a slight British accent when he was feeling aristocratic, for example
– were more than **(4)** .... by his disarming sincerity. We became friends. I felt **(5)** ....
to watch him work and play up-close. It soon became clear that, like his music, his personal life was
(6) .... with dramatic contradictions, a combination of charm and chaos. Because he was a
hero of mine, and because his art was so dazzlingly beautiful – so self-contained, so accomplished, so
(7) .... slick – it took me a **(8)** .... to realise my hero was drowning.

1	**A** distant	**B** faint	**C** secluded	**D** far-away
2	**A** prompt	**B** impulsive	**C** abrupt	**D** quick
3	**A** type	**B** self	**C** like	**D** own
4	**A** set against	**B** weighed up	**C** made up for	**D** settled up with
5	**A** advantageous	**B** privileged	**C** indulgent	**D** gainful
6	**A** inundated	**B** filled	**C** plentiful	**D** dense
7	**A** appreciably	**B** fully	**C** utterly	**D** sorely
8	**A** while	**B** phase	**C** length	**D** course

Before you check your answers to Part 1 of the test, go on to pages 9–10.

WHAT'S TESTED

Part 1 of the Reading and Use of English paper focuses on vocabulary. Questions may test any of the following:

- **semantic precision** – choosing the word with the right meaning in the context. This does not involve completing a phrase or deciding according to grammatical structure; you must simply decide which option has the correct meaning in relation to the meaning of the sentence or the text as a whole.

- **collocation** – choosing which word goes together with another or others to form a phrase. It may be possible to fill the gap with another word that is not an option in the question, but only one of the words given as an option correctly completes the phrase.

- **complementation** – choosing the option that fits grammatically. More than one of the options may have the right meaning but only one will form a grammatically correct structure.

- **idioms** – phrases that have a special meaning, which may differ substantially from the meaning of the individual words in them. Questions testing idioms involve choosing which single word completes the idiom.

- **fixed phrases** – phrases in which the individual parts are always used together, and in which the meaning can be logically worked out from the meaning of the individual words in them. Questions testing fixed phrases involve knowing which single word completes them.

- **phrasal verbs** – phrases consisting of a verb followed by a preposition and/or an adverb which have a special meaning that cannot be worked out simply from the meaning of the verb. Questions may involve choosing which single word completes a phrasal verb or choosing from a set of complete phrasal verbs.

- **linkers** – words or phrases that connect sentences or parts of sentences. Questions testing linkers involve choosing from single-word linkers, deciding which word completes a linking phrase or choosing from complete linking phrases.

TIPS

- Read the text very carefully to make sure that the options you choose make sense in terms of the meaning of the text. If you only focus on a few words immediately before or after a gap, you may incorrectly choose an option that might seem to fit grammatically and in isolation, but does not fit in the context of the text.

- Make sure that the option you choose fits grammatically. It may be that more than one of the options fits the meaning of the text but that only one fits in grammatically.

- Don't choose an option simply because it looks like the 'hardest' word or because it is the only one that you don't know. The correct option may be a relatively simple word, though not used in a simple phrase or with its simplest meaning.

In each of the exercises below, choose which of the four options fits into each of the four sentences. Each exercise relates to the question with the same number in the test, and the options are the same as those given for that question in the test. This will help you to eliminate some of the incorrect options in the test or to confirm that you have selected the correct option.

1   *distant   faint   secluded   far-away*
     A   It is hard to warm towards someone who is so .... with everyone else.
     B   They gave me only a .... outline of the project they had in mind.
     C   Fame caused her to lead a rather .... life, in her own private world.
     D   She had a .... look in her eyes, as if something was troubling her.

2 *prompt   impulsive   abrupt   quick*

    A Frank is .... to blame other people when something goes wrong.

    B He's .... and makes promises without thinking about the consequences.

    C Hazel has a very .... manner, which many people find rude.

    D I think it's important to be .... in replying to letters and messages.

3 *type   self   like   own*

    A There was amazing scenery, the .... of which I had never seen before.

    B People of his .... would lie to anyone if it was to their advantage.

    C The island is unlike any other, as it has an atmosphere all its ....

    D After a bad patch, Helen is back to her old .... again, I'm glad to say.

4 *set against   weighed up   made up for   settled up with*

    A When I'd .... both sides of the argument, I made my decision.

    B I hope this present has .... the fact that I forgot your birthday.

    C When the cost was .... the benefits, the scheme looked good.

    D She paid for both of us and I .... her when we got home.

5 *advantageous   privileged   indulgent   gainful*

    A Doing this course might prove .... to me in my future career.

    B She has rather .... parents, who give her everything she asks for.

    C He said he felt .... when he was made captain of the national team.

    D It took James some time to find .... employment when he left college.

6 *inundated   filled   plentiful   dense*

    A It's a rather .... novel and certainly not an easy read.

    B Her work was .... with errors and she had to do it all again.

    C When they advertised the job, they were .... with applications.

    D He decided to move to a place where cheap accommodation was ....

7 *appreciably   fully   utterly   sorely*

    A When Sally leaves this department she will be .... missed.

    B I think they're .... brilliant and they're my favourite group.

    C I was .... expecting to have a bad day, but it turned out all right.

    D Her health is .... better than it was a week or so ago.

8 *while   phase   length   course*

    A The situation remained serious for a considerable .... of time.

    B The first .... of the plan was carried out successfully.

    C For a .... life was difficult but then things began to improve.

    D During the .... of his stay, he met a lot of interesting people.

Now check your answers to these exercises. When you have done so, decide whether you wish to change any of your answers to Part 1 of the test. Then check your answers to Part 1 of the test.

PART 2

For questions 9–16, read the text below and think of the word which best fits each space. Use only one word in each space. There is an example at the beginning (0).

In the exam you will write your answers in CAPITAL LETTERS on a separate answer sheet.

Example: **0** *THAT*

Laughing is Good for You – Seriously

It is a sad fact **(0)** .....THAT..... adults laugh far less than children, sometimes **(9)** .... as much as

a couple of hundred times a day. Just take a **(10)** .... at people's faces on the way to work or in

the office: you'll be lucky to see a smile, let **(11)** .... hear a laugh. This is a shame – especially in

(12) .... of the fact that scientists have proved that laughing is good for you. 'When you laugh,'

says psychologist David Cohen, 'it produces the feel-good hormones, endorphins. It counters the effects

of stress **(13)** .... enhances the immune system.'

There are many **(14)** .... why we might laugh less in adult life: perhaps we are too work-obsessed,

or too embarrassed to **(15)** .... our emotions show. Some psychologists simply believe that

children have more naive responses, and as adults we naturally grow **(16)** .... of spontaneous

reactions.

Now check your answers to Part 2 of the test.

PART 3

*For questions **17–24**, read the text below. Use the word given in capitals at the end of some of the lines to form a word that fits in the space in the same line. There is an example at the beginning (**0**).*

In the exam you will write your answers in CAPITAL LETTERS on a separate answer sheet.

Example: **0**   NECESSITY

Tube Inspired a Book

For many people, the London Underground is a grim **(0)** NECESSITY....... that   **NECESSARY**

gets them from A to B. But for **(17)** .... author Preethi Nair, it is a   **BUD**

source of inspiration. She has just published her first novel, *Gypsy Masala* –

a tale she dreamt up whilst commuting on the Metropolitan Line. 'Have

you observed people on the tube?' she asks **(18)** .... 'Everyone   **ENTHUSE**

is in their own little world. I just used to sit there and imagine what

kind of lives they led.'

Gypsy Masala charts the adventures and **(19)** .... thoughts of   **INNER**

three members of an Indian family living in London, as they search for

happiness. 'It is a story about following your dreams,' says Preethi,

who gave up her high-pressure job as a management **(20)** .... in   **CONSULT**

order to go in **(21)** .... of her ambition of becoming a writer.   **PURSUE**

'It was a big risk but it was definitely the right decision in terms of peace

of mind and **(22)** .... ,' she explains.   **CONTENT**

Preethi was born in a small village in the Indian state of Kerala and

moved to London with her parents at the age of three. She says

the striking contrast in cultures made a **(23)** .... impression   **LAST**

and is reflected in her story, which flits between the suburbs of London

and **(24)** .... India. Many of the scenes in the book are based   **FAR**

on the place where she was born and spent long summer holidays.

Now check your answers to Part 3 of the test.

PART 4

For questions 25–30, complete the second sentence so that it has a similar meaning to the first sentence, using the word given. **Do not change the word given.** *You must use between* **three** *and* **eight** *words, including the word given.*

Here is an example (0).

0   Robert was offended when he was left out of the team.

   exception

   Robert .... left out of the team.

0	took exception to being

In the exam you will write **only** *the missing words on a separate answer sheet.*

---

25 So that he would be able to leave the room quickly, Matthew stood by the door.

   positioned

   Matthew .... as to be able to leave the room quickly.

26 In my opinion, it was an absolute miracle that they survived the accident.

   short

   The fact that they survived the accident was .... , in my opinion.

27 I tried as hard as I could to make sure that this problem would not arise.

   power

   I .... this problem from arising.

28 I don't think it was reasonable of you to complain so much about the service.

   justified

   I don't think you .... fuss about the service.

29 Laura was faced with a lot of problems during her childhood.

   contend

   Laura had a .... during her childhood.

30 The audience suddenly started to applaud loudly.

   sudden

   All .... from the audience.

Now check your answers to Part 4 of the test.

PART 5

You are going to read an extract from a book about comedy.

*For questions **31–36**, choose the answer (**A, B, C** or **D**) which you think fits best according to the text.*

In the exam you will mark your answers on a separate answer sheet.

Comedians

What drives moderately intelligent persons to put themselves up for acceptance or disparagement? In short, what sort of individual wants to be a comedian? When we hear the very word, what does the label suggest? Other professions, callings and occupations attract separate and distinct types of practitioner. Some stereotypes are so familiar as to be cheaply laughable examples from the world of travesty, among them absent-minded professors, venal lawyers, gloomy detectives and cynical reporters. But what corny characteristics do we attribute to comedians? To a man or woman, are they generally parsimonious, vulgar, shallow, arrogant, introspective, hysterically insecure, smug, autocratic, amoral, and selfish? Read their superficial stories in the tabloids and so they would appear.

Rather than look at the complete image, perhaps we need to explore the initial motives behind a choice of career. Consider first those who prefer a sort of anonymity in life, the ones who'd rather wear a uniform. The psychological make-up of individuals who actively seek to resign their individuality is apparent among those who surrender to the discipline of a military life. The emotional and intellectual course taken by those who are drawn to anonymity is easily observed but not easily deflected. They want to be told what to do and then be required to do it over and over again in the safety of a routine, often behind the disguises of a number of livery. If their egos ache with the need for recognition and praise, it's a pain that must be contained, frustrated or satisfied within the rut they occupy. The mere idea of standing up in front of an audience and demanding attention is abhorrent.

Nor will we find our comics among the doormats and dormice, the meek. There's precious little comedy in the lives of quiet hobbyists, bashful scholars, hermits, anchorites and recluses, the discreet and the modest, ones who deliberately select a position of obscurity and seclusion. Abiding quietly in this stratum of society, somewhere well below public attention level, there is humour, yes, since humour can endure in the least favourable circumstances, persisting like lichen in Antarctica. And jokes. Many lesser-known comedy writers compose their material in the secret corners of an unassuming existence. I know of two, both content to be minor figures in the civil service, who send in topical jokes to radio and TV shows on condition that their real names are not revealed.

In both cases I've noticed that their comic invention, though clever, is based upon wordplay, puns and similar equivoques, never an aggressive comic observation of life. Just as there may be a certain sterility in the self-effacement of a humble life, so it seems feasible that the selection process of what's funny is emasculated before it even commences. If you have no ginger and snap in your daily round, with little familiarity with strong emotions, it seems likely that your sense of fun will be limited by timidity to a simple juggling with language.

If the comedian's genesis is unlikely to be founded in social submission, it's also improbable among the top echelons of our civilisation. Once again, humour can be found among the majestic. Nobles and royals, statesmen and lawmakers, have their wits. Jokes and jokers circulate at the loftiest level of every advanced nation, but being high-born seems to carry no compulsion to make the hoi polloi laugh. Some of our rulers do make us laugh but that's not what they're paid to do. And, so with the constricted comedy of those who live a constricted life, that which amuses them may lack the common touch.

Having eliminated the parts of society unlikely to breed funnymen, it's to the middle ranks of humanity, beneath the exalted and above the invisible, that we must look to see where comics come from and why. And are they, like nurses and nuns, called to their vocation? As the mountain calls to the mountaineer and the pentameter to the poet, does the need of the mirthless masses summon forth funsters, ready to administer relief as their sole raison d'être? We've often heard it said that someone's a 'born comedian' but will it do for all of them or even most of them? Perhaps we like to think of our greatest jesters as we do our greatest painters and composers, preferring to believe that their gifts are inescapably driven to expression. But in our exploration of the comedy mind, hopefully finding some such, we are sure to find some quite otherwise.

31 What does the writer imply about comedians in the first paragraph?
    A People in certain other professions generally have a better image than them.
    B It is possible that they are seen as possessing only negative characteristics.
    C It is harder to generalise about them than about people in other professions.
    D They often cannot understand why people make negative judgements of them.

32 What does the writer say about people who wear uniforms?
    A They criticise performers for craving attention.
    B It is unusual for them to break their normal patterns of thought.
    C They are more aware of their inadequacies than others may think.
    D The desires they have are never met when they are at work.

33 The writer says in the third paragraph that shy people
    A may be able to write humorous material but could not perform it.
    B are capable of being more humorous than they realise.
    C fear that what they find humorous would not amuse others.
    D do not get the recognition they deserve even if they are good at comedy.

34 In the fourth paragraph, the writer criticises the kind of comedy he describes for its lack of
    A originality.
    B coherence.
    C sophistication.
    D spirit.

35 The writer says that people at the top of society
    A have contempt for the humour of those at lower levels of society.
    B take themselves too seriously to wish to amuse anybody.
    C are unaware of how ridiculous they appear to others.
    D would not be capable of becoming comedians even if they wanted to.

36 What does the writer wonder in the last paragraph?
    A whether people's expectations of comedians are too high
    B whether comedians can be considered great in the way that other people in the arts can
    C whether it is inevitable that some people will become comedians
    D whether comedians realise how significant they are in the lives of ordinary people

Before you check your answers to Part 5 of the test, go on to pages 16–19.

WHAT'S TESTED

The questions in Part 5 of the Reading and Use of English paper test you on your ability to understand and interpret the content and subtleties of a longer text. Questions may focus on any of the following:

- **detail** – understanding of complex pieces of information and/or ideas that are clearly stated in the text.

- **opinion** – understanding of opinions expressed or referred to by the writer.

- **attitude** – understanding of feelings described in the text which either the writer or someone the writer refers to expresses.

- **tone** – identifying from the style of the text or a section of it the impression the writer wishes to create.

- **purpose** – identifying what the writer is trying to achieve in the text or a section of it.

- **main idea** – identifying the gist or the main topic of what is said in the text or a section of it, as opposed to minor points or details which exemplify general points.

- **implication** – interpreting what is not directly stated in the text but which instead is strongly suggested in such a way that it is clear that the writer intends the reader to make certain inferences.

- **exemplification** – understanding how a point made in the text is illustrated with examples.

- **imagery** – understanding why certain images are used, or how certain effects are achieved by the writer in order to indicate similarities and differences between things.

- **reference** – understanding of what words, phrases or sentences in the text refer to or relate to elsewhere in the text.

TIPS

- In multiple-choice questions such as those in this part of the paper, it is essential to remember that more than one of the options given may be correct according to what is stated in the text, but only one of the options will correctly answer the question that is asked. Don't choose the most appealing option; superficially it may be true, but it may not answer the question you have been asked.

- The questions follow the order of the text and often each question relates to each succeeding paragraph. Sometimes, though, questions may relate to the whole of the text.

- Before you attempt to answer any questions, skim through the whole text quickly. This will give you an idea of what it is about and enable you to approach the questions with some understanding of the text. If you start answering the questions too hastily, you may become confused by what you discover later in the text and have to start again, thus wasting valuable time.

The following exercises will help you to eliminate the incorrect options in the questions in the test or to confirm that you have selected the correct options.

Question 31   *Look at the first paragraph.*

1   Does the writer say that generalisations are made about people in other professions? If so, where?

....

2   Does the writer mention the view comedians have of other people's opinions of them? If so, where?

....

3   Match these adjectives from the first paragraph with the definitions.

Adjectives		Definitions
absent-minded	*G*	**A** lacking confidence
venal	*F*	**B** incapable of serious thought
gloomy	*H*	**C** too self-confident
cynical	*L*	**D** too self-satisfied
parsimonious	*K*	**E** expecting to be obeyed at all times
vulgar	*I*	**F** corrupt
shallow	*B*	**G** forgetful
arrogant	*C*	**H** miserable
introspective	*N*	**I** rude and likely to offend
insecure	*A*	**J** having no principles
smug	*D*	**K** mean
autocratic	*E*	**L** tending to see only negative aspects
amoral	*J*	**M** thinking only of your own wishes
selfish	*M*	**N** tending to analyse yourself

Question 32   *Look at the second paragraph.*

1   Does the writer mention the view that people who wear uniforms hold concerning performing in public? If so, where?

....

2   If you are 'not easily deflected' from something,
   A   it is hard to stop you from continuing with it.
   B   it is hard for you to make others understand it.
   C   it is hard for you to be satisfied with it.
   D   it is hard for you to see the point of it.

3   Does the writer refer to the way in which people in uniforms see themselves? If so, where?
....

4   Does the writer say that people who wear uniforms may be treated well at work? If so, where?

....

Question 33   *Look at the third paragraph.*

1   What is meant by the word 'comics' in the context of the third paragraph?
   A   people who write comedy
   B   people who appreciate comedy
   C   people who perform comedy

2   What two things does the writer imply should be distinguished from comedy?
....

3   Does the writer mention what the two 'lesser-known comedy writers' he refers to think of the material they write? If so, where?

....

4 Does the writer give a reason why those writers don't want their names to be revealed? If so, what is it?

....

5 Which six words in the paragraph mean 'shy' or 'not wishing to attract attention'?

....

6 Does the writer refer to the success or otherwise of the comedy material written by shy people? If so, where?

....

Question 34   *Look at the fourth paragraph.*
1 What do 'puns' involve?
   A humour that focuses on nonsense
   B witty manipulation of the meanings of words   ✓
   C jokes that may be regarded as being in bad taste

2 Which two words in the fourth paragraph are used with the meaning 'vigour' or 'liveliness'?

.... *pizzazz and energy* ....

3 What is meant in the context by 'emasculated'?
   A complicated
   B weakened   ✓
   C pre-determined
   D made less acceptable

4 Which of the following does 'self-effacement' involve?
   A vulgarity
   B repetition
   C modesty   ✓
   D determination

Question 35   *Look at the fifth paragraph.*
1 What is meant by the phrase 'the hoi polloi'?
   A the elite
   B the masses   ✓
   C one's peers

2 Does the writer refer to the opinions those at the top of society have of the sense of humour of people at other levels of society? If so, where?

....

3 Does the writer refer to those at the top of society being amusing? If so, where?

....

4   Does the writer say that people at the top of society do not realise that others laugh at them?
    If so, where?   *no*
    ....

5   What is meant by 'constricted'?
    A   disrespectful
    B   limited ✓
    C   unconscious
    D   solemn

6   What is meant by the phrase 'the common touch'?
    A   the sense of responsibility required of those at the top of society
    B   the ability to relate to people at lower levels of society ✓
    C   the ability to make general points about life
    D   the attitudes shared by the majority of society

Question 36   *Look at the last paragraph.*
1   What four words are used in the last paragraph with the meaning 'comedians'?
    ....

2   Does the writer refer to what comedians do for people? If so, what?
    ....

3   The writer compares comedians with other figures in the arts with regard to
    A   their popularity.
    B   how much talent they require.
    C   what motivates them.

4   If someone has a 'vocation', they
    A   feel compelled to take up a particular kind of work because of the expectations of others.
    B   feel that there is one particular type of work that they are naturally suited to.
    C   feel strongly attracted to a particular kind of work because others regard it as important.

5   What does the writer say about the expression 'a born comedian'?
    A   It highlights the importance of comedy.
    B   It is often used inaccurately.
    C   It may not apply to the majority of comedians.
    D   It suggests that comedians are different from other people in the arts.

Now check your answers to these exercises. When you have done so, decide whether you wish to change any of your answers to Part 5 of the test. Then check your answers to Part 5 of the test.

PART 6

*You are going to read an extract from a novel. Seven paragraphs have been removed from the extract. Choose from the paragraphs **A–H** the one which fits each gap (**37–43**). There is one extra paragraph which you do not need to use.*

In the exam you will mark your answers on a separate answer sheet.

Husband and Wife

Detective Inspector Luke Thanet was a happy man. He had an interesting job, no pressing financial worries, two healthy, lively children and, perhaps best of all, a wife who was all that any man could wish for.

| 37 |

Reaching for his pipe, he tapped it out, scraped it, inspected it, blew through it, then filled it with loving care. 'It's nine o'clock,' Joan said. 'D'you want the news?' 'I don't think so. Do you?' 'Not particularly.'

| 38 |

Now she fidgeted, crossed and re-crossed her legs, fiddled with her hair, chewed the tip of her thumb. Eventually, 'Book no good?' Thanet enquired. She looked up at once. 'Mmm? Oh, it's all right. Very interesting, in fact.' 'What's the matter, then?' She hesitated, gave him a speculative look. He laid down his newspaper. 'Come on, love. Out with it.'

| 39 |

'Oh?' he said, warily. She looked at him with something approaching desperation. 'It's just that ... oh dear ... Look, you know we've said all along that when Ben starts school I'll go back to work? Well, that's only six months away now. So I really ought to start thinking about what I want to do.' 'I see,' Thanet said slowly. 'There you are. I knew you wouldn't like it.' 'Darling, don't be silly. It's just that, well, the idea will take a bit of getting used to after all this time, that's all.' 'Don't pretend,' she said. 'You're dead against it really, aren't you? I can tell.'

| 40 |

Now, in a flash, he saw all of that changing. Uncomfortable adjustments would have to be made, there would be inconvenience, irritation, arguments. Theory and practice, he now realised, were very different matters. All very well, in the past, to contemplate with equanimity the prospect of Joan returning to work one day, but to accept that that day was almost here ... No, he didn't like it at all.

| 41 |

'No. Oh, I did consider it seriously, at one time. I'm very interested, as you know. But ... I don't know, I'd like to feel I was doing something, well, less self-indulgent, more useful. Oh, dear, does that sound horribly priggish?'

| 42 |

'Not in the least. What sort of thing did you have in mind?' 'Well, that's the trouble. I'm just not qualified for anything. That's why I feel I ought to start thinking about it now, so that if I have to do a course, or any special training, I can get organised for September.' 'Yes, I can see that. You haven't gone into it yet, then?'

| 43 |

Very much later, he told himself, as he drove to work next morning. And preferably not at all.

A Not very inspiring, he thought guiltily, assessing the situation in the light of Joan's projected foray into the world of work. 'I meant it, you know. You go ahead, make enquiries, find out the sort of thing you'd enjoy.' But the false heartiness in his tone did not deceive and she bit her lip, glanced away from him.

B 'Nonsense,' he said. 'We've always said you would, when the children were old enough.' 'Oh, I know you've always said you wouldn't mind. But that's very different from not minding when it actually happens,' she replied. 'Anyway, I thought you'd more or less made up your mind to do an art course.'

C She went back to her book. Thanet picked up the newspaper. He hadn't been reading for more than a few minutes, however, when he realised that Joan was unusually restless. Normally, when she was reading, she plunged at once into total absorption. On one occasion, Thanet had counted up to a hundred from the time he asked her a question to the moment when she looked up, eyes unfocused, and said, 'What did you say?'

D 'I wanted to speak to you about it first. Oh, darling,' and she came to kneel before him, took his hands, 'you're sure you don't mind?' 'No,' he lied valiantly, 'I knew, of course, that the time would come, sooner or later ...'

Now check your answers to Part 6 of the test.

E He grinned. 'To be honest, yes. But I know what you mean.' 'Do you?' she said eagerly. 'You don't think I'm being stupid?'

F And so it was that on this blustery March evening, blissfully unaware of the nasty little shock that Fate was preparing for him, he stretched his toes out to the fire, settled back into his armchair and reflected that he wouldn't change places with any man in the world.

G And she was right, of course, he was. They had been married for eight years now and for all that time Joan had been the good little wife who stayed at home, ran the house efficiently and without fuss, coped with two children and made sure that everything was geared to Thanet's convenience. Unlike the wives of so many of his colleagues, Joan had never complained or nagged over the demands of his job, the irregular hours.

H To his surprise, she still did not respond. 'Joan?' He was beginning to feel the first faint stirrings of alarm. She shook her head slowly then, a fierce little shake. 'Oh, it's all right. There's nothing wrong, not really. It's just that I've a nasty feeling you aren't going to like what I'm trying to pluck up the courage to say.'

PART 7

You are going to read an extract from an article about archaeological discoveries in a cave in the south of Britain. For questions 44–53, choose from the sections (A–F). The sections may be chosen more than once.

In the exam you will mark your answers on a separate answer sheet.

In which section are the following mentioned?

surprise about the location of some findings   44 ....

the present and possible future significance of the cave   45 ....

the danger of drawing attention to certain contents of the cave   46 ....

subjects that people previously had no information on   47 ....

a reaction to what the presence of something in the cave indicated   48 ....

a revised assessment of something found in the cave   49 ....

the different aims of people investigating the cave   50 ....

the disproving of a theory by a body of evidence   51 ....

a sign of previous activity in the cave   52 ....

the physical appearance of the cave   53 ....

Now check your answers to Part 7 of the test.

Kents Cavern: Inside the Cave of Stone-Age Secrets

A

The entrance to the cave was narrow and no more than 1.5 metres high. Only one person at a time could enter, head stooped, a flickering light held in one hand, pickaxe in the other. They were a group of 12 explorers on that summer's day in 1825, including local coastguards, a man determined to discover an ancient Roman temple, and a young Roman Catholic priest with an interest in fossils. Father John MacEnery had recently arrived from Limerick as private chaplain to the Cary family at nearby Torre Abbey. He was the last to enter this strange world of darkness – of vast chambers, narrow fissures and magical stalactites that formed crystalline chandeliers and pillars, glinting in the lantern light.

B

Breaking off from the rest of the party, who were vainly trying to break through the calcified floor, Father MacEnery investigated areas of the cave where the ground had already been disturbed. Beneath the stalagmites, in reddish brown earth, the priest saw something gleam. His candle reflected off the enamel of fossil teeth. He wrote later: 'As I laid my hand on these relics of distant races... I shrank back involuntarily... I am not ashamed to own that, in the presence of these remains, I felt more awe than joy.' The priest continued his search in silence, keeping 'my good fortune a secret, fearing that amidst the press and avidity of the party to possess some fossil memorial of the day, my discoveries would be damaged.'

C

If he had known what he had stumbled upon, he might have held his finds even closer. For the teeth and other remains found in the cave are rewriting human prehistory. It is now known that this cave, called Kents Cavern, outside Torquay in Devon, had been home to prehistoric hominids and animals extinct for half a million years. In 2011, Professor Chris Stringer of the Natural History Museum announced that a human jaw found in the cave in 1927 is 7,000 years older than was thought and, at 42,000 years, this makes it the oldest Homo sapiens in northwest Europe. This is yet more evidence that modern humans must have lived side-by-side with Neanderthals, an extinct cousin species, for tens of thousands of years.

D

But back in the 1820s, science knew nothing of humanity's origins – or of what Britain was like millennia ago. Between 1825 and 1829, Father MacEnery made more astonishing discoveries. He unearthed the bones of extinct and exotic creatures, among them elephants, rhinos, sabre-tooth tigers, cave lions, bears and hyenas, from beneath the stalagmite cave floor. For the early 19th century, this was momentous. It was just four years since the professor of the new science of geology at Oxford, William Buckland, had discovered similar fauna in a cave in Yorkshire. Science – and society as a whole – were barely coming to grips with the idea that animals which now existed only in tropical countries could once have tramped over the Dales in northern England. Now it seemed they had also lived in the south of the country.

E

But Father MacEnery found something even more astonishing. As he dug, he discovered, on a bed of dirty red colour, 'the singular phenomenon of flint instruments intermingled with fossil bones!' They were the unmistakeable tools of Stone Age humans. 'This,' he wrote – his intellectual shock palpable – 'electrified me'. Father MacEnery was enthused by his momentous discovery and his realisation that it implied the co-existence of man and extinct beasts.

F

The 19th century was a frenzy of the new. Rapid developments in transport, industry and technology were paralleled by radical new philosophies and a revolution in the understanding of the age and nature of the Earth. The belief that our planet was just 6,000 years old was fatally undermined by the geologists who were revealing the great antiquity of our world. Now it is acknowledged that Kents Cavern is one of the most important archaeological and palaeontological sites in Britain. Furthermore, although now a splendid show cave, it is still producing wonders. With the advance of new dating techniques, this vast warren that has already revealed astonishing fossils and artefacts may again revolutionise our understanding of our origins.

PAPER 2 WRITING 1 hour 30 minutes

PART 1

Read the two texts below.

Write an essay summarising and evaluating the key points from both texts. Use your own words throughout as far as possible, and include your own ideas in your answer.

*Write your answer in **240–280 words**.*

1

Perceptions of Crime

In many places all over the world, surveys again and again show that crime is, if not top of the list, very high up amongst most people's concerns. The response from the authorities is often to pull out sets of statistics aimed at showing that crime, or at any rate certain kinds of crime, has in fact fallen. Such pronouncements do very little to allay the public's fears, however, since these are based not only on an impression of how serious a problem crime is arising from media reports, but also on personal experience and anecdotal evidence they get from people they talk to.

Rising Crime

The idea that crime is rising is commonplace among vast swathes of the population. Statistics from the forces of law and order frequently tell a different story, but these tend to be dismissed as untrustworthy, especially since these are often seen as being highly selective and leaving out inconvenient truths. Statistics, goes the popular view, can be manipulated to show almost anything. But is the assumption that crime is rising necessarily true? There is certainly historical evidence that crime rates were higher for certain kinds of crime decades ago. Such comparisons are of little relevance, however – what naturally concerns people is how likely they are to be victims of crime today or tomorrow.

Write your **essay**.

Before you write your essay, go on to pages 25–27.

WHAT'S TESTED

In Part 1 of the Writing paper you are required to write an essay based on two short texts. In this essay you must:

- **summarise the key points in the two short texts**

- **give your own opinions on the topic**

The texts

- The two texts present opinions on the same topic.

- Each text contains two main points/opinions that you must include in your answer.

- The two texts may present contrasting opinions or they may make points that are consistent with each other.

Your essay

- The content of your essay does not have to follow any particular order.

- You can summarise the main points of the text and then give your own opinions.

- You can give your opinion on each point from the text as you summarise it.

- You can summarise the points in a different order from how they appear in the text.

- You must include your own opinions but you can put them anywhere in the essay as long as they connect closely with the points made in the texts.

TIPS

When planning and writing your answer there are a number of aspects to consider, as it will be judged according to the following criteria:

- **content** – you must make sure that you identify and summarise all the key points/opinions in the two texts (two for each text) and that you also give your own opinions on what is stated in the two texts. As the opinions given in the texts are closely related to each other, you will not need to use a lot of words to summarise them – try to do this briefly, while making sure you have not left out a key point. When you give your own opinions, you can agree or disagree with what is stated in the texts.

- **communicative achievement** – your essay should be suitably neutral or fairly formal in register but it does not have to be extremely formal. In it, you need to demonstrate that you have fully understood the main points, by summarising them in your own words, not copying large parts from the texts. The opinions that you give must be closely related to those main points so that your essay is both informative and makes clear sense as a whole.

- **organisation** – make sure that your essay flows well and logically and is divided appropriately into paragraphs. Make sure that there is a clear connection between your opinions and the content of the two texts, and that these features are linked using appropriate linking words and phrases, both between sentences and between paragraphs. It is not necessary to have a separate introduction and/or conclusion but your essay must begin and end in a clear way so that it is a coherent piece of writing.

- **language** – the language that you use needs to be both accurate and not simple/basic. You need to demonstrate that you have a high level of English by using a range of grammatical structures and appropriate vocabulary correctly. Don't use only simple words and structures throughout your answer, try to think of ones that show a more advanced level, without making sentences too complicated for the reader to understand. It is advisable to check very carefully for accuracy when you have completed your answer, as well as making sure that everything you have written makes clear sense.

SUMMARISING THE TEXTS

In the part of your essay in which you summarise the texts you must:

• **identify** two main points/opinions for each text

• **paraphrase** these key points in your own words rather than copying long parts of the texts

1   Read the first text carefully. Then decide which of A–E are paraphrases of the two main points.

In many places all over the world, surveys again and again show that crime is, if not top of the list, very high up amongst most people's concerns. The response from the authorities is often to pull out sets of statistics aimed at showing that crime, or at any rate certain kinds of crime, has in fact fallen. Such pronouncements do very little to allay the public's fears, however, since these are based not only on an impression of how serious a problem crime is arising from media reports, but also on personal experience and anecdotal evidence they get from people they talk to.

A   Some crime statistics are regarded as being more reliable than others.
B   Both the media and members of the public have a tendency to exaggerate about crime.
C   Official statistics that show that crime is falling do not stop people worrying about it.
D   There are a number of reasons why people have fears about crime.
E   Many members of the public worry more about crime than any other issue.

2   Read the second text carefully. Then decide which of A–E are paraphrases of the two main points.

The idea that crime is rising is commonplace among vast swathes of the population. Statistics from the forces of law and order frequently tell a different story, but these tend to be dismissed as untrustworthy, especially since these are often seen as being highly selective and leaving out inconvenient truths. Statistics, goes the popular view, can be manipulated to show almost anything. But is the assumption that crime is rising necessarily true? There is certainly historical evidence that crime rates were higher for certain kinds of crime decades ago. Such comparisons are of little relevance, however – what naturally concerns people is how likely they are to be victims of crime today or tomorrow.

A   People today worry about whether crime will have a direct effect on them.
B   Evidence shows that people are right to think that crime is higher than in the past.
C   Differences between different sets of crime statistics confuse the public.
D   People believe that crime statistics are generally false.
E   The public pay too much attention to what they are told about crime.

Now check your answers to these exercises.

Then write your essay, summarising the key points from the texts and including your own opinions.

When you have written your answer, assess it in accordance with the mark scheme.

SAMPLE ANSWER

Now read this sample answer for Part 1 and answer the questions that follow it.

In these texts, the authors talk about the issue of crime and how society feels affected by it.

Constant leaks of information about crimes in the media, and word of mouth between people, is often covered by statistics from the authorities which show the rate of crime falling. These statistics and reports may be often faked, and can show anything to reassure the society that the problem doesn't exist as big as they see it. The author of the second text asks the question if the concern about rising crime is really true. Some past events may have been worse than what happens nowadays, but crime is in the spotlight and is a main topic of the media, and today people's real concern is how likely they are to be the victims of crime.

The biggest concern now is the youth crime, in particular stabbings, gang activities and the resulting deaths of young people. Does it take to be in the wrong place at the wrong time to be attacked, or do these crimes happen only between youths? This issue makes everyone worry, because there is a great deal of clear evidence of so much visible and brutal misconduct. The authorities certainly won't be able to pull out trustworthy statements, covering the truth about rising youth crime. It seems like adults are losing the authority to stop these crimes, and parents are failing to show youngsters what is right and what is wrong.

Content

Are the two main points for each text summarised in the essay?

Where are the main opinions from the text summarised? Are any key points missing?

Are any additional but irrelevant points included? Are the writer's own opinions included? If so, where?

Communicative achievement

Is the style and tone of the essay suitably neutral/formal or is it too informal?

Are the key points from the texts expressed in the writer's own words or are large parts of the texts simply copied?

Are the writer's opinions clear and are they logically connected with the points made in the texts?

Organisation

Does the essay flow well and is it coherent as a whole? Is it divided appropriately into paragraphs?

Is there appropriate linking between points made and opinions expressed? If there is an introduction and/or a conclusion, is it appropriate/clear?

Language

Is there a good range of grammatical structures that are not just simple? Are grammatical structures used accurately?

Is there a good range of vocabulary, both single words and phrases that are appropriate for the topic? Is the vocabulary used accurately? Are there any language errors in the essay? If so, try to correct them.

Now check your assessment of this sample answer with the assessment.

PART 2

*Write an answer to **one** of the questions 2–5 in this part. Write your answer in **280–320** words in an appropriate style.*

2   As part of a course assignment you have been asked to write a report analysing the organisation where you work, or the institution where you study. Write your report, commenting on the organisational structure of the place, its strengths and weaknesses, and the performance and attitude of those who are in charge and those who work or study there.

Write your **report**.

3   A recent article in a travel magazine presented unflattering views of people of a variety of different nationalities. Write a letter to the magazine giving your views on some typical national stereotypes and describing what image you think people of your nationality have to outsiders, together with whether you think this image is accurate or not.

Write your **letter**. Do not write any postal addresses.

4   A local newspaper is running a competition for the most interesting review of an exhibition or museum. Write a review, describing the exhibition or museum you have chosen and commenting on why it is particularly worth visiting or why you would not recommend it to other people.

Write your **review**.

5   Set book questions – a choice from **(a)** or **(b)**.

In the exam you may choose to answer a question on one of the two set books.

When you have written your answer, assess it in accordance with the mark schemes.

PAPER 3 LISTENING approximately 40 minutes

PART 1

You will hear three different extracts.

For questions 1–6, choose the answer (A, B or C) which fits best according to what you hear. There are two questions for each extract.

In the exam you will hear each extract twice.

Extract One

You hear a reviewer on a radio programme talking about a book.

1   The speaker says that the book's title refers to the point at which
    A   social epidemics are at their height.
    B   something becomes a social epidemic. – *takes off widespread.*
    C   people become concerned about social epidemics.

2   The speaker says, that in her opinion, the book
    A   presents some challenging conclusions. –
    B   is less complex than it may appear.
    C   uses terminology that may confuse readers.

Extract Two

You hear a reporter on a radio programme talking as he climbs a big rock.

3   One question the speaker asks himself is
    A   why he feels the way he does.
    B   where his climbing partner has gone.
    C   what has motivated him to climb the rock. *why am I up here?*

4   The speaker says that at this exact moment
    A   he doesn't care about the risk he is taking.
    B   he is relishing the experience. *would be anywhere else*
    C   he feels that age is irrelevant.

Extract Three

You hear part of a radio programme about literary festivals.

5   The interviewer says that when writers appear at events at literary festivals,
    A   they dislike being asked difficult questions.
    B   they find the experience easier if they read their own work. _
    C   they seldom prepare as thoroughly as they should.

6   Why, according to William, do writers like meeting readers?
    A   Writers are made to feel they have succeeded in their aim. –
    B   Writers want readers to know what they are really like.
    C   Readers give writers ideas for future work.

Stop the recording when you hear 'That's the end of Part 1'.

Before you check your answers to Part 1 of the test, go on to pages 30–32.

WHAT'S TESTED

The questions in Part 1 of the Listening paper test your ability to understand and interpret often complex points made and information given by speakers in three separate short pieces. Questions may focus on any of the following:

- **gist** – the general meaning of what a speaker says, based on more than one sentence or phrase.

- **detail** – a specific piece of information given or point made by a speaker, contained in a single phrase or sentence.

- **main idea** – the main point made by a speaker, rather than more minor points made or examples given.

- **function** – what a speaker is doing when speaking, for example, criticising or apologising.

- **purpose** – what a speaker is trying to achieve, what a speaker wants to happen as a result of speaking.

- **topic** – the subject matter of what a speaker says.

- **feeling** – the feeling expressed by a speaker.

- **attitude** – the way a speaker regards something or someone, as conveyed by what the speaker says.

- **opinion** – a view expressed or strongly implied by a speaker.

TIPS

- Don't rush into choosing the option that appears superficially to be the most plausible – what speakers say is often fairly complex and subtle.

- It is possible that more than one option in a question may be correct according to what the speaker says, but only one option will correctly answer the question that has been asked, so make sure that you read the question carefully.

- The two questions for each extract are likely to follow the sequence of what is said, with the first question about the first part of the piece and the second question about the second part. On occasions, however, a question may focus on the piece as a whole.

- If you find one of the extracts very difficult and are struggling with the questions on it, don't spend too much time on them so that you do not concentrate sufficiently on the next piece. If you do that, you may fail to answer questions on the next piece and lose marks unnecessarily.

- Use the pauses before and between the extracts to read the questions in advance, so that you are aware of the aspects of each piece that you will be tested on. Read the rubrics carefully too – they will give you the context for each of the pieces.

- Use the second listening to check your answers, even if you were confident of them on the first listening.

- Write your answers on the question paper as you listen. In the exam you will have five minutes at the end of the test to transfer your answers onto a separate answer sheet.

The exercises below will help you to eliminate the incorrect options in the questions in the test or to confirm that you have selected the right options.

Listen to each of the three extracts again and after each one, tick one or more boxes for the relevant questions.

Question 1   *Stop the recording when you hear 'take us by surprise'.*
Which of the following does the speaker say about the 'tipping point'?
A   It is a phrase that is used for the book's title.   ☐
B   It refers to the sudden growth of a phenomenon.   ☐
C   After it, social epidemics cease to become more widespread.   ☐
D   It can be applied more to inventions than to ideas.   ☐
E   It is mostly associated with unwelcome social developments.   ☐
F   It refers to something becoming unexpectedly widespread.   ☐

Question 2   *Stop the recording at the end of the first extract.*
Which of the following does the speaker say about the book?
A   It presents a detailed analysis of the causes of social epidemics.   ☐
B   It does not make clear exactly what 'connectors' and 'mavens' are.   ☐
C   It would be wrong to regard its analysis as a simplistic one.   ☐
D   Not all the ideas in it are original.   ☐
E   It suggests ways of dealing with social problems.   ☐
F   It contains unorthodox ideas about what should be done about social problems.   ☐

Question 3   *Stop the recording when you hear 'somewhere far above your head'.*
Which of the following does the speaker refer to?
A   being close to the top   ☐
B   what the point of climbing the crag is for him   ☐
C   the fact that he normally feels bad when he is high up   ☐
D   the fact that there is nothing solid below him   ☐
E   no longer being able to see his climbing partner   ☐
F   the fact that his climbing partner is further up than him   ☐

Question 4   *Stop the recording at the end of the second extract.*
Which of the following does the speaker mention?
A   the physical appearance of the object he is climbing   ☐
B   the physical effects that climbing is having on him   ☐
C   being glad that he is where he is   ☐
D   regretting not having looked closely at his life insurance policy   ☐
E   the appeal of danger to men of his age   ☐
F   a belief that men of his age are good at dangerous activities   ☐

Question 5   *Stop the recording when you hear 'every couple of sentences'.*

Which of the following does the interviewer mention about literary festivals?

A   something that writers seldom say about them ☐

B   the amount of preparation required of writers before reading from their work ☐

C   a misunderstanding writers have concerning what is expected of them ☐

D   questions of a kind that writers are happy to be asked ☐

E   questions which are not about the writer's own work ☐

F   that writers are repeatedly asked the same questions ☐

Question 6   *Stop the recording at the end of the third extract.*

Which of the following does William say?

A   Writers are not as miserable as people think they are. ☐

B   Some writers never lose confidence in themselves. ☐

C   Writers need to talk to people in order to get ideas. ☐

D   Writers write with readers in mind. ☐

E   Readers are sometimes surprised by what writers are really like. ☐

F   Writers like to know that someone has read their work. ☐

Now check your answers to these exercises. When you have done so, listen again to Part 1 of the test and decide whether you wish to change any of the answers you gave. Then check your answers to Part 1 of the test.

PART 2

You will hear someone called Karen Williams talking about her career.

For questions 7–15, complete the sentences with a word or short phrase.

In the exam you will hear the piece twice.

At the end of her first work experience, Karen spent two days [7] and checking rooms with the floor housekeeper.

Her last work experience was spent in the hotel's [8] .

The subject of Karen's next course was [9] .

During her HND course, the subjects she had to study were business studies, hotel management, human resource management and [10] .

The topic of her report was [11] in hotels.

In her report, she wrote reviews of various [12] .

She joined an organisation with the initials [13] .

She got information from a magazine called [14] .

page 66

In her present job, she has to deal with problems caused by the hotel being [15] .

Stop the recording when you hear 'That's the end of Part 2'.

Now check your answers to Part 2 of the test.

PART 3

You will hear an interview with someone who consulted a 'life coach' to improve her life.

For questions 16–20 choose the answer (A, B, C or D) which fits best according to what you hear.

In the exam you will hear the piece twice.

16 Brigid says that she consulted a life coach because
    A she had read a great deal about them.
    B both her work and home life were getting worse.
    C other efforts to improve her life had failed.
    D the changes she wanted to make were only small ones.

17 What did Brigid's coach tell her about money?
    A It would be very easy for Brigid to get a lot of it.
    B Brigid's attitude towards it was uncharacteristic of her.
    C Brigid placed too much emphasis on it in her life.
    D Few people have the right attitude towards it.

18 What does Brigid say about her reaction to her coach's advice on money?
    A She felt silly repeating the words her coach gave her.
    B She tried to hide the fact that she found it ridiculous.
    C She felt a lot better as a result of following it.
    D She found it difficult to understand at first.

19 What does Brigid say happened during the other sessions?
    A She was told that most people's problems had the same cause.
    B Her powers of concentration improved.
    C Some things she was told to do proved harder than others.
    D She began to wonder why her problems had arisen in the first place.

20 What has Brigid concluded?
    A The benefits of coaching do not compensate for the effort required.
    B She was too unselfish before she had coaching.
    C She came to expect too much of her coach.
    D It is best to limit the number of coaching sessions you have.

Stop the recording when you hear 'That's the end of Part 3'.

Now check your answers to Part 3 of the test.

PART 4

You will hear five short extracts in which people are talking about cities they have visited.

You will hear the recording twice. While you listen, you must complete both tasks.

TASK ONE

For questions 21–25, choose from the list (A–H) why each speaker visited the city.

A   for an interview

B   as part of a holiday

C   to see friends

D   for a conference

E   to show it to others

F   to see it again

G   to see a particular building

H   for research purposes

Speaker 1		21
Speaker 2		22
Speaker 3		23
Speaker 4		24
Speaker 5		25

TASK TWO

For questions 26–30, choose each speaker's opinion of the city from the list (A–H).

A   friendly

B   ugly

C   exciting

D   overcrowded

E   too big

F   well-organised

G   frightening

H   overrated

Speaker 1		26
Speaker 2		27
Speaker 3		28
Speaker 4		29
Speaker 5		30

Stop the recording when you hear 'That's the end of Part 4'.

In the exam you will have five minutes at the end of the test to copy your answers onto a separate answer sheet.

Now check your answers to Part 4 of the test.

PAPER 4 SPEAKING 16 minutes

PART 1 (2 minutes)   GENERAL AND SOCIAL

Questions that may be addressed to either candidate:

- Where do you live?
- Could you describe the area/city you live in?
- What do you like/dislike about the area/city you live in?
- Can you describe the building you live in?
- Who do you live with and do you get on well with them?

- What's your favourite kind of music/performer/band?
- What's the best concert you've ever been to?
- What's the worst concert you've ever been to?
- What kind(s) of music/artist(s) is/are popular in your country at the moment?
- Do fashions in music change rapidly in your country?

PART 2 (4 minutes)   CAREERS

Discussion between candidates:

Look at pictures A and B on page 132 and discuss the kinds of career shown in these pictures.

(1 minute)

Now look at all of the pictures.

Imagine that a school is producing a webpage giving advice to its students about possible future careers. These pictures are being considered for the webpage.

Discuss how appealing the careers shown in the pictures are for young people. Then decide which picture would be the most suitable to include in the webpage for school students.

(3 minutes)

PART 3 (10 minutes)   CHANGE AND STABILITY

In Part 3 each candidate is given a card and talks alone for two minutes about the topic on the card. After each candidate has spoken, the other candidate is asked a question and the candidate who spoke alone is invited to respond (1 minute).

Prompt Card (a)   *(Given to Candidate A, and a copy to Candidate B)*

> Is change always a good thing?
> * social change
> * changes in personal life
> * technological developments

One of the following questions for Candidate B:

* Is there something which you believe will never change?
* What would you most like to change in your life?
* What change in society would you most like to see?

One of the following questions for Candidate A:

* What do you think?
* Do you agree?
* How about you?

Prompt Card (b)   *(Given to Candidate B, and a copy to Candidate A)*

> Is a certain amount of stability essential in life?
> * childhood
> * work
> * society

One of the following questions for Candidate A:

* What is generally regarded as a stable childhood?
* Is there now more or less stability in people's working lives?
* Is society now more or less stable than it used to be?

One of the following questions for Candidate B:

* What do you think?
* Do you agree?
* How about you?

Part 3 finishes with a discussion between the two candidates and the examiner on the general topic (4 minutes).

General questions for both candidates on the topic of change and stability:

> * Describe a change which you think has particularly benefited you personally.
> * Describe a change which you think has been particularly bad for society.
> * What changes have happened recently in the place where you live?
> * Describe a situation which you think is particularly unstable.
> * What are the causes of instability in society?
> * Are there any disadvantages to growing up in a stable environment?

WHAT'S TESTED

In the Speaking paper you are required to do the following:

Part 1

- with the examiner, talk about yourself and general social matters

Part 2

- with the other candidate taking the test with you, talk about pictures you are shown, discuss a topic arising from them and make a decision connected with them

Part 3

- talk on your own about another topic based on a question and some ideas printed on a card that is given to you by the examiner
- answer a question based on the topic on the other candidate's card
- discuss the same topic in general with the other candidate and the examiner

TIPS

Your performance in the Speaking paper is judged according to the following criteria:

- **grammatical resource** – your ability to use a wide range of grammatical structures appropriately and accurately.

- **lexical resource** – your ability to use a wide and appropriate range of vocabulary accurately in order to convey your precise meaning and to express attitudes, opinions and abstract ideas.

- **discourse management** – your ability to say things which form coherent speeches and make relevant and logical contributions to conversations. What you say should link together well, both with other things you say, and with what the other candidate and the examiner say.

- **pronunciation** – your ability not only to pronounce what you say so that it can easily be understood (although you do not have to try to sound exactly like a native speaker) but also to link words and phrases together smoothly. You should speak in such a way that appropriate words and phrases are emphasised, and the appropriate intonation is used to convey clearly the meaning of what you are saying.

- **interactive communication** – your ability to demonstrate conversation skills, such as knowing when you should speak and when it is someone else's turn to speak and keeping a conversation going by not hesitating too much. Coming up with something to say that enables the discussion to develop when it appears to be coming to an end before the subject has been fully covered is also important, as is making points of your own or responding to those made by others, so that you play a full part in the conversation.

- **global achievement scale** – your general performance in the paper as a whole.

Part 1: General and Social

Although this involves talking about yourself and general social matters it is not simply a pleasant chat that doesn't really matter – you will be assessed on your performance in this part of the paper in just the same way that you will be assessed in the other two parts.

You may feel that this is the only part of the Speaking paper that you can really prepare for. However, beware! Do not prepare a fixed speech, learn it by heart and try to repeat it. Firstly, it will not sound natural and the examiners will know immediately that you are simply repeating something you have learnt – this will affect their assessment of your performance. Secondly, you cannot be sure what areas of discussion will come up – you may not be able to say anything that you prepared and therefore be unable to give natural or coherent answers to the questions that you are asked.

However, it is worth practising talking about a range of personal and general areas of conversation that may come up in the paper.

With a partner, ask and answer questions about the following:

• where you live • your aims for the future • places you have travelled to	• your occupation • learning languages • spare time activities
• your own personality • your preferences in the arts • employment	• friends and family • the media • your social life

Part 2: Talking About Pictures

1   To talk coherently about a picture without having to point constantly to various parts of it, it is essential to know appropriate words and phrases for describing parts of a picture.

Look at the pictures on page 132 and describe them using the phrases below. With a partner, take it in turns to describe the content of each picture.

• in the foreground • in the background • in the top left-hand corner • in the bottom left-hand corner • in the top right-hand corner • in the bottom right-hand corner • on the right-hand side • on the left-hand side • on/to the right of …	• on/to the left of … • at the top • at the bottom • in front of … • behind • next to/close to … • between • facing … • opposite

2   When you are talking about a picture, you may need to guess or deduce what the situation is in the picture because you cannot be completely sure. Instead of constantly using very simple phrases for doing this, such as *Maybe* or *I think*, try to vary the way in which you speculate on the content of the picture.

Look again at the pictures on page 132 and try to use as many as possible of the phrases below to introduce comments on them. With a partner, take it in turns to guess or deduce what is happening in each picture.

- I get the impression that ...
- The impression I get is that ...
- My impression is that ...
- It looks (to me) as if/as though ...
- I'd say ...
- I reckon ...
- I suppose ...
- I assume ...
- I expect ...
- I guess ...
- I imagine ...
- I suspect ...
- It would appear that ...
- I should think ...
- I've got a feeling that ...
- It's hard to say, but ...

- He/She/They seem(s) to ...
- He/She/They must/can't ...
- He/She/They seem(s) to have ...
- He/She/They must/can't have ...
- He/She/They seem(s) to be ...-ing
- He/She/They must/can't be ...-ing
- In my opinion/view ...
- He/She/They might/could ...
- The way I see it ...
- He/She/They might/could have ...
- If you ask me ...
- He/She/They might/could be ...-ing
- Judging by ...
- As far as I can tell/see ...
- It's (quite/fairly/highly) likely that ...
- ... is quite/fairly/highly likely to ...

TEST TWO

PAPER 1 READING AND USE OF ENGLISH 1 hour 30 minutes

PART 1

*For questions **1–8**, read the text below and decide which answer (**A**, **B**, **C** or **D**) best fits each gap.*
In the exam you will mark your answers on a separate answer sheet.

*There is an example at the beginning (**0**).*

0	**A** gather	**B** acquire	**C** collect	**D** possess

0	A ☐	B ☐	C ▇	D ☐

A Message for Lisa

It was nearly two weeks later that Lisa arrived at college to find there was a message for her. The voice teacher, Pete, said she'd have to go up to the head office to (**0**) .....C..... it. Lisa wanted to know what was in the message and who it was from, but the voice teacher insisted it was (**1**) .... 'Can't you just tell me?' Lisa (**2**) .... , but Pete jutted his chin and said he was only (**3**) .... the rules. Lisa stretched her eyes at him. She had been brought up to be (**4**) .... of anyone who believed in rules.

The head office was on the third floor. Lisa's fantasies grew with each turn of the stairs. Each flap of swing door (**5**) .... sweeter and sweeter thoughts of her and Quentin's reconciliation. It (**6**) .... to her only a second before she slid through into the dusty light of the office that Quentin had no (**7**) .... of knowing that she was at college, and even if he did, it was unlikely he would know which college she was at. 'Lisa.' The head of department was talking to her. 'Someone has been looking for you.' Lisa's change of heart was so severe it (**8**) .... her breath away.

1	**A** confidential	**B** intimate	**C** clandestine	**D** undercover
2	**A** pleaded	**B** asserted	**C** craved	**D** pledged
3	**A** fulfilling	**B** obeying	**C** conforming	**D** complying
4	**A** guarded	**B** uneasy	**C** wary	**D** edgy
5	**A** led	**B** arose	**C** brought	**D** put
6	**A** struck	**B** occurred	**C** dawned	**D** sprang
7	**A** access	**B** route	**C** scope	**D** way
8	**A** caught	**B** drew	**C** held	**D** took

Now check your answers to Part 1 of the test.

PART 2

*For questions 9–16, read the text below and think of the word which best fits each space. Use only **one** word in each space. There is an example at the beginning (0).*

In the exam you will write your answers in CAPITAL LETTERS on a separate answer sheet.

Example: *0*   IT

Advertising in Britain

What does (0) ....IT...... say about a nation that when a national newspaper recently set (9) ....

to establish the best television adverts of all time, as (10) .... as 10,000 people responded? The

answer lies (11) .... the fact that the British have developed an intense admiration for a genre that

has developed into an art form in its (12) .... right. In 1955, when Gibbs SR toothpaste broadcast

the first TV commercial, it was inconceivable that ads would ever end (13) .... being considered

as sophisticated and innovative as the programmes surrounding (14) .... Yet by 1978, the author

Jonathan Price was able to declare: 'Financially, commercials represent the pinnacle of our popular

culture's artistic expression. More money and thought per second goes into (15) .... making

and more cash flows from their impact than (16) .... the case for any movie, opera, stage play,

painting or videotape.'

Before you check your answers to Part 2 of the test, go on to page 43.

WHAT'S TESTED

Part 2 of the Reading and Use of English paper is primarily a test of grammar, with many questions involving the completion of grammatical structures. Some questions may involve the completion of collocations, fixed phrases, idioms, phrasal verbs and complementation (for explanations of these terms, see the Further Practice and Guidance pages for Test 1, Paper 1, Part 1 on page 9).

TIPS

- Read the whole text quickly before attempting to fill the gaps, as this will give you an idea of what it contains and will help you to know what kind of answers will be required.

- Before deciding on an answer, read the whole sentence with the gap in it, and the sentences both before and after that – many answers may require you to see the flow and connections between ideas and information in the text. If you simply consider each gap in isolation, you may produce an answer that appears to make sense within the narrow context of the few words either side of the gap but in fact does not make sense within the context of the text.

- Remember that the majority of the answers will be what might be considered 'simple' words, although they will be placed within a relatively complex setting.

Look again at Part 2 of the test on page 42 and for each question decide which of the four choices below best expresses the meaning of the part of the text in which the gap appears.

9   A succeeded in establishing
    B started trying to establish
    C proposed the establishment of
    D devised a way of establishing

10 A approximately 10,000
    B almost 10,000
    C the high number of 10,000
    D only 10,000

11 A contradicts the fact
    B can be found by looking at the fact
    C is concealed by the fact
    D is the cause of the fact

12 A that can be regarded as distinct from others
    B that is highly regarded
    C as it should be
    D despite opposition

13 A have the aim of being considered
    B and not be considered
    C no longer be considered
    D be considered later

14 A that the adverts came in the middle of
    B that the adverts tried to copy
    C that were sophisticated and innovative
    D that were popular at that time

15 A and creating commercials
    B for example, creating commercials
    C while creating commercials
    D the creation of commercials

16 A than results from any movie, etc
    B in contrast with what is said of movies, etc
    C than anything else concerning movies, etc
    D with the exception of the occasional movie, etc

Now check your answers to this exercise. You may wish to change some of the answers you gave in the test after you have done this. Then check your answers to Part 2 of the test.

PART 3

For questions 17–24, read the text below. Use the word given in capitals at the end of some of the lines to form a word that fits in the space in the same line. There is an example at the beginning (0).

In the exam you will write your answers in CAPITAL LETTERS on a separate answer sheet.

Example: **0**   *REFUSAL*

Captain Webb

Captain Matthew Webb is fortunate in being remembered as the first man to

swim the English Channel, rather than the one who later tried, and failed, to

plunge through the Niagara Falls. If ever a man possessed an abundance of

self-confidence, it was Webb; but it was his stubborn **(0)** ..REFUSAL........   **REFUSE**

to give up that eventually proved his **(17)** .... Unwilling to   **UNDO**

recognise the Channel crossing as the peak of his career, he went on and on,

addicted to glory, literally swimming himself to death.

Webb astonished the British nation on August 25, 1875, with a Channel

crossing that took a mammoth 21 hours and 45 minutes. He had entered

the sea a merchant-ship captain living in **(18)** .... , but he emerged   **OBSCURE**

in France, stung by jellyfish and half-dead with **(19)** .... ,   **EXHAUST**

a national hero. He was feted, mobbed and cheered wherever he went. But all

this **(20)** .... was too much for him, and he made the   **STAR**

fatal error of many a pop star in later years. Craving **(21)** .... ,   **APPLAUD**

he very nearly dissolved himself in a series of marathon swims for money, including

a six-day **(22)** .... contest. Then he sailed for America, where he had a   **ENDURE**

(23) .... schedule of long swims. It was America that lured Webb   **PUNISH**

to the final act in his tragedy; his crazed attempt to swim the Niagara River beneath

the Falls in June 1883. **(24)** .... of all advice, he dived in from a boat   **REGARD**

and subsided forever into the boiling rapids.

Now check your answers to Part 3 of the test.

PART 4

*For questions **25–30**, complete the second sentence so that it has a similar meaning to the first sentence, using the word given. **Do not change the word given.** You must use between **three** and **eight** words, including the word given.*

*Here is an example (**0**).*

0   Robert was offended when he was left out of the team.

   exception

   Robert .... left out of the team.

0	took exception to being

*In the exam you will write **only** the missing words on a separate answer sheet.*

---

25 David played the main role when the proposal was drafted.

   instrumental

   David .... of the proposal.

26 If you hadn't changed our original agreement, everything would have been fine.

   stuck

   Had .... agreed, everything would have been fine.

27 I think you should have some consideration for those who don't have lives as privileged as yours.

   spare

   I think you should .... lives aren't as privileged as yours.

28 I didn't want to give up while some hope of success remained.

   defeat

   I was loath .... some hope of success.

29 After a long hard journey, I cheered up when I saw my home again.

   sight

   After a long hard journey my spirits .... of my home again.

30 Your attitude to life would be greatly improved by regular exercise.

   wonders

   Regular exercise would .... at life.

Now check your answers to Part 4 of the test.

PART 5

You are going to read an extract from a novel.

*For questions 31–36, choose the answer (**A**, **B**, **C** or **D**) which you think fits best according to the text.*

In the exam you will mark your answers on a separate answer sheet.

Piper and Buxxy

It was a great double act. Piper looking relaxed but dependable in a conservative, lightweight suit. Art Buxxy, the showman, doing what he did well. It was a big moment for both of them. They had to secure $200 million from their audience.

Piper warmed up the crowd. In a reasonable, persuasive voice he talked in abstract terms about the remarkable financial opportunity that the Tahiti represented. There was talk of numbers, strategy, competitive analysis. Enough to make us think that the Tahiti was in safe hands, not enough to bore us. Despite the outward reserve, as he warmed up to his presentation, Piper did let some of the excitement he felt for the project show through. Standing there, tall, tanned, elegantly but conservatively dressed, speaking in a manner that was more suited to the Harvard Club than a casino, he gave his audience reassurance. Despite appearances, the Tahiti must be a respectable, conservative investment, or why would someone like Irwin Piper be involved with it?

Then it was Art Buxxy's turn. Buxxy was a small man with a nut-brown face, longish blow-dried grey hair and bundles of enthusiasm. He was hardly ever still, and when he was, it was for a melodramatic pause, to let the full consequence of what he had just said sink in. His abrasive, rough-edged manner jolted his audience after the smooth Piper, but within a minute his energetic charm had already bewitched us all. Selling was his calling, and the Tahiti was the love of his life. He used all his skills. We were captivated. And I think most of us were sold.

They took us on a tour of the complex. Seen through Buxxy's eyes, the tackiness and the loneliness of a big casino disappeared. We saw the glamour, the glitter, the amazing technological effects. He took us to see the private rooms where the high-rollers played, wallowing in sophistication, power and money. By the time we had returned to the conference room where he had started his pitch, I could feel the majority of the audience would write out a cheque there and then.

'Any questions?'

Silence. No difficult questions about Piper's background. No tedious questions about percentage drop of slots against tables, high-roller comps, or blue-collar busing costs. Even the most cynical investor was under the spell of the greatest casino on earth. At least temporarily.

I had thought through this moment carefully. I stood up. Piper's eyebrows pulled together slightly, in the barest trace of a frown. 'Yes?'

'I have two questions for Mr Piper.' The audience were looking at me with mild interest. My English accent jarred in the glitzy Las Vegas surroundings. Piper was staring at me hard. 'First – has the Nevada Gaming Commission scrutinised your previous investments?' The audience stirred a little, but not much. Piper stiffened. 'Second – can you comment on an investment you made in a clinic for executive stress in Britain?'

I sat down. The audience reaction was mixed. Some faces bore disapproval; I was a spoil-sport to try and take cheap shots at these great guys and their great casino. A few sat up and took notice.

Piper rose to his feet. He was as unruffled and urbane as ever. 'I would be happy to answer those questions. First, the Commission checks out all applicants for gambling licences very thoroughly. Second, I have a large portfolio of investments. I believe a few years ago these included some properties in England, but I don't have the details at my fingertips. Any other questions?' He looked around the audience quickly.

This was a dangerous moment for Piper. Until now he had had his listeners eating out of his hand. But he hadn't answered my questions properly. If anyone pursued him on this, then doubts might creep in. But I wasn't going to push it any further. I had achieved my objective. He knew I knew, and he knew I would tell.

Half an hour later, I was having a cup of coffee in the atrium, when a bellboy came over to me. 'Excuse me sir, Mr Piper would like you to join him in his suite.' That didn't take him long, I thought, as I put down my cup and followed the bellboy to the elevators.

Piper's suite was on the top floor of the hotel. Piper was alone in the room. He beckoned me to a seat. I perched on the flimsy-looking Georgian sofa, whilst he sat in one of the high-backed mahogany armchairs. Gone was all the civilised politeness. Piper was angry.

'What the hell do you think you were doing out there?' he said. 'I am not some two-bit bond salesman you can play games with. I am a powerful man in this town. I've got money, and I've got lawyers. And if you mention Bladenham Hall one more time, or even allude to it, I will sue. I will sue you for so much that your great-grandchildren will still be paying off your debts a hundred years from now.'

Piper, angry, was impressive. For a moment he had me on the defensive. If I had upset such a powerful man, I had surely made a mistake. The moment passed.

31 When he addressed the audience, Irwin Piper gave the impression that
    A   it was not his primary purpose to get the audience to invest in the project.
    B   he was less comfortable talking about details than about general principles.
    C   he was not the sort of person who would normally associate himself with such a project.
    D   there were already plenty of people who were keen to invest in the project.

32 The narrator says that Art Buxxy's style of addressing the audience
    A   contained certain elements he may not have been aware of.
    B   came as something of a shock to them.
    C   involved making his most important points first.
    D   contrasted with his physical appearance.

33 When they went on a tour of the complex,
    A   it appeared that some members of the audience had never been inside a casino before.
    B   Buxxy diverted the audience's attention away from the less attractive aspects of casinos.
    C   it was clear the project was at a more advanced stage than the audience had realised.
    D   Buxxy encouraged the audience to picture themselves playing there.

34 When the narrator asked his questions,
    A   he feared that the audience would not take him seriously because of his accent.
    B   Piper reacted initially as if he had been expecting the questions to be asked.
    C   he did so because he was surprised by the audience's apparent trust in the project.
    D   it seemed that some of the audience considered he had no right to ask such questions.

35 When Piper stood up and answered the narrator's questions,
    A   he knew that the audience would not be convinced by his reply.
    B   he claimed that the questions concerned trivial matters.
    C   the narrator decided that he had conveyed a clear message to Piper.
    D   it was clear to the audience that he was ill at ease.

36 When the narrator went to see Piper in his suite,
    A   he had been expecting Piper to seek a confrontation with him.
    B   he briefly feared that he had been wrong to doubt Piper's honesty.
    C   what Piper first said to him was what he had expected him to say.
    D   Piper made it clear that other people had regretted underestimating him.

Now check your answers to Part 5 of the test.

PART 6

*You are going to read a newspaper article. Seven paragraphs have been removed from the article. Choose from the paragraphs **A–H** the one which fits each gap (37–43). There is one extra paragraph which you do not need to use.*

In the exam you will mark your answers on a separate answer sheet.

The Perils of Pizza Making

It looks easy but it really isn't, says Chandos Elletson, whose efforts turned out far from perfect.

My first pizza was cremated. I hadn't even got to the toppings, let alone the tossing stage. I was stuck on the rolling-out bit. I fast discovered that specialist pizza chefs – pizzaioli – don't use rolling pins, they use their hands to shape the dough into perfect circles. Francesco Sarritzu, the pizzaiolo at The Park restaurant in Queen's Park, London, where I went to be trainee for the evening, took one look at my sorry effort and sighed.

37	

Real, or original, pizza is an art: the pizzaiolo is baker, fire stoker and cook. A wood-burning oven is an essential part of the proceedings. However, before the pizzas get to the fire, they have to be properly shaped and it was this procedure that was causing me all the grief.

38	

From here it was all hands. He pressed out the dough with his fingers, all the time working in flour and pressing the edges out until a small round circle had emerged. He then threw it into his hands, twirling it to shake off the excess flour. He did not toss it in the air. 'Tossing is for show,' he said disdainfully. 'It is not necessary.' Once the flour was shaken off, he put the dough onto the steel work surface with one half of it hanging over the edge. One hand pressed and stretched and the other pulled in the opposite direction. Before you could say 'pizza Margherita' there was a perfect circle ready to be topped.

39	

The object is to press out the edges, not the centre, using the flour to dry out the stickiness. However, the temptation to press everything in sight to make it stretch into a circular shape is too strong; before I knew it, I had thick edges and a thin centre.

40	

Then I noticed, to my horror, that some customers were watching me. 'Shall we watch the man make the pizza?' a man asked his young daughter, who he was holding in his arms.

41	

A hole appeared in the centre. 'Look, Daddy. There's a hole,' the little girl said. I looked up from my work, crestfallen. I was defeated. 'It's my first evening,' I admitted. Francesco stepped in with the paddle and my second pizza went where the first one had gone: on the fire. We all watched it go up in flames.

42	

Francesco noticed and applauded. I wanted to call back the little girl and tell her: 'I can do it! It's just like swimming!' My base was not perfectly round but it was not bad. It wasn't perfectly even but it was certainly an improvement. We decided to top it. We put on a thin smear of tomato sauce and some mozzarella.

43	

When I got there, Francesco showed me where to put it. There was a point in the deep oven away from the fire, where the pizzas go when they are first put into the oven. I put the long handle deep into the oven and, feeling the heat on my arms, brought it back sharply. The pizza slid onto the floor of the oven. My first pizza was in the oven and not being burnt alive.

A To put those things right, I did as Francesco had done and slapped it with the palm of my hand. This made me feel better and I slapped it again. Next, I did some twirling and the flour showered everywhere.

B Instead, Francesco quickly made one of his own to act as a comparison. When they were done and brought from the oven, we had a tasting. The result was astonishing. Mine was tough and crunchy in places, not bad in others. His was perfectly crispy and soft everywhere.

C Having done that, it was time to get it on to the paddle, which felt like a pole vault. With one determined shove, the pizza went on halfway. Another shove forward got it on completely but put an ugly buckle in it. I turned and headed for the oven.

D Francesco made it look easy. He showed me what to do again and I tried to take it in. The chilled dough balls, pre-weighed at 170g, were all ready in a special fridge below the work counter. The dough was sticky and Francesco worked fast. First it was dropped into a large pile of flour and then it was mixed with a small handful of polenta.

E Clearly, the stage was all mine. I had been told to concentrate on the edges using the flat edge of my hand under my little finger. I started to work the dough and tried to stretch it. It did begin to take shape, but as soon as I let it go it just went back again and didn't get any bigger. I felt more and more eyes on me. Then the worst thing happened.

F That was because it wasn't so much a circle as an early map of the world. Silently, Francesco reached for his pizza paddle, scooped it up and threw it disdainfully into the red-hot stone oven, where it burnt rapidly on top of a funeral pyre of burning wood. I made up my mind that my future efforts would be good enough to be spared the death sentence.

G I was baffled and embarrassed as it did so, but I thought I was onto something. On my next attempt, I quickly got to the shaping stage with half the pizza hanging over the edge. This was where I had gone wrong. Using only the bottom edge of my hands with my fingers working the edges, I started to do the breast stroke: fingers together, fingers apart, working and stretching. It began to work.

H I moved nervously into position to have a go at achieving the same result myself. I scooped up a piece of dough from its snug tray. It immediately stuck to my fingers and when I threw it at the flour, it just remained stuck. I had to pull it off. The first bit is easy, or so it seems, but unless you follow the right procedure you sow the seeds of later failure.

Before you check your answers to Part 6 of the test, go on to pages 51–54.

WHAT'S TESTED

In Part 6 of the Reading and Use of English paper you are required to work out how the various parts of a text fit together. This involves making sure that each paragraph you choose fits into the gap that you place it in for the following reasons:

- **cohesion** – each paragraph must fit in because there is a grammatical match with something in the paragraph before it and/or after it.

- **coherence** – each paragraph must fit in because it makes sense in terms of the meaning of the previous and/or next paragraph.

- **text structure** – each paragraph must fit in because it flows logically at that point in the text in terms of its line of development (for example, the argument being put forward, the series of events being described).

- **global meaning** – each paragraph must fit in because it can only be put in that place in terms of the meaning of the text as a whole.

TIPS

- There are two key issues for identifying the correct paragraph to fill a particular gap. The paragraph must fit grammatically in terms of pronouns, verb forms, linking words and phrases and it must fit in with the sense of what went before and what comes after the gap. Several options may superficially appear to fit a given gap because they meet one of these two requirements but only one will meet them both. For example, a paragraph may seem to fit in perfectly in terms of what is happening in the text, but be incorrect because it contains a pronoun that cannot refer to anything in the previous paragraph.

- Before you start trying to fill any of the gaps, read quickly through the whole of the text with gaps in it. This will give you a general idea of what the whole text is about and what might be missing from it. As a result, you may well have an idea of what you are looking for when you come to select from the missing paragraphs. If you simply plunge in and start trying to fill gaps immediately, you may well find that you have to keep changing your answers because what you discover further on in the text shows you that answers you have given are wrong. This, of course, wastes time.

- Remember that if you decide to change an answer, this may well have a knock-on effect on other answers you have given, which may also need changing.

The exercises below will help you to see whether you have given the correct answers for each of the questions in this Part of the test.

For each of the questions in these exercises, two of the choices given are correct and two are not. Check your answers to each question in each exercise as soon as you have given them. When you have answered question 3 in each exercise check that the answer that you gave in the test conforms with the answers that you gave to question 3.

Question 37

1   Read the first paragraph. Which of the following are mentioned?
    A   Francesco's reaction to a pizza that the writer had prepared ☐
    B   a task successfully completed by the writer ☐
    C   the writer's failure to do something well ☐
    D   a series of mistakes made by the writer ☐

2 Read the paragraph after gap 37. Which of the following are mentioned?
   A the way in which a pizza should be prepared before it is cooked
   B a pizza made by the writer being eaten
   C the writer's difficulty in carrying out an operation
   D the writer preparing a pizza that was ready to go into the oven

3 Which of the following would the missing paragraph most logically contain?
   A something Francesco did with a pizza prepared by the writer
   B the writer feeling encouraged that he was improving
   C a description of a pizza prepared by the writer
   D a reference to correcting a number of errors

Question 38

1 Read the paragraph before gap 38 again. Which of the following are mentioned?
   A the writer managing to prepare a pizza properly
   B the writer doing something according to Francesco's instructions
   C the fact that there are certain rules to preparing a pizza
   D a particular skill that the writer could not master

2 Read the paragraph after gap 38. Which of the following are mentioned?
   A the writer beginning an attempt at something
   B Francesco showing the writer how something is done
   C various elements in the preparation of a pizza
   D the writer's reaction to doing something badly

3 Which of the following would the missing paragraph most logically contain?
   A the writer taking a completed pizza to the oven
   B a description of one stage of preparing a pizza
   C something that happened to a pizza the writer was preparing
   D the writer observing Francesco in action

Question 39

1 Read the paragraph before gap 39 again. Which of the following are mentioned?
   A the way to prepare a pizza of a certain shape
   B the writer's own efforts at preparing a pizza
   C the writer being observed by others
   D the successful completion of a process

2 Read the paragraph after gap 39. Which of the following are mentioned?
   A a mistake that it is easy to make
   B the writer correcting previous errors
   C the writer's feelings about a pizza he had prepared
   D how to achieve a certain result

3 Which of the following would the missing paragraph most logically contain?

    A the writer's reaction to a disaster

    B the writer attempting to copy something

    C the fact that it was now the writer's turn to do something

    D Francesco deciding on an alternative course of action

Question 40

1 Read the paragraph before gap 40 again. Which of the following are mentioned?

    A the writer correcting a previous error

    B a reason why it is hard to perform a particular operation

    C Francesco observing what the writer was doing

    D ways in which what the writer was doing went wrong

2 Read the paragraph after gap 40. Which of the following are mentioned?

    A the writer starting a process

    B the writer looking at the pizza he was preparing

    C the writer's reaction to becoming aware of something

    D the writer being observed by strangers

3 Which of the following would the missing paragraph most logically contain?

    A a reference to solving more than one problem

    B the writer doing something that might look foolish

    C the writer sampling a pizza he had made

    D the writer taking over from Francesco

Question 41

1 Read the paragraph before gap 41 again. Which of the following are mentioned?

    A the writer feeling some pressure

    B the writer feeling encouraged

    C the writer completing a pizza so that it could go into the oven

    D a sense of expectation on the part of someone else

2 Read the paragraph after gap 41. Which of the following are mentioned?

    A a reason for the writer to give up

    B a description of what happened to a pizza the writer had made

    C the writer's pizza being repaired

    D a movement made by the writer

3 Which of the following would the missing paragraph most logically contain?

    A a reference to a pizza being eaten

    B a reference to something disastrous

    C the writer's inability to do what he knew he should do

    D a reference to pizzas the writer would subsequently prepare

Question 42

1   Read the paragraph before gap 42 again. Which of the following are mentioned?

    A   a repetition of events ☐

    B   Francesco making a pizza himself ☐

    C   Francesco attempting to rectify an error ☐

    D   the destruction of something the writer had done ☐

2   Read the paragraph after gap 42. Which of the following are mentioned?

    A   a decision to proceed with a pizza prepared by the writer ☐

    B   the fact that the writer had made too many mistakes ☐

    C   the writer feeling dispirited ☐

    D   a positive reaction from Francesco ☐

3   Which of the following would the missing paragraph most logically contain?

    A   an improvement made by the writer ☐

    B   the writer tasting a pizza he had made ☐

    C   something that suddenly went wrong with the writer's pizza ☐

    D   a reference to the writer's feelings about a failure of his ☐

Question 43

1   Read the paragraph before gap 43 again. Which of the following are mentioned?

    A   the end of part of a process ☐

    B   confusion on the part of the writer ☐

    C   the writer's sense of satisfaction ☐

    D   the beginning of a process again ☐

2   Read the final paragraph. Which of the following are mentioned?

    A   problems that always affect the cooking of pizzas ☐

    B   something the writer learnt about the cooking of pizzas ☐

    C   an improvement on a previous event ☐

    D   something Francesco did that was unlike common practice ☐

3   Which of the following would the missing paragraph most logically contain?

    A   the writer's failure to prepare a pizza correctly ☐

    B   a reference to the early stages of preparing a pizza ☐

    C   the next stage of a process ☐

    D   a movement in a certain direction ☐

Now check your answers to these exercises. When you have done so, decide whether you wish to change any of your answers to Part 6 of the test. Then check your answers to Part 6.

PART 7

You are going to read some extracts from an article about places of natural beauty in Britain. For questions 44–53, choose from the places (A–D). The places may be chosen more than once.

In the exam you will mark your answers on a separate answer sheet.

Of which place are the following stated?

It combines the old and the new.	44 ....
A piece of information about it may be open to doubt.	45 ....
A popular activity led to the introduction of new items.	46 ....
Some people are unwilling to go there all year round.	47 ....
Action taken there led to wider similar action.	48 ....
Its name isn't strictly accurate.	49 ....
It is a good place for energetic people.	50 ....
Certain favourable conditions have enabled it to flourish.	51 ....
Official actions have not changed its fundamental character.	52 ....
It underwent rapid change over a short period.	53 ....

Now check your answers to Part 7 of the test.

A Wander through Britain's Woodlands

The President of the Woodland Trust, an organisation which encourages people to enjoy the woodlands of Britain, selects his favourite places for an autumn walk.

A   Hampstead Heath

Where better for a country walk in autumn than north London? Hampstead Heath is just a few kilometres from the centre of town, but it is one of the capital's best-known beauty spots. And covering very nearly 325 hectares, certainly one of the largest. It is called a heath, although it is in fact a patchwork of not just heath but also parkland and hedgerow, laid out paths, open hillside and overgrown thickets, lakes and ponds – and plenty of woods and trees. The City of London Corporation is now responsible for its upkeep. They fuss about the swimming, designate cycle paths, regulate the fishing, and put up notices about all such dangerous activities. But despite their best efforts, the Heath still feels quite wild. From one popular vantage point there is a panoramic view of central London, where visitors stop to admire the crowded streets and skyscrapers they have come to the Heath to get away from. It's at its best later in the year. When it's warm and sunny it can feel too crowded with casual visitors. But frosts and mist, rain and snow deter the Heath's fair-weather friends.

B   Hainault Forest

This remnant of what was once the vast Forest of Essex is now an attractive stretch of woodland easily reached by the London Underground. The woods around here were a royal forest, but an Act of Parliament of 1851 authorised the cutting down and removal of its trees. And removed they were, grubbed up by all too efficient men and machines – hectare upon hectare laid waste within weeks of the passing of the Act. The devastation stirred the beginnings of the modern conservation movement – local people led by a politician called Edward North Buxton saved and restored Hainault. It is now owned and managed by the Woodland Trust. Hainault is a unique site, which features open heathland, some of which has been recently planted up with native trees by the Woodland Trust, and the dense woodland of the ancient forest.

C   Glen Finglas

Far away from London and the South East, the Trossachs is a strikingly beautiful corner of Scotland. Among the best of the Trossachs is Glen Finglas, the Woodland Trust's 4,000-hectare estate, which can truly take the breath away, particularly during the late autumn when the frosted peaks and still, cold lochs take on an ethereal splendour. For the enthusiastic hill walker, there is a challenging 25-kilometre trail around the hill called The Mell, which takes you on a meander through woodland, alongside a reservoir and into the upper part of the glen, where the remnants of an ancient royal hunting forest give way to the open hillsides of Meall Cala, reaching a height of 600m. It's certainly not a gentle stroll, but is worth the effort as the views are spectacular. For those after a slightly less arduous journey there are many shorter routes around the site too.

D   Ardkinglas Woodland Gardens

For a slightly different woodland walk in the west of Scotland, head for the Ardkinglas. In addition to native species it features many specimens of firs and pines and other trees from overseas planted in the 19th century, when plant hunting was all the rage. There is plenty of scope for a good walk around its ten hectares. Ardkinglas's sheltered location, high rainfall and warm temperatures all encourage spectacular tree growth, and they claim to have the tallest tree in Britain – a Grand Fir, Abies grandis – standing at last time of measuring 64.5 metres high. If you are sceptical of such claims, bring a tape measure and a long ladder. There are many other mighty trees that are impressive all year round but on a clear November day the views towards the loch are fantastic. A couple of miles away on Loch Fyne itself, next to the famous oyster restaurant, Ardkinglas runs a tree shop. So if you want to create your own forest you can buy it and plant it, tree by tree.

PAPER 2 WRITING 1 hour 30 minutes

PART 1

Read the two texts below.

Write an essay summarising and evaluating the key points from both texts. Use your own words throughout as far as possible, and include your own ideas in your answer.

*Write your answer in **240–280 words**.*

1

The Importance of the Aeroplane

When people discuss the most important inventions of the last hundred years, how many of them pick the aeroplane? While they might acknowledge its importance, they would seldom choose it in preference to, say, television, or the computer. But a case could be made for the aeroplane having had more influence on the world than anything else. After all, it is responsible for mass tourism, enabling people to see for themselves places they could previously only have read about in books. And it has played a major role in mass emigration – such numbers of people simply could not have gone to settle in far-away countries without the aeroplane.

Attitudes Towards the Aeroplane

The image of the aeroplane has undergone massive changes since its first appearance only a matter of decades ago. It rapidly went from a miraculous culmination of man's obsession with flight, the realisation of what had hitherto been mere fantasy, to the instrument of death and destruction in two world wars and beyond. And air travel has subsequently gone from a luxury only available to a privileged few to a common experience for almost everyone, for whom flight is taken for granted as a routine way of getting from A to B.

Write your **essay**.

When you have written your answer, assess it in accordance with the mark scheme.

PART 2

*Write an answer to **one** of the questions 2–5 in this part. Write your answer in **280–320** words in an appropriate style.*

---

2   The authorities at the place where you study or work have decided to look into the possibility of a student or staff representative group being set up. You have been asked to write a report on the setting up of such a representative group. Write your report, outlining reasons for setting it up, how it should be set up, what issues it could deal with and what the advantages of having such a group would be.

      Write your **report**.

3   A magazine you read has asked readers to send in reviews of particular TV channels or radio stations. Write a review of a TV channel or radio station, commenting on the type and/or mixture of programmes it broadcasts, the standard of its broadcasts, which people it generally appeals to and how it compares to other TV channels or radio stations.

      Write your **review**.

4   You have read a magazine article entitled *Too Much Too Young*, in which the writer says that some young people today are given too much by their parents and therefore have the impression that life is easier than it really is. Readers have been invited to send in their own articles on this subject, with the same title. Write your article, addressing the points made in the original article and giving your own views.

      Write your **article**.

5   Set book questions – a choice from **(a)** or **(b)**.

      In the exam you may choose to answer a question on one of the two set books.

Before you write your answer, go on to pages 59–63.

WHAT'S TESTED

Questions 2–4

In Part 2 of the Writing paper you may choose one of three different types of writing. The choices you are given may include any of the following:

- **an article** – a piece of writing on a given topic that would be suitable for the specified type of publication.

- **a letter** – probably a formal or fairly formal letter, in which you may be required to give opinions, explain reasons for writing the letter, describe events or request actions.

- **a review** – this may be about anything that gets reviewed in publications, from films to hotels, and it should include both a description of the subject of the review and your views on it. You will obviously need to include a range of vocabulary associated with that particular subject, and the review should be written in a style that is appropriate for the specified type of publication.

- **a report** – this involves the presentation and analysis of information in clear and logical sections, perhaps with section headings. The report must be in a style suitable for the specified reader or readers of it, for example a boss or colleagues. It may involve making recommendations and justifying them.

Question 5

In Part 2 of the Writing paper, you may prefer to write about one of the two set books. If so, you may choose one of two questions, which are each about one of the books. Questions on the set books may require you to write any of the following:

- **an essay** – a composition on a given topic connected with the book, organised into an introduction, the expansion of points and a conclusion, so that it is a coherent whole.

- **an article** (see notes above for questions 2–4)

- **a letter** (see notes above for questions 2–4)

- **a review** (see notes above for questions 2–4)

- **a report** (see notes above for questions 2–4)

TIPS

Answers to Part 2 of the Writing paper are judged according to the same criteria as those for Part 1, as follows (for details on these criteria, see page 138):

- **content**
- **communicative achievement**
- **organisation**
- **language**

Also remember the following:

- marks will be reduced for answers that are significantly shorter than the specified number of words.

- spelling and punctuation are taken into consideration in the marking – a significant number of spelling mistakes will affect your marks, as will insufficient or inappropriate punctuation.

- handwriting should be as neat as possible – if the examiner has trouble reading your answers, your marks will be affected.

To plan your answer for question 3 in Part 2, complete the following notes.

1   Note down as briefly as possible the **topic** of your review.

    ....

2   List as briefly as possible the following:

    • the **main points** in the question which you will have to cover in your review

    • the **comments and opinions** you wish to give with regard to these points

    • any **examples** you plan to give to support or illustrate these comments/opinions

Main point	Comments/Opinions	Example
Main point	Comments/Opinions	Example
Main point	Comments/Opinions	Example

3   List briefly any additional points you wish to make, which are not mentioned in the question but which you think are relevant to the topic. You may not wish to include any additional points.

Additional point	Comments/Opinions	Example
Additional point	Comments/Opinions	Example

4   Now note briefly how your review will be organised by deciding what each part of it will contain. You may not wish to have as many paragraphs as are listed below.

Introduction
Paragraph 1
Paragraph 2
Paragraph 3
Paragraph 4
Paragraph 5
Ending

5   Now use these notes to write your review.

When you have written your answer, assess it in accordance with the mark scheme.

SAMPLE ANSWER

Now read this sample answer for question 3 in Part 2 and answer the questions that follow it.

> As a keen reader of your magazine, I noticed the appeal in your last issue for writing a review of my favourite TV channel or radio station, which is here to follow.
>
> The radio channel I've chosen to write about is called FIZZ FM. Many of your other readers may not have heard about this channel. The reason is that it's only on air between 11pm and 4am. It's a private channel only run by five people.
>
> The main aim of FIZZ FM is to entertain people who have to work or get up either late at night or early in the morning. So it does not appeal to a certain social or age group, but to particular work groups such as nurses, bakers, etc. Nevertheless, it's very popular with people from 14 to 25 who, even if they don't have to, get up in the middle of the night just to listen to that programme.
>
> Concerning their mixture of programmes, they don't have a fixed schedule. It's a 'colourful' mix of music (from the 60s, 70s, 80s, 90s, ...), news and discussions. Everything is very easy going, so it can happen that there is a whole night of music, followed by a night of discussions about anything. The coordinators of FIZZ FM want to make it easier for working people who have to face a long day full of work.
>
> Though it's not a very busy or (sometimes) interesting station, it is able to compete against bigger stations, because a broad range of people enjoy listening to it. To my mind, this is because of its unique style and appearance. These people have successfully filled a gap in the market without having the problem of competing against others, just because other stations don't care about that time of day.
>
> Perhaps now more people will tune in to FIZZ FM, who knows?

Content

Are all the main points mentioned in the question covered? Where are these points covered? If any are not covered, which are missing? Are any additional points included? If so, what are they, and are they relevant?

Communicative achievement

Are the style and tone of the review appropriate? How would you describe them? Why are they appropriate or inappropriate? Is the format suitable for a review? If so, why? If not, why not?

Do you feel that someone reading this review would be clear about what the writer is describing and the writer's views on it? If so, summarise the writer's review briefly. If not, say what you feel is unclear in the review.

Organisation

Is the review well-organised in terms of the beginning, the middle and the end? Is it divided into paragraphs appropriately? Describe briefly the content of each paragraph.

Does the review flow well in terms of the linking of points and ideas within paragraphs and between paragraphs? Give examples of places where the linking is good. If there are occasions when the linking is inadequate or inappropriate, suggest improvements.

Language

Is there a wide range of vocabulary and grammatical structures? If so, give examples. If there are occasions when the vocabulary or grammar is too simple, suggest alternatives.

Are there any mistakes in the use of vocabulary or grammar? Correct any that you find.

Now check your assessment of this sample answer with the assessment.

To plan your answer for question 4 in Part 2, complete the following notes.

1 Note down as briefly as possible the **topic** of your article.

....

2 List as briefly as possible the following:

- the **main points** raised in the original article which you will have to cover in your article

- the **views** you intend to express with regard to those points

- any **examples** you wish to give to support or illustrate your views

Main point	Comments/Opinions	Example
Main point	Comments/Opinions	Example
Main point	Comments/Opinions	Example

3 List briefly any additional points you wish to make that are relevant to the topic. You may not wish to include any additional points.

Additional point	View	Example
Additional point	View	Example

4 Now note briefly how your article will be organised by deciding what each part of it will contain. You may not wish to have as many paragraphs as are listed below.

Introduction
Paragraph 1
Paragraph 2
Paragraph 3
Paragraph 4
Paragraph 5
Paragraph 6
Conclusion

4 Now use these notes to write your review.

When you have written your answer, assess it in accordance with the mark scheme.

SAMPLE ANSWER

Now read this sample answer for question 4 in Part 2 and answer the questions that follow it.

> I think it is very difficult to generalise the topic because it depends mainly on the environment the youngsters live in. The upbringing in a rich family is very different to growing up in a poor family. Children with rich parents have more opportunities to live an easier life.
>
> I hold the view that many youngsters are spoilt because their parents try to calm their bad conscience (caused by too much work and less time, for example) by giving money or presents to them. They want to do as much as they can for their loved children and they want them to be happy and satisfied. And money and presents seem to be a good way to solve problems.
>
> Parents want to support their children by giving money to them and make a good way of life possible (good education, ...). But this behaviour can cause difficulties for the spoilt youngsters. On the one hand they want to be independent as soon as possible, but on the other hand they can't manage their life on their own, because their caring parents 'did almost everything' for them so far. It is possible that young adults can't overcome financial problems or challenges which are common during their lifetime. It seems to be easier to live with money, but children can't live from their parents' support all the time. They have to learn that life is a hard struggle which includes big challenges they have to deal with.
>
> All in all, I think that the upbringing is very important. A proper mixture of financial support, independence and struggle for life would be the best way to prepare youngsters for the 'hard life' outside their homes.

Content

Are the main points raised in the original article covered? Where are these points covered? If any are not covered, which are missing? Are any additional points included? If so, what are they, and are they relevant?

Communicative achievement

Are the style and tone of the article appropriate? How would you describe them? Why are they appropriate or inappropriate? Is the format suitable for a magazine article? If so, why? If not, why not?

Do you feel that someone reading this article in a magazine would be clear what the writer's point of view is throughout it? If so, summarise the writer's point of view briefly. If not, say what you feel is unclear in the article.

Organisation

Is the article well-organised in terms of the beginning, middle and end? Is it divided into paragraphs appropriately? Describe briefly the content of each paragraph.

Does the article flow well in terms of the linking of points and ideas within paragraphs and between paragraphs? Give examples of places where the linking is good. If there are occasions when the linking is inadequate or inappropriate, suggest improvements.

Language

Is there a wide range of vocabulary and grammatical structures? If so, give examples. If there are occasions when the vocabulary or grammar is too simple, suggest alternatives.

Are there any mistakes in the use of vocabulary or grammar? Correct any that you find.

Now check your assessment of this sample answer with the assessment.

PAPER 3 LISTENING approximately 40 minutes

PART 1

You will hear three different extracts.

For questions 1–6, choose the answer (A, B or C) which fits best according to what you hear. There are two questions for each extract.

In the exam you will hear each extract twice.

Extract One

You hear part of a talk about negotiating with others.

1   The speaker says that both soft and hard ways of negotiating
   A   are more suitable in some situations than in others.
   B   tend to result in outcomes that were not anticipated.
   C   indicate a lack of confidence on the part of those using them.

2   The speaker says that principled negotiation involves
   A   accepting that life can be unfair.
   B   greater effort from both sides.
   C   the use of objective criteria.

Extract Two

You hear part of a radio programme about a pottery.

3   What does the reporter emphasise about the pottery?
   A   how seldom anyone visits it these days
   B   how deceptive its appearance is
   C   how much it seems to belong to a previous era

4   When describing the history of the pottery, Roly Curtis
   A   mentions a problem common to many potteries.
   B   refers to a mistake he believes was made.
   C   expresses support for what his father did.

Extract Three

You hear part of a radio programme about the stars of silent films.

5   The speaker says that Harold Lloyd became very successful because he
   A   acted on a suggestion made by a colleague.
   B   changed the character he portrayed in films.
   C   became more ambitious than he had previously been.

6   The speaker says that Lloyd's career suffered because
   A   his character's attitude ceased to be appealing.
   B   he was reluctant to make films with sound.
   C   he lost confidence in his abilities as a performer.

Stop the recording when you hear 'That's the end of Part 1'.

Now check your answers to Part 1 of the test.

PART 2

You will hear part of a radio programme, in which the history of Ty-Phoo Tipps – a brand of tea that is well-known in Britain – is described.

For questions 7–15, complete the sentences with a word or short phrase.

In the exam you will hear the piece twice.

In 1835, William Sumner appeared in a publication called the [**7**].

At the beginning of the 20th century, the Sumners' business sold [*and*   **8**] in addition to groceries.

Mary found that a certain type of tea was good for [**9**].

John was told that people would not wish to buy tea that resembled [**10**].

John thought that the name he chose for the tea sounded like a word that was [**11**].

The name of the tea has a double 'p' because of a [**12**].

To promote the tea, customers were offered a big [**13**].

John wanted people to know his tea came from the [**14**].

John was given an honour for his [**15**].

Stop the recording when you hear 'That's the end of Part 2'.

Before you check your answers to Part 2 of the test, go on to pages 66–67.

WHAT'S TESTED

Part 2 of the Listening paper is the productive task, in which you have to write words and phrases to complete sentences with information that you hear in the piece.

TIPS

- You will normally be required to write only words and phrases that are actually said in the piece. If you attempt to rephrase what you hear, for example by using different vocabulary or changing the grammatical structure, you may make unnecessary mistakes and lose marks, even though you understood perfectly what was said in the piece.

- Don't spend too much time on a question you are having difficulty with – this may mean that you miss the information required for subsequent questions, which you may have been able to answer more easily.

- Use the pause of 45 seconds before the piece is heard to look carefully at the questions so that you are prepared for the kind of answer that will be required in each case. This will also give you a good idea of the kind of information the piece will contain.

- Pay close attention to any words that appear after the gap in a question, as these will affect the nature of the answer that is required.

- Use the second listening to check answers you were confident about on the first listening and to fill in answers to questions you were unable to answer then.

Listen to Part 2 of the test again and do the exercises below. They will give you clues to the answers to each question in the test.

Question 7   *Stop the recording when you hear 'came from China'.*
The gap should be filled by a title referring to
    A   a particular region.
    B   a list of businesses.
    C   certain kinds of shop.

Question 8   *Stop the recording when you hear 'life was good'.*
The gap should be filled by words describing
    A   food and drink.
    B   types of drink.
    C   drinks and household goods.

Question 9   *Stop the recording when you hear 'why Sumner did not sell it'.*
The gap should be filled by a word or phrase describing
    A   an illness.
    B   a mood.
    C   a physical feature.

Question 10   *Stop the recording when you hear 'under a brand name'.*
The gap should be filled by a word or phrase describing
    A   a block of something.
    B   the colour of something.
    C   small particles of something.

Question 11   *Stop the recording when you hear 'Ty-Phoo could and was'.*
The gap should be filled by a word or phrase referring to
  A   a type of product.
  B   a region.
  C   the length of words.

Question 12   *Stop the recording when you hear 'stick with this spelling'.*
The gap should be filled by a word or phrase describing
  A   a sound.
  B   a decision.
  C   an action.

Question 13   *Stop the recording when you hear 'cream and biscuits'.*
The gap should be filled by a word or phrase describing
  A   an object.
  B   a sum of money.
  C   an event.

Question 14   *Stop the recording when you hear 'inserted them in the packets of tea'.*
The gap should be filled by a word or phrase describing
  A   a geographical area.
  B   part of a plant.
  C   a process.

Question 15   *Stop the recording at the end of the piece.*
The gap should be filled by a word or phrase connected with
  A   commercial success.
  B   helping others.
  C   employment.

Now check your answers to these exercises. When you have done so, listen again to Part 2 of the test and decide whether you wish to change any of the answers you gave. Then check your answers to Part 2 of the test.

PART 3

You will hear an interview with someone whose family spent a year living without television.

For questions 16–20 choose the answer (A, B, C or D) which fits best according to what you hear.

In the exam you will hear the piece twice.

---

16 One reason why the family decided not to have a television was that
    A the reception from the communal aerial was often poor.
    B they did not think the satellite technician would do the job properly.
    C linking up with the communal aerial was complicated.
    D they preferred to enjoy the beauty of their new surroundings.

17 One thing that Miranda enjoyed about not having a television was
    A telling other people about what they did instead.
    B returning to hobbies they had previously given up.
    C observing the reaction of others when they found out.
    D feeling more energetic during the evening.

18 Miranda says that one disadvantage of not having a television was
    A the fact that they could not follow their favourite series.
    B a constant desire to be more up-to-date with the news.
    C being unable to discuss topics they had previously discussed.
    D feeling out of touch with what other people talked about.

19 What does Miranda say about getting connected again?
    A She felt it would be of some benefit to the whole family.
    B She agreed because her attitude towards television had changed.
    C She initially disagreed with her husband about doing so.
    D She felt that they were doing so because they were lazy people.

20 Miranda says that since they got a television again, her children
    A are more able to distinguish good programmes from rubbish.
    B sometimes refuse to watch it when she suggests they do so.
    C have decided not to return to the habit of watching it.
    D never watch it simply because they are feeling lazy.

Stop the recording when you hear 'That's the end of Part 3'.

Now check your answers to Part 3 of the test.

PART 4

You will hear five short extracts in which people are talking about hearing some unexpected news.
You will hear the recording twice. While you listen, you must complete both tasks.

TASK ONE

For questions 21–25, choose from the list (A–H) what the news involved.

A   a chance to travel

B   a job application

C   a request for a favour

D   the cancellation of an arrangement

E   a financial matter

F   an offer of accommodation

G   someone's anger

H   an invitation to an event

Speaker 1 [ ] 21
Speaker 2 [ ] 22
Speaker 3 [ ] 23
Speaker 4 [ ] 24
Speaker 5 [ ] 25

TASK TWO

For questions 26–30, from the list (A–H) how each speaker feels with regard to the news.

A   embarrassed

B   uninterested

C   curious

D   disappointed

E   relieved

F   envious

G   annoyed

H   amused

Speaker 1 [ ] 26
Speaker 2 [ ] 27
Speaker 3 [ ] 28
Speaker 4 [ ] 29
Speaker 5 [ ] 30

Stop the recording when you hear 'That's the end of Part 4'.

In the exam you will have five minutes at the end of the test to copy your answers onto a separate answer sheet.

Now check your answers to Part 4 of the test.

PAPER 4 SPEAKING 16 minutes

PART 1 (2 minutes)   GENERAL AND SOCIAL

Questions that may be addressed to either candidate:

- What is your purpose in taking this exam?
- What are your short-term and long-term aims?
- What will you have to do to achieve them?
- What are your friends' aims for the future?
- Do you think they will achieve them?

- Do you tend to get nervous, and if so, in what circumstances?
- What are the best ways of overcoming nervousness?
- What aspect(s) of your personality do you particularly like?
- What aspect(s) of your personality do you like the least?
- Do you think your personality has changed over the years?

PART 2 (4 minutes)   GOOD AND BAD MOODS

Discussion between candidates:

Look at pictures A and B on page 133 and discuss what may have caused the feelings shown in these pictures.

(1 minute)

Now look at all of the pictures on pages 133 and 134.

Imagine that you are taking part in a project about what causes people in modern society to feel good or bad. These pictures show feelings that the project could focus on.

Discuss the feelings represented in the pictures and what causes people to have them. Then decide which feeling should be the focus of the project.

(3 minutes)

PART 3 (10 minutes)   CONFLICT AND COOPERATION

In Part 3 each candidate is given a card and talks alone for two minutes about the topic on the card. After each candidate has spoken, the other candidate is asked a question and the candidate who spoke alone is invited to respond (1 minute).

Prompt Card (a)   *(Given to Candidate A, and a copy to Candidate B)*

What are the most common causes of conflict?

- greed/envy

- personality clashes

- desire for superiority

One of the following questions for Candidate B:
- Describe an occasion when you were in conflict with someone else. What was the outcome?
- Are you good at handling conflicts or do you try to avoid them?
- What sort of people are you most likely to come into conflict within your life?

One of the following questions for Candidate A:
- What do you think?
- Do you agree?
- How about you?

Prompt Card (b)   *(Given to Candidate B, and a copy to Candidate A)*

In what ways are cooperation essential?

- problem-solving

- between nations

- team games

One of the following questions for Candidate A:
- Describe an occasion when cooperation had a positive effect for you.
- Describe an experience you have had as a member of a team.
- Is there something that you would be or have been unwilling to cooperate on?

One of the following questions for Candidate B:
- What do you think?
- Do you agree?
- How about you?

Part 3 finishes with a discussion between the two candidates and the examiner on the general topic (4 minutes).

General questions for both candidates on the topic of conflict and cooperation:

- Is it simply human nature for conflicts to arise?

- Describe a conflict which you think could have been avoided.

- What typically makes people uncooperative?

- Can people be taught to cooperate with others and if so, how?

- Describe a problem which you think could be solved by cooperation.

- Are there any situations in which cooperation is simply impossible?

Part 2: Describing Feelings

In the Speaking paper you may need to talk about your own or other people's feelings. To do this, you will need to know and use a wide range of words connected with feelings appropriately.

To check or add to your vocabulary on this subject, look at the adjectives below, decide whether each one is used for describing a feeling of sadness, anger, anxiety, shock or confusion and list them in the appropriate columns.

agitated	concerned	distressed	irate	stunned
appalled	cross	downcast	mad	taken aback
apprehensive	dejected	edgy	outraged	tense
astounded	despondent	enraged	perplexed	thrown
baffled	devastated	flabbergasted	petrified	touchy
bemused	dismayed	flustered	resentful	unnerved
bewildered	dispirited	harassed	speechless	worked up
bothered	distraught	infuriated	staggered	wound up

Sadness	Anger	Anxiety	Shock	Confusion

Now check your answers to this exercise.

TOPIC VOCABULARY

In Part 3 of this test, you are required to talk about the topic of conflict and cooperation. To check or add to your vocabulary on this subject, look at the words and phrases below. Group them together under the headings given. Then decide whether they are verbs, adjectives or nouns and label them appropriately. Then note down the precise meaning of each one (you may need to consult a dictionary) and try to think of sentences in which you could use them.

accommodating	bad blood	defuse	in concert	rivalry
acknowledge	band together	enmity	incompatible	see eye to eye
acquiesce	bicker	fall out	intervene	set-to
acrimonious	bone of contention	feud	join forces	showdown
allow	camaraderie	friction	mediate	squabble
altercation	collaborate	give-and-take	mollify	strife
animosity	concede	grant	pacify	take issue with
antagonise	concerted effort	harmony	placate	unanimous
antipathy	conciliatory	hostility	pool	win over
appease	consensus	in accord	reconcile	wrangle

Conflict	Cooperation	Agree	Try to create agreement

Now check your answers to this exercise.

TEST THREE

PAPER 1 READING AND USE OF ENGLISH 1 hour 30 minutes

PART 1

For questions 1–8, read the text below and decide which answer (A, B, C or D) best fits each gap.

In the exam you will mark your answers on a separate answer sheet.

There is an example at the beginning (0).

0   **A** resided   **B** settled   **C** dwelt   **D** inhabited

0	A	B	C	D
	▭	▭	▭	▬

Horses

Of the more than 4,000 species of mammals that have **(0)** .....D........ our earth over the past 10,000 years, the horse is one of fewer than a dozen which have been successfully domesticated. Domestication is not simply a **(1)** .... of human intention. If it were, it is possible that we would now be sitting in our fireside chairs with a hyena curled at our feet.

Much of what we take for **(2)** .... as useful in the modern horse – speed, size and intelligence, for example – can be explained through the evolutionary changes it has **(3)** .... in response to a changing diet. As the Ice Age advanced and forests **(4)** .... away, to be replaced by windswept savannah, many herbivores were **(5)** .... to change their diets from leaves to grass. The little leaf-browsing predecessor of our modern horse – the ur-horse – began to change and adapt to a new ecological niche on the plains. The head **(6)** .... longer, with the eye positioned at some **(7)** .... from the mouth, so that in exposed spaces it could keep a careful **(8)** .... for predators while it grazed. A larger brain began to develop, probably because, as a grazer, it needed greater tactile sensitivity in its lips to choose its food.

1	**A** concern	**B** business	**C** point	**D** matter
2	**A** assumed	**B** granted	**C** given	**D** read
3	**A** subjected	**B** undergone	**C** submitted	**D** committed
4	**A** died	**B** passed	**C** dwindled	**D** vanished
5	**A** coerced	**B** enforced	**C** compelled	**D** necessitated
6	**A** expanded	**B** increased	**C** grew	**D** enlarged
7	**A** space	**B** extent	**C** stretch	**D** distance
8	**A** lookout	**B** heed	**C** vigilance	**D** alert

Now check your answers to Part 1 of the test.

74

PART 2

For questions 9–16, read the text below and think of the word which best fits each space. Use only **one** *word in each space. There is an example at the beginning (0).*

In the exam you will write your answers in CAPITAL LETTERS on a separate answer sheet.

Example: **0**   *AND*

Celebrity Crossover

It is not surprising that actors want to be pop stars, **(0)** .....AND..... vice versa. **(9)** .... deep in a

part of our brain that most of us manage to keep **(10)** .... control, we all want to be pop stars and

actors.

Sadly, there's nothing about the **(11)** .... profession that automatically qualifies you for the other.

Some stars do display a genuine proficiency in both disciplines, and a few even maintain successful

careers in both fields, but this just **(12)** .... a bad example for all the others. **(13)** .... every

success, there are two dozen failures. And most of them have no idea **(14)** .... terrible they are.

(15) .... as power tends to corrupt, so celebrity tends to destroy the ability to gauge whether or

not you're making a fool of **(16)** ....

Now check your answers to Part 2 of the test.

PART 3

For questions 17–24, read the text below. Use the word given in capitals at the end of some of the lines to form a word that fits in the space in the same line. There is an example at the beginning (0).

In the exam you will write your answers in CAPITAL LETTERS on a separate answer sheet.

Example: *0*   CONSIDERABLE

King of the Watchmakers

For a period of its history, the city of Coventry had a (0) *CONSIDERABLE* .... **CONSIDER**

reputation as the main centre of clock and watchmaking in Britain and Coventry

timepieces made then were (17) .... with both quality and **SYNONYM**

(18) .... Few people in the city today will have heard of **RELY**

Samuel Watson, but he almost (19) .... paved the way for Coventry's **HAND**

involvement in the clock and watch business.

Watson made his name in 1682 when he sold a clock to King Charles II. The

following year he began work on an astronomical clock for the king, complete with

planets and signs of the zodiac, which took seven years to build. It not only told the

time of day but also the (20) .... changes of the planets. Queen Mary **POSITION**

acquired it in 1691 and it is still in the (21) .... of the Royal Family. **OWN**

He built several other clocks, and by 1690 the clamour for Watson's clocks was

such that he left Coventry and took up (22) .... in London. He **RESIDE**

became Master of the London Clockmakers' Company in 1692, which is testament

to his (23) .... in the growing industry. In 1712, Samuel Watson's **STAND**

name disappears from the records of the London Clockmakers' company, and

the (24) .... is that he died in that year. **LIKELY**

Before you check your answers to Part 3 of the test, go on to pages 77–78.

WHAT'S TESTED

Part 3 of the Reading and Use of English paper is primarily a vocabulary test, in which you have to form words in different parts of speech from the words given. Questions may involve any of the following:

- changing or adding to the end of the word given, for example to form a noun from a given verb or an adjective from a given noun – the majority of the questions usually fall into this category.

- the use of prefixes, for example when a negative form of a word has to be formed.

- forming a compound word, either by adding another word to the word given, or by both adding a word to the word given and changing the form of the word given.

TIPS

- First of all, decide from the context what part of speech the word you have to form must be – do you have to form a noun, an adjective, an adverb, a verb?

- Then decide what the meaning of that word is most likely to be and whether it will require a prefix or be a compound word.

- If you are sure that your decisions about both the above are correct but do not know the actual word required, use your knowledge of the language to produce a word which you feel sounds correct. Your guess may be right, and if you put no answer at all, you certainly won't get a mark!

Look again at Part 3 of this test on page 76 and then for each question, decide which of the choices A–D best expresses the meaning of the word that should fill the gap.

Then decide which of the words listed could fill the gap for that question. Some of the words listed do not exist at all.

You may wish to change some of the answers you gave in the test after you have done these exercises.

17 **A** incomparable objects
    B always made to the same standard
    C considered to mean automatically
    D in the same way

    synonymatic
    synonymists
    synonymous
    synonymally
    synonymised

18 **A** in such a way that they could be relied upon
    B being in a position of relying on
    C dependence
    D the fact of being something that can be relied upon

    reliance
    reliability
    reliably
    reliant
    reliableness

19 A earlier
   B in an authoritarian way
   C conveniently
   D alone

single-handedly
handfully
handily
high-handedly
beforehand

20 A having a certain position
   B putting into positions
   C relating to position
   D forcing someone/something into a position

positionalised
positional
positionful
imposition
postionalising

21 A the person owning
   B the act of becoming owned by
   C the fact of being owned by
   D something owned

ownering
owning
ownerdom
ownership
ownerhood

22 A connected with the place where someone lives
   B a person who lives in a particular place
   C the situation of living in a particular place
   D employment

resident
residential
residency
residence
residentity

23 A reputation
   B extraordinary
   C being able to endure
   D attitude

standpoint
standing
withstanding
outstanding
standence

24 A evidence
   B explanation
   C guess
   D probability

likelihood
likeliness
likelibility
likeliance
likeliment

Now check your answers to these exercises and to Part 3 of the test.

PART 4

*For questions **25–30**, complete the second sentence so that it has a similar meaning to the first sentence, using the word given. **Do not change the word given.** You must use between **three** and **eight** words, including the word given.*

*Here is an example (**0**).*

0   Robert was offended when he was left out of the team.

exception

Robert .... left out of the team.

0	took exception to being

*In the exam you will write **only** the missing words on a separate answer sheet.*

---

25 If Tony hadn't interfered, there would have been no problems yesterday, I'm sure.

smoothly

Without Tony's .... yesterday, I'm sure.

26 He didn't want to get into a position where he might lose all his money.

possibility

He didn't want to expose .... all his money.

27 The company received an enormous number of calls responding to the advert.

deluged

The company .... response to the advert.

28 The manager said that he had paid attention to my complaints and would take the appropriate action.

note

The manager said that he had .... accordingly.

29 His behaviour at the conference gave him the bad reputation he now has.

conducted

The way .... in the bad reputation he now has.

30 Her work didn't meet the standards that were considered acceptable.

conform

Her work .... acceptable standards.

Now check your answers to Part 4 of the test.

PART 5

You are going to read an extract from a magazine article about a chess champion.

For questions 31–36, choose the answer (A, B, C or D) which you think fits best according to the text.

In the exam you will mark your answers on a separate answer sheet.

The Chess Player

In the corner of the room sits the pub champion. He looks like the classic chess bum. Untidy hair. Big beard. His possessions in a white polythene bag by his feet. The chess board is also made of polythene, and the pieces of plastic. The 'table' is an up-ended keg of beer. The pub champion is playing some kid genius from out of town who has just won a London grandmaster tournament. He is called David R. Norwood. (I know. The boy wonder, all of 19, gave me his business card. It said 'David R. Norwood. International Chess Master'.) Now David R. Norwood is, as he will be the first to admit, one of the hottest properties on the international chess circuit.

But something funny is happening in his games – played at the rate of about one every ten minutes – against the pub champion. David R. Norwood is not winning any. And he is not merely losing. He is being taken apart. In the argot of the chess player, he is being 'busted'. But David R. does not seem too worried about this denouement. Occasionally he will say, with a smile, 'Hey, you're not such a bad player.' His opponent, Jonathan Speelman, the pub champion, only laughs and sets up the pieces for the next act of slaughter. It is a joke, of course. He is not merely 'not a bad player'. He is possibly the best player in the Western world.

After Jon had finally exhausted David R. Norwood's enthusiasm, I asked whether he would mind playing me. Not at all, he said, and played game after game against me until I became more bored by losing than he did by winning. 'Why,' I asked, 'do you put up with playing chess jerks like me?' 'Because I like to play with the pieces,' was the instant and unanswerable reply. My impression while playing Jon was slightly different, namely that the pieces enjoyed playing with him. He gives them the time of their life. These plastic pieces, property of the pub, had probably never before experienced more than the intellectual equivalent of being cooped up in a shed. With Jon, they were roaming free across vast expanses.

His friends, incidentally, do not call him Jon. They do not call him Speelman either. They call him 'Spess'. This stems from a report in *The Times* about ten years ago of a tournament in which Speelman was taking part. But, *Times* sub-editors being *Times* sub-editors, his name inadvertently came out as 'Specimen'. In view of his rather weird appearance, fellow chess players decided that this was, if not his real name, at least descriptively accurate, and so Specimen, and then later Spess, he became.

On many personal matters, Jon Speelman is difficult to interview. He is very self-conscious, a keen practitioner of self-psychoanalysis. The result is that he is only too aware of the implications which might be drawn from anything he might say. Worse, he was so concerned about what I was writing down that he would stare at my pad when I noted anything, attempting to read my scribble upside-down. In an effort to counter this awkward turning of the tables, I began deliberately to write in messier and messier scrawl.

Afterwards I was quite unable to read many of my own notes. Later I surmised that the chess player in Speelman had calculated that his scrutiny of my notepad would have this effect, and that it was a deliberate attempt to reduce the number of personal details I would be able to decipher. If that sounds convoluted, it is quite in character with Speelman's way of playing chess. Some great players reveal their greatness through the simplicity of their methods. Others, more unusually, have a genius to confuse, an ability to generate chaos, out of which only they can perceive a clear path to victory. This is Speelman's method.

But such a style is one which makes enormous demands on the exponent's nervous system. When he plays, Speelman is all nervous, twitchy movement. His hands play with his beard, his glasses, anything he can reach. He makes strange clicking noises. He will get up from the board and stand over it and his opponent, nodding his head as if checking through the variations. ('He goes there, I go there, he goes there ...') I asked him how many moves he can see ahead. 'It's a silly question,' he replied, 'but it's not too difficult to imagine a position in which one could calculate 25 moves ahead.' 25 moves on each side, he means. That is 50 moves in total. Try saying 'he goes there, I go there' 25 times. Now you get the picture.

31 In the first paragraph, the writer implies that
    A he found David R. Norwood rather arrogant.
    B it is strange for chess players to have business cards.
    C the best chess players tend to be scruffy in appearance.
    D he likes to see chess played in informal surroundings.

32 What does the writer say about the games between David R. Norwood and Jonathan Speelman?
    A They might have different outcomes if they were being played in a real tournament.
    B They indicate that Jonathan Speelman does not have a high regard for David R. Norwood.
    C They involve David R. Norwood making jokes to cover his embarrassment.
    D They indicate that there is a huge gulf between the standard of the two players.

33 When the writer played Jonathan Speelman, he felt that Speelman
    A preferred just to play than to indulge in polite conversation as well.
    B had an approach to the game that made other approaches seem limited in comparison.
    C was doing his best not to let the games bore him.
    D was adopting an approach he would not use if he was playing in a serious game.

34 What does the writer say about Speelman's nickname?
    A It indicates that he is regarded as a rather distant figure.
    B It is not very flattering.
    C It is connected with his style of playing.
    D It was first used as a joke.

35 The writer says that Speelman tried to read the notes he was making because
    A he saw it as the kind of thing the writer would expect of him.
    B he felt that he could get a clear picture of a person from the way they wrote.
    C he was aware that this would put the writer off while he was making them.
    D he wanted to make sure that certain complex points he made were correctly understood.

36 When the writer says 'Now you get the picture' (final line), he is emphasising
    A how complex a serious game of chess can be.
    B how extraordinary Speelman believes his style of play is.
    C how incredible the mental feat Speelman performs is.
    D how peculiar Speelman might appear to others to be.

Now check your answers to Part 5 of the test.

PART 6

*You are going to read an extract from an autobiography. Seven paragraphs have been removed from the extract. Choose from the paragraphs **A–H** the one which fits each gap (37–43). There is one extra paragraph which you do not need to use.*

In the exam you will mark your answers on a separate answer sheet.

The Hammond Organ

It's September 1995 and I'm on my way home to Austin, Texas from Bangkok. Breaking the journey in Los Angeles, I spot an ad for an organ in the classifieds. It's a 1954 Hammond B2. I can't resist this little gem, so I buy it – sight unseen – and arrange to have it collected, crated and trucked to Texas.

37	

Ever since I heard *Green Onions* by Booker T. and the MG's on the radio, the sound of a Hammond organ has moved me. Although at the time I didn't know exactly what Booker T. was playing, I knew I wanted to make that noise. I didn't even know how to play an organ, but the way it swirled and swam and bit your ears off, I knew somehow I had to have one. So I did my research in the music shops, and found out that the coolest-sounding organs were all Hammonds, but that the L100, while it still had that special sound, was lighter and cheaper than the other models. Not that any of them were cheap, which didn't much matter, because I had no money.

38	

But when I called them up, they were very helpful. There was no drawback. The only thing I could not do was move it, once they'd set it up. That wasn't going to be a problem. The problem would be explaining the arrival of this beautiful monster to Mum and Dad. But I wasn't thinking that far ahead. I wasn't really thinking at all, apart from wondering – when could it be delivered? 'Tomorrow.' 'Okay.' And that was it. The next morning at about 10am there was a knock at the door and two men in white coats were standing on the doorstep. After I'd signed papers and promised not to move it, we pushed the dining table and chairs back against the wall.

39	

It was all polished and shiny and made our dining-room suite look quite tatty. They showed me how to start it up and we shook hands. It couldn't have been simpler. 'See you in two weeks then.' 'Yes,

okay, bye.' Slam. 'Aarrgh!' I screamed and ran upstairs to get the record player from the bedroom, set it up on top of the bookcase, plonked *Green Onions* on the turntable and cranked it up! Yes, yes, yes, nothing could stop me now. I had lost my mind and I'd never find it again.

40	

The next thing to master was the Leslie cabinet. This was where the sound came out. The Leslie is a combined amplifier and speaker cabinet, but it has two speakers which point up and down. The sound travels through revolving rotors, which throws the music out in waves. It's what makes the sound of every Hammond bite and swim in your ears. You can regulate the speed it rotates and it's very powerful.

41	

When Dad came whistling his way up the path after work, I went to the door to head him off. 'Hello Dad.' 'What's up?' 'Nothing much. Well, I've got something to tell you.' 'Yes.' 'Er, Dad, you'll never guess what I've got.' 'What have you got?' 'A Hammond organ.'

42	

He was down the hall and peering round the door suspiciously before I could stop him. 'Blimey,' he said. 'Well, I'm blowed. Where's the dining-room table gone?' He was in the doorway, trying to squeeze past the monster organ and the Leslie. 'It's great, isn't it?' 'Well, it's big … how are we going to eat with this thing in here, and why didn't you ask me or your mum?' 'Sorry, but it'll only be here for a couple of weeks, listen to this.' I played the first part of *Green Onions* on it. 'Not bad, eh?' 'I dunno.' He was thinking. 'Here, don't say a word, let me break it to your mum.'

43	

I bought it on the 'never never'. Dad co-signed the hire purchase forms for me because I was under age.

A This meant that there was now enough room. Very carefully, they wheeled in a brand new Hammond organ and matching bench with the Playing Guide and connecting cables tucked inside the lid, and a brand new Leslie 147 speaker cabinet, which filled up the entire room. My face must have been a picture. This was the gear!

B I found all that out by fiddling around with it for hours that day until I got some results. Basically, I just taught myself. The wonderful thing about the Hammond is it sounds good without too much effort. It's not like the bagpipes or the violin, where even after a lot of work it can still sound bad!

C However, I never had any ambition as a kid to play the piano, let alone the organ. It was all my mum's fault. She'd had a dream of playing the piano since she was a kid, but growing up in the little town of Mountrath in the centre of Ireland, as one of 11 kids, there was hardly money for shoes let alone piano lessons. And as she hadn't been able to afford them when she was young, I was going to get them whether I wanted them or not.

D 'What's a Hammond organ?' 'It's free. I've got it for two weeks, then they'll come and take it away and no charge whatsoever.' 'Where is it then?' 'It's in the back room, it's fantastic and it's not costing a penny.'

E Then, thumbing through the back pages of the *Melody Maker*, I noticed an ad for Boosey and Hawkes, in Regent Street, who were offering to let me: 'Try a Hammond Organ in your own home on two weeks' free approval.' 'Yeah, right,' I thought. 'Pull the other one.' I tried to figure out what the catch could be, because I couldn't believe they'd let me get my sweaty hands on a genuine Hammond without money changing hands or at least making a promise to buy.

F Somehow I knew that meant it was going to be all right. The men in white coats came to take it away two weeks later and my new mahogany Hammond organ and matching Leslie cabinet arrived the following week.

G Sometimes, a smell can trigger a memory so strong and true it unravels years in an instant, like the smell of oil paint, which takes me straight back to my art school days. So, as they unbolt the container, even before I get to see how beautiful the instrument is, the combination of furniture polish and Hammond oil wafts up my nose and I get a flashback to 1964, when I caught that odd mixture for the first time.

H Now I had to figure out how to play the beast and get the same sound as that. Carefully listening to sustained notes on the record, I pushed and pulled the drawer bars in and out until I got the same sound. Then, if I played the part right, the sound would change – just like the record.

Now check your answers to Part 6 of the test.

PART 7

You are going to read an extract from an article about a man who was involved in the development of computing. For questions 44–53, choose from the sections (A–F). The sections may be chosen more than once.

In the exam you will mark your answers on a separate answer sheet.

In which section are the following mentioned?

the speed at which McCarthy made progress in his career   44 .... *D? E√*

an opinion McCarthy had which proved to be mistaken   45 .... *F*

McCarthy's belief that one of his ideas could have a widespread function   46 .... *B*

McCarthy's attention to the moral aspects of an area of research   47 .... *D*

what inspired McCarthy to go into a certain area of research   48 .... *E*

McCarthy's view of what was the cause of a certain problem   49 .... *A*

McCarthy's attempt to introduce a rival to something commonly used   50 .... *F/E √*

McCarthy's continuing belief in the importance of a certain field   51 .... *F*

a common belief about McCarthy   52 .... *A*

McCarthy's criticism of an area of research he had been involved in   53 .... *C*

Before you check your answers to Part 7 of the test, go on to pages 86–87.

John McCarthy – Computer Pioneer

A

John McCarthy was often described as the father of 'artificial intelligence' (AI), a branch of computer science founded on the notion that human intelligence can be simulated by machines. McCarthy, who coined the term in 1956, defined it as 'the science and engineering of making intelligent machines' and created the Lisp computer language to help researchers in the AI field. He maintained that there were aspects of the human mind that could be described precisely enough to be replicated: 'The speeds and memory capacities of present computers may be insufficient to simulate many of the higher functions of the human brain,' he wrote in 1955, 'but the major obstacle is not lack of machine capacity but our inability to write programs taking full advantage of what we have.'

B

McCarthy went on to create AI laboratories at the Massachusetts Institute of Technology, and later at Stanford University where he became the laboratory's director in 1965. During the 1960s he developed the concept of computer time-sharing, which allows several people to use a single, central, computer at the same time. If this approach were adopted, he claimed in 1961, 'computing may some day be organised as a public utility'. The concept of time-sharing made possible the development of so-called 'cloud computing' (the delivery of computing as a service rather than a product). Meanwhile, his Lisp programming language, which he invented in 1958, underpinned the development of voice recognition technology.

C

McCarthy's laboratory at Stanford developed systems that mimic human skills – such as vision, hearing and the movement of limbs – as well as early versions of a self-driving car. He also worked on an early chess-playing program, but came to believe that computer chess was a distraction, observing in 1997 that it had developed 'much as genetics might have if the geneticists had concentrated their efforts starting in 1910 on breeding racing Drosophila. We would have some science, but mainly we would have very fast fruit flies.'

D

The concept of AI inspired numerous books and sci-fi films, notably Stanley Kubrick's dystopian *2001: A Space Odyssey* (1968). In the real world, however, the technology made slow progress, and McCarthy later admitted that there was some way to go before it would be possible to develop computer programs as intelligent as humans. Meanwhile he applied himself to addressing theoretical issues about the nature of human and robotic decision-making and the ethics of creating artificial beings. He also wrote a sci-fi story, *The Robot and the Baby*, to 'illustrate my opinions about what household robots should be like'. The robot in the story decides to simulate love for a human baby.

E

McCarthy taught himself mathematics as a teenager by studying textbooks at the California Institute of Technology. When he arrived at the institute to study the subject aged 16, he was assigned to a graduate course. In 1948 a symposium at Caltech on 'Cerebral Mechanisms in Behaviour', that included papers on automata and the brain and intelligence, sparked his interest in developing machines that can think like people. McCarthy received a doctorate in Mathematics from Princeton University in 1951 and was immediately appointed to a Chair in the subject. It was at Princeton that he proposed the programming language Lisp as a way to process more sophisticated mathematical concepts than Fortran, which had been the dominant programming medium until then. McCarthy joined the Stanford faculty in 1962, remaining there until his official retirement in 2000.

F

During the 1970s he presented a paper on buying and selling by computer. He also invited a local computer hobby group, the Homebrew Computer Club, to meet at the Stanford laboratory. Its members included Steve Jobs and Steven Wozniak, who would go on to found Apple. However, his own interest in developing time-sharing systems led him to underestimate the potential of personal computers. When the first PCs emerged in the 1970s he dismissed them as 'toys'. McCarthy continued to work as an emeritus professor at Stanford after his official retirement, and at the time of his death was working on a new computer language called Elephant. Despite his disappointment with AI, McCarthy remained confident of the power of mathematics: 'He who refuses to do arithmetic is doomed to talk nonsense,' he wrote in 1995.

WHAT'S TESTED

Part 7 of the Reading and Use of English paper requires you to match information or points with different sections of a text or different short texts. The text may be a continuous text divided into sections (like this one) or it may consist of a series of short texts (about different people, places, etc, as in Test 2). You have to decide which section or short text contains the exact information that is in the statement or question. You will be required to match the following:

- **specific information/details** included in the text

- **opinions and attitudes** expressed in the text

TIPS

- Begin by reading quickly through the whole text (or all of the short texts). This will give you a general idea of what the whole text or each short text contains and the differences between the content of each section/text, which will help you when you come to answer the questions. If you start with the questions, you may quickly become confused.

- There are two approaches you can take:

    1 matching information/points to sections/texts: you can look at each numbered question and then look through the sections/texts to find the lettered section/text that matches it.

    2 matching sections/texts to information/points: you can read each lettered section/text and then go through all of the numbered questions to find which one or ones match it. A section/text may match more than one of the numbered questions.

- If you use approach 1, be careful. More than one section/text may contain something closely related to the question. But only one will contain something that precisely matches the question.

- If you use approach 2, be careful. A question may relate closely to something in the section/text you are dealing with, but not be the correct answer. To be the correct answer, a question must match exactly something stated in that section/text.

- The numbered questions rephrase what is stated in the text. Do not try to match exact words and phrases in the question with the same words and phrases in the text. Words and phrases used in the question may appear in a section/text, but that section/text may not be the correct answer. What you have to do is to match ideas. So look for the place in the text where the same idea is expressed in different words and phrases.

*The following exercises will help you to answer questions you were unable to do in the test or to confirm answers that you gave. For each exercise, **there may be more than one correct answer**.*

Section A

Read section A of the text carefully. Which of the following are mentioned about McCarthy?
1 his reputation among other people
2 why he got involved in AI
3 a false belief he had
4 something he believed to be preventing progress in AI

Section B

Read section B of the text carefully. Which of the following are mentioned?
1   how quickly McCarthy was promoted at Stanford
2   a prediction made by McCarthy
3   McCarthy's concern about the possible bad effects of computers on people
4   something that McCarthy hoped to compete with

Section C

Read section C of the text carefully. Which of the following are mentioned?
1   claims McCarthy made about the future benefits of one of his ideas
2   a difficulty associated with developing a chess-playing program
3   McCarthy's view of the importance of genetics as an area of research
4   something McCarthy regarded as a waste of time and effort

Section D

Read section D of the text carefully. Which of the following are mentioned about McCarthy?
1   his disapproval of computer programs developed by others
2   two aspects of technology that he focused on in his research
3   a solution that he came up with concerning the creation of robots
4   something concerning robots that he was wrong about

Section E

Read section E of the text carefully. Which of the following are mentioned?
1   an event that had a huge influence on McCarthy
2   what people at various academic institutions thought of McCarthy
3   how quickly McCarthy rose in status at Princeton
4   an alternative to something established

Section F

Read section F of the text carefully. Which of the following are mentioned about McCarthy?
1   his fears about the effects of computers on people
2   his incorrectly negative view of a certain development
3   his view of the commercial possibilities of a language he developed
4   a statement he made about a particular area of study

Now check your answers to these exercises. When you have done so, decide whether you wish to change any of your answers to Part 7 of the test. Then check your answers to Part 7 of the test.

PAPER 2 WRITING 1 hour 30 minutes

PART 1

Read the two texts below.

Write an essay summarising and evaluating the key points from both texts. Use your own words throughout as far as possible, and include your own ideas in your answer.

Write your answer in 240–280 words.

1

Views on Adolescence

One of the most irritating conventional wisdoms of recent times is that adolescence is a horrendously traumatic and stressful phase of life, characterised by rebellion and dissent. A somewhat unholy alliance of therapists, advertising moguls, pop pundits and preachers pontificates about the rupture that occurs with the entry into adolescent status, the special and separate culture, the bewildering biological and psychological changes. The expectation is of trouble. This is not to suggest that adolescence is a golden age, a wondrous period of growth, self-exploration and self-discovery. It can be these things but it is also a time of pain, embarrassment, self-doubt and loss.

Parents and Adolescence

If you've got a teenager who is loud, moody, distant and rebellious, it won't make your life any more comfortable to know that this is normal, but it may at least put your mind at rest that you haven't gone badly wrong somewhere. The processes that teenagers go through, physical and emotional, are unavoidable if they are ever to reach maturity. There are no short cuts, no cryogenic miracles that will suspend them in ice between the ages of 13 and 20. And in terms of their psychological development, it does appear that the more you try to hijack it, or delay it, or mould it in your very own image, the bigger the problems will be, especially for your child.

Write your essay.

Before you write your essay, go on to pages 89–90.

PART 1

For information on What's Tested and Tips, see page 25.

SUMMARISING THE TEXTS

1   Read the first text carefully. Then decide which of A–E are paraphrases of the two main points.

One of the most irritating conventional wisdoms of recent times is that adolescence is a horrendously traumatic and stressful phase of life, characterised by rebellion and dissent. A somewhat unholy alliance of therapists, advertising moguls, pop pundits and preachers pontificates about the rupture that occurs with the entry into adolescent status, the special and separate culture, the bewildering biological and psychological changes. The expectation is of trouble. This is not to suggest that adolescence is a golden age, a wondrous period of growth, self-exploration and self-discovery. It can be these things but it is also a time of pain, embarrassment, self-doubt and loss.

A   Adolescents dislike what is said about them by a range of adults.

B   According to experts, adolescence is a very difficult time for both teenagers and parents.

C   Different individuals experience adolescence in different ways.

D   There is disagreement among experts on the subject of adolescence.

E   There are both positive and negative aspects to adolescence.

2   Read the second text carefully. Then decide which of A–E are paraphrases of the two main points.

If you've got a teenager who is loud, moody, distant and rebellious, it won't make your life any more comfortable to know that this is normal, but it may at least put your mind at rest that you haven't gone badly wrong somewhere. The processes that teenagers go through, physical and emotional, are unavoidable if they are ever to reach maturity. There are no short cuts, no cryogenic miracles that will suspend them in ice between the ages of 13 and 20. And in terms of their psychological development, it does appear that the more you try to hijack it, or delay it, or mould it in your very own image, the bigger the problems will be, especially for your child.

A   Parents should be careful not to make problems associated with adolescence even worse.

B   Different parents respond to the problems of adolescence in very different ways.

C   Not all teenagers are difficult for their parents to deal with during adolescence.

D   Parents can be very helpful to their children during adolescence.

E   Parents should realise that difficult behaviour among teenage children is to be expected.

Now check your answers to these exercises.

Then write your essay, summarising the key points from the texts and including your own opinions.

When you have written your answer, assess it in accordance with the mark scheme.

SAMPLE ANSWER

Now read this sample answer for Part 1 and answer the questions that follow it.

> The texts state how irritating and emotionally demanding it can be for both parents and their growing up children. When the time comes for teenagers to step into the adulthood, the emotional discomfort and the chemical reactions in the body can cause trouble. It is a very traumatic and stressful experience, but it is a very vital time of any growing up teenager. The time of growing into responsibilities, becoming mature, exploring your personality, discovering your body from an adult point of view. As good as it sounds, it is also the time for confusion, an emotional roller-coaster, and often pain.
>
> The side effects of the chemical processes in the body often reveal themselves in anger, mood swings, loud expression of feelings, tears, sometimes even violence. Awareness for parents might not bring any solutions, but it is important for them to try to understand that what is happening to their adolescent children is an unavoidable way to adulthood, and there is no other way.
>
> In my opinion, adolescence is a time when parents are the people who should set an example to their children. They should help the children through hard times, and guide them into the right path. A young person during that adolescence time is more likely to soak up any bad influences from the world around them and therefore parents should look after their children with a special approach and extra care to make sure that such influences do not have a bad effect.

Content

Are the two main points for each text summarised in the essay? Where are the main opinions from the text summarised? Are any key points missing? Are any additional but irrelevant points included? Are the writer's own opinions included? If so, where?

Communicative achievement

Is the style and tone of the essay suitably neutral/formal or is it too informal? Are the key points from the texts expressed in the writer's own words or are large parts of the texts simply copied?

Are the writer's opinions clear and are they logically connected with the points made in the texts?

Organisation

Does the essay flow well and is it coherent as a whole? Is it divided appropriately into paragraphs? Is there appropriate linking between points made and opinions expressed? If there is an introduction and/or a conclusion, is it appropriate/clear?

Language

Is there a good range of grammatical structures that are not just simple? Are grammatical structures used accurately? Is there a good range of vocabulary, both single words and phrases that are appropriate for the topic? Is the vocabulary used accurately? Are there any language errors in the essay? If so, try to correct them.

Now check your assessment of this sample answer with the assessment.

PART 2

*Write an answer to **one** of the questions 2–5 in this part. Write your answer in **280–320** words in an appropriate style.*

2   A magazine is running a competition for the best article entitled *The Day That Changed My Life*. Write an article for this competition, explaining the background to what happened, the details of what happened and the effect it had on your life.

         Write your **article**.

3   An arts magazine has started a section called *Answer The Critics*, in which readers are invited to respond to the reviews written by the magazine's critics with reviews of their own. Write a review of something you have seen (a film, show, play or TV programme) or read, giving your own opinions on it and comparing your views with those of the critics.

         Write your **review**.

4   You recently stayed at one of a chain of large hotels and encountered a number of problems during your stay which you feel were the fault of the company. Write a letter to the company's head office, detailing the problems that you had, describing what happened when you complained to the hotel staff about them and suggesting ways in which the hotel group could improve its service to customers.

         Write your **letter**. Do not write any postal addresses.

5   Set book questions – a choice from **(a)** or **(b)**.

         In the exam you may choose to answer a question on one of the two set books.

Before you write your answer, go on to pages 92–93.

PART 2

For information on What's Tested and Tips, see page 59.

To plan your answer for question 4 in Part 2, complete the following notes.

1   Note down as briefly as possible the **topic** of your letter.

   ....

2   List as briefly as possible the following:

   • the **problems** that you had at the hotel

   • **what happened** when you complained at the time

   • your **suggestions** as to how the hotel could improve

Problem	What happened	Suggestion
Problem	What happened	Suggestion
Problem	What happened	Suggestion

3   List briefly any additional points you wish to make about the hotel which you think are relevant to the topic. You may not wish to include any additional points.

Additional point	What happened	Suggestion
Additional point	What happened	Suggestion

4   Now note briefly how your letter will be organised by deciding what each part of it will contain. You may not wish to have as many paragraphs as are listed below.

Opening
Paragraph 1
Paragraph 2
Paragraph 3
Paragraph 4
Paragraph 5
Paragraph 6
Ending

5   Now use these notes to write your letter.

When you have written your answer, assess it in accordance with the mark scheme.

SAMPLE ANSWER

Now read this sample answer for question 4 in Part 2 and answer the questions that follow it.

Dear Sir or Madam,

I'm writing to complain about your Hotel Blue Star, where I was staying for two nights on 24th–25th of November during my business trip. Despite of recommendations of a friend of mine, I encountered three major problems that made my stay rather unpleasant and unnecessarily complicated. Although the hotel facilities were of high standard, I certainly cannot say the same about your service.

For the first night I reserved a table for four people in your hotel restaurant. For some reason the reservation had not been made and my business partners and I had to wait at the lobby for more than half an hour to get a table. Considering that my guests were some of the most important business partners of mine, this was most unpleasant.

The next evening I arrived at the hotel very tired at 7pm, hoping that my dinner, which I ordered in the morning, will be delivered to my room at 7.30pm. At 8 o'clock, starving, I rang the restaurant. They knew nothing about my order. Therefore I had to wait for my dinner for another 45 minutes to be ready.

The same evening I rang the reception, asking them to prepare my bill for the following morning as I was about to leave at 6am for the airport and could not wait. This had not been done either, which meant another wait for me. It took more than 20 minutes to get my bill ready. Not mentioning that my taxi booking was omitted too.

I strongly advise you to inform your hotel staff in the reception as well as in the restaurant about the appalling service I had to endure and instruct them in the service they should provide, especially for business people, who usually lack the time for waiting. I don't require any financial compensation, although your apology and information about steps that have been taken to avoid such a situation in the future is awaited.

Yours faithfully,

Content

Are all the main points mentioned in the question covered? Where are these points covered? If any are not covered, which are missing? Are any additional points included? If so, what are they, and are they relevant?

Communicative achievement

Are the style and tone of the letter appropriate? How would you describe them? Why are they appropriate or inappropriate? Is the format suitable for a letter of this kind? If so, why? If not, why not?

Do you feel that someone reading this letter would be clear what the writer's point of view is throughout it? If so, summarise the writer's point of view briefly. If not, say what you feel is unclear in the letter.

Organisation

Is the letter well-organised in terms of the beginning, middle and end? Is it divided into paragraphs appropriately? Describe briefly the content of each paragraph.

Does the letter flow well in terms of the linking of points and ideas within paragraphs and between paragraphs? Give examples of places where the linking is good. If there are occasions when the linking is inadequate or inappropriate, suggest improvements.

Language

Is there a wide range of vocabulary and grammatical structures? If so, give examples. If there are occasions when the vocabulary or grammar is too simple, suggest alternatives.

Are there any mistakes in the use of vocabulary or grammar? Correct any that you find.

Now check your assessment of this sample answer with the assessment.

PAPER 3 LISTENING approximately 40 minutes

PART 1

You will hear three different extracts.

For questions 1–6, choose the answer (A, B or C) which fits best according to what you hear. There are two questions for each extract.

In the exam you will hear each extract twice.

Extract One

You hear part of a radio programme about British attitudes.

1   The speaker says that one example of British people's pessimism is their
   A   calm response to problems that affect them personally.
   B   acceptance of what they are told by administrators.
   C   tendency to exaggerate potential problems.

2   What does the speaker say about British children?
   A   They come to appreciate irony later in life.
   B   It comes naturally to them to be pessimistic.
   C   They are aware of having a peculiar sense of humour.

Extract Two

You hear the introduction to a radio science programme.

3   The speaker describes a process by which the brain
   A   changes previous perceptions about events.
   B   discards irrelevant information about events.
   C   waits before focusing on events.

4   What does the speaker say about the research he mentions?
   A   It has been influenced by the methods used for live TV broadcasts.
   B   It adds useful information to what is already known.
   C   It is likely to be disproved by other research.

Extract Three

You hear the introduction to a radio programme about inventors.

5   The speaker says that Edison's comment
   A   reflects the naivety of inventors.
   B   sums up the unpredictability of an inventor's life.
   C   is as true today as when he made it.

6   What does the speaker say about the rules concerning English patents?
   A   He can understand why they remain in force.
   B   They have always put inventors at a disadvantage.
   C   Some inventors do not abide by them.

Stop the recording when you hear 'That's the end of Part 1'.

Now check your answers to Part 1 of the test.

PART 2

You will hear part of a radio report about interactive science and technology centres in Britain.
For questions 7–15, complete the sentences with a word or short phrase.
In the exam you will hear the piece twice.

The area on which the National Stone Centre stands has been used for a long time for the mining of

[*and* | **7**] .

Visitors to the centre are surprised to discover how much stone people

[| **8**] .

Examples of the use of stone in construction shown are [*and* | **9**] .

The headmaster describes the centre as an excellent [| **10**] .

The first interactive gallery in Britain was called [| **11**] .

At Techniquest, there are structures which [| **12**] .

At Techniquest, a special [| **13**] is used for teaching people about
centrifugal force.

People can learn about the effect that [| **14**] can have on each
other at Techniquest.

A dragon is used for teaching people about [| **15**] at Techniquest.

Stop the recording when you hear 'That's the end of Part 2'.
Now check your answers to Part 2 of the test.

PART 3

You will hear an interview with someone who reviews hotels.

For questions 16–20 choose the answer (A, B, C or D) which fits best according to what you hear.

In the exam you will hear the piece twice.

16 What does Paddy say about some readers of her column?
    A   They suspect that she enjoys criticising hotels.
    B   Her attitude to hotels has changed because of their response.
    C   Her comments match their experiences of hotels.
    D   They prefer reading about hotels they would not want to visit.

17 What does Paddy say about some hotel-keepers?
    A   They sometimes have to force themselves to have a sense of humour.
    B   They would be more suited to a different profession.
    C   They expect to receive negative comments about their hotels.
    D   They are surprised that they become friends of hers.

18 Paddy says that some hotel-keepers she has contacted about the book have
    A   realised that she does not really have an assistant called Emily.
    B   corrected inaccuracies that were in her review of their hotels.
    C   responded favourably despite criticisms she had made.
    D   made her wonder whether her reviews of their hotels were unfair.

19 Paddy says that one hotel-keeper she spoke to told her that
    A   other people are unlikely to be treated in the same way in hotels as she is.
    B   he was unwilling to discuss some of the comments in her review.
    C   her reviews did not have as much influence as she believed.
    D   he no longer wanted his hotel to appear in the book.

20 The same owner also told her that
    A   he had passed information about her to other hotels.
    B   he resented her description of him in her review.
    C   he did not understand why she wanted to put his hotel in her book.
    D   there was nothing distinctive about her physical appearance.

Stop the recording when you hear 'That's the end of Part 3'.

Before you check your answers to Part 3 of the test, go on to pages 97–98.

WHAT'S TESTED

The questions in Part 3 of the Listening paper test you on your ability to understand and interpret often complex points made and information given by speakers in conversation, particularly in an interview situation. Questions may focus on any of the following:

- **opinion** – a view expressed by a speaker.
- **gist** – the general meaning of what a speaker says, or the main point a speaker makes.
- **detail** – specific information given or a particular point made by a speaker.
- **inference** – something which is not directly stated by a speaker but which is strongly implied.

TIPS

- Questions follow the order of what is said in the piece – for example, questions in an interview may cover each succeeding answer given by the person being interviewed.
- Don't rush into choosing the option that appears superficially to be the most plausible – what speakers say is often fairly complex and subtle.
- It is possible that more than one option in a question may be correct according to what the speaker says, but only one option will correctly answer the question that has been asked, so make sure that you read the question carefully.
- If you find a question particularly difficult, don't linger on it so that you do not concentrate sufficiently on what comes next in the piece. If you do that, you may fail to answer the next question, which may have presented you with considerably less difficulty.
- Use the pause of one minute before the piece to read the questions in advance, so that you are aware of the aspects of it that you will be tested on.
- Use the second listening to check your answers even if you were confident of them on the first listening, as well as to answer questions you were unable to do then.

Listen to Part 3 of the test again and do the exercises below. They will help you to eliminate the incorrect options in the questions in the test or to confirm that you have selected the right options. In each exercise, tick one or more boxes.

Question 16 *Stop the recording when Paddy says 'some awful ones too'.*
Which of the following does Paddy mention in her first speech?
A   a feeling of optimism whenever she goes to a hotel ☐
B   hotels whose appearances are deceptive ☐
C   a desire on her part to find things wrong with hotels ☐
D   the influence that readers' letters have had on her ☐
E   a reference to highly critical reviews of hotels she has written ☐
F   readers' own opinions of hotels she has reviewed ☐
G   a comment on how enjoyable her critical reviews of hotels are ☐
H   a comment about hotels she approves of in her reviews ☐

Question 17 *Stop the recording when Paddy says 'have become friends'.*
Which of the following does Paddy refer to in her second speech?

A   hotel-keepers who are aware of reasons why their hotels deserve criticism   ☐

B   circumstances in which she does not feel good about criticising a hotel   ☐

C   hotel-keepers who would prefer to be in a different line of work   ☐

D   hotel-keepers she thinks would make excellent performers   ☐

E   the kind of hotel-keepers most likely to have a sense of humour   ☐

F   the reaction of hotel-keepers when she gives their hotels bad reviews   ☐

G   hotel-keepers who she thinks disguise their true feelings about her reviews   ☐

H   how strange it is that she has become friends with certain hotel-keepers   ☐

Question 18 *Stop the recording when Paddy says 'behind-the-scenes stories'.*
Which of the following does Paddy mention in her third speech?

A   realising that some details in her original reviews were inaccurate   ☐

B   the fact that she has enjoyed getting into contact with hotel owners   ☐

C   the reason why she sometimes pretends to be someone else   ☐

D   occasions when she has regretted pretending to be someone else   ☐

E   hotel owners protesting about the reviews she wrote about their hotels   ☐

F   asking hotel owners whether their hotels have got better since her review   ☐

G   changing her mind about whether some hotels were really as bad as she said   ☐

H   hotel owners who have been pleased to give her further information   ☐

Question 19 *Stop the recording when Paddy says 'the last thing that I want'.*
Which of the following does Paddy mention concerning the hotel owner in her fourth speech?

A   why he did not want his hotel to be included in her book   ☐

B   a particular comment she had made that he strongly disagreed with   ☐

C   his reluctance to discuss her review of his hotel in detail   ☐

D   why his hotel had originally been included in the book but then removed   ☐

E   occasions when people have told him that Paddy's reviews were wrong   ☐

F   a comment he made about the effect that her reviews have on people   ☐

G   his belief that she only likes hotels where she is treated as important   ☐

H   a belief he has about what she likes about hotels that is not true   ☐

Question 20 *Stop the recording at the end of the interview.*
Which of the following does Paddy refer to concerning the hotel owner in her final speech?

A   people wanting to know what Paddy looked like   ☐

B   details he gave that would enable hotels to know when she was visiting them   ☐

C   his opinion of the way she looked   ☐

D   people telling him that his description of Paddy was inaccurate   ☐

E   his realisation that appearing in the book would be free   ☐

F   his confusion as to the purpose of her book   ☐

G   the possibility that he found her description of him flattering   ☐

H   a comment he made on her description of him   ☐

Now check your answers to these exercises. When you have done so, listen again to Part 3 of the test and decide whether you wish to change any of the answers you gave. Then check your answers to Part 3 of the test.

PART 4

You will hear five short extracts in which people are talking about leisure activities they take part in. You will hear the recording twice. While you listen, you must complete both tasks.

TASK ONE

For questions 21–25, choose from the list (A–H) what the leisure activity involves for the speaker.

A   organising events

B   raising money

C   travelling to many places

D   performing

E   attending regular meetings

F   spending significant sums of money

G   doing a course

H   spending a lot of time

Speaker 1	21
Speaker 2	22
Speaker 3	23
Speaker 4	24
Speaker 5	25

TASK TWO

For questions 26–30, choose from the list (A–H) what each speaker particularly enjoys about the leisure activity.

A   returning to a previous interest

B   being better at something than other people

C   being part of a group

D   taking part in something useful

E   doing something that contrasts with work

F   acquiring a skill

G   receiving praise from others

H   meeting a variety of new people

Speaker 1	26
Speaker 2	27
Speaker 3	28
Speaker 4	29
Speaker 5	30

Stop the recording when you hear 'That's the end of Part 4'.

In the exam you will have five minutes at the end of the test to copy your answers onto a separate answer sheet.

Now check your answers to Part 4 of the test.

PAPER 4 SPEAKING 16 minutes

PART 1 (2 minutes)   GENERAL AND SOCIAL

Questions that may be addressed to either candidate:

- Describe your journey here today.

- What do you like/dislike about a journey you regularly take?

- Describe a typical day for you.

- What do you like most about the routines in your life?

- What do you like least about the routines in your life?

- What is the employment situation like where you live?

- Do you think it is likely to change in the future?

- Has it changed in comparison with the past?

- What would make/has made you move away from the place you come from?

- Is it common for people to leave the place you come from?

PART 2 (4 minutes)   HEALTH AND EXERCISE

Discussion between candidates:

Look at pictures A and B on page 135 and discuss how common these scenes are among people of different ages in your country.

(1 minute)

Now look at all of the pictures on pages 135 and 136.

Imagine that you are involved in producing a leaflet to promote good health. These pictures are being considered for the front of the leaflet.

Discuss the different aspects of health and exercise shown in the pictures. Then decide which picture would be the most effective for the front of the leaflet.

(3 minutes)

PART 3 (10 minutes)   **RULES AND REGULATIONS**

In Part 3 each candidate is given a card and talks alone for two minutes about the topic on the card. After each candidate has spoken, the other candidate is asked a question and the candidate who spoke alone is invited to respond (1 minute).

Prompt Card (a)   *(Given to Candidate A, and a copy to Candidate B)*

In what ways is it important to have rules and regulations?

* order rather than chaos in society

* children/school

* crime and punishment

One of the following questions for Candidate B:

* Are you someone who is happy to conform or are you rebellious?

* Is there a rule or law that you find particularly ridiculous?

* Have you ever broken the rules when playing a game or sport? What happened as a result?

One of the following questions for Candidate A:

* What do you think?

* Do you agree?

* How about you?

Prompt Card (b)   *(Given to Candidate B, and a copy to Candidate A)*

What are the most important rules of personal behaviour?

* politeness/rudeness

* honesty/dishonesty

* being reliable/unreliable

One of the following questions for Candidate A:

* Describe an occasion when you did not act according to your own rules of behaviour. What happened as a result?

* Describe someone whose general behaviour you particularly disapprove of.

* What kind of bad behaviour particularly annoys you?

One of the following questions for Candidate B:

* What do you think?

* Do you agree?

* How about you?

Part 3 finishes with a discussion between the two candidates and the examiner on the general topic (4 minutes).

General questions for both candidates on the topic of rules and regulations:

* Which laws are the most commonly broken ones in your society?

* What is the common attitude towards the law and order authorities in your society?

* If you could introduce one rule or law, what would it be?

* Are ideas about personal behaviour changing in your society?

* Do young people in general in your society behave in a conventional way?

* What rules of behaviour in your society do/would foreigners find it hard to conform to?

DESCRIBING MOVEMENT

In the Speaking paper, you may need to describe movements, perhaps of people in the pictures. To check or add to your vocabulary on that subject, look at the list of verbs below and put them into the categories given. Then note down the precise meaning of each one (you may need to consult a dictionary) and try to think of sentences in which you could use them.

amble	limp	shove	tear
chuck	nudge	shudder	thump
dash	poke	shuffle	toss
dig	prod	slap	totter
fling	punch	sling	tremble
hobble	quiver	sprint	trot
hop	rock	stagger	wander
hurl	shiver	stroll	whack

Walk/Run	Shake	Hit	Throw

Now check your answers to this exercise.

DESCRIBING VOCAL SOUNDS

You may need to describe the sounds that people make, perhaps the sounds you think people in the pictures are making. To check or add to your vocabulary on that subject, look at the list of verbs below and put them into the categories given. Then note down the precise meaning of each one (you may need to consult a dictionary) and try to think of sentences in which you could use them.

babble	groan	murmur	wail
bellow	grumble	mutter	weep
cackle	holler	natter	whimper
chatter	howl	roar	whine
chuckle	jabber	shriek	whinge
drone	jeer	snigger	whisper
gibber	moan	sob	whoop
giggle	mumble	titter	yell

Shout	Speak/Talk	Laugh	Sound unhappy / Complain

Now check your answers to this exercise.

TOPIC VOCABULARY

In Part 3 in this test, you are required to talk about the topic of rules and regulations. To check or add to your vocabulary on this subject, look at the words and phrases below. Group them together under the headings given. Then decide whether they are verbs, adjectives or nouns and label them appropriately. Then note down the precise meaning of each one (you may need to consult a dictionary) and try to think of sentences in which you could use them.

abide by	contravene	insubordinate	rebel
adhere to	defy	middle-of-the-road	sin
binding	dissent	naughty	stick-in-the-mud
breach	eccentric	observe	toe the line
cheeky	enforce	offbeat	unorthodox
comply	etiquette	petty	unruly
conform	idiosyncratic	protocol	
conservative	infringe	reactionary	

Obeying rules	Not obeying rules	Conventional	Unconventional

Now complete this table for forming words connected with this subject.

Verb	Adjective	Noun	Adverb	Opposites
1 behave	–		–	(verb) (noun)
2 conform	–	(noun) (person)	–	(person)
3 –	cheeky			–
4 defy				–
5 obey				(verb) (adj) (noun) (adv)
6 rebel		(noun) (person)		–

Now check your answers to these exercises.

TEST FOUR

PAPER 1 READING AND USE OF ENGLISH 1 hour 30 minutes

PART 1

For questions 1–8, read the text below and decide which answer (A, B, C or D) best fits each gap.

In the exam you will mark your answers on a separate answer sheet.

There is an example at the beginning (0).

0   **A** understatement   **B** misinformation   **C** incomprehension   **D** distortion

0	A	B	C	D
	▬	▭	▭	▭

The Rejected Novel

'You've not had much luck with the book, I hear.'

That had to be the (0) ......A........ of the year. My novel had been rejected four times (1) .... far. I've no doubt that behind my (2) .... the family were having a good snigger. Rhona of course had been the loyal (3) .... , though I admit that her piteous expressions when the thing limped home battered by franking stamps were harder to (4) .... than her sister's outright sarcasm: 'Has your boomerang got back yet, Patton?' she'd enquire, while her husband Jack would give the knife an extra twist by asking if I'd managed to sell any of my daubs. Which meant that he presumed I'd (5) .... my job on the railways to pursue a painting career. Maybe I should have. The manuscript had begun to show bruises from its days, weeks and months (6) .... in the 'slush pile' of various publishing firms. Actual criticism of the novel by its rejectors was very (7) .... on the ground, although the consensus of opinion seemed to indicate that its main weakness (8) .... in its apparent 'lack of plot'.

1	**A** yet	**B** thus	**C** hence	**D** by
2	**A** back	**B** head	**C** ears	**D** face
3	**A** omission	**B** exclusion	**C** difference	**D** exception
4	**A** bear	**B** defy	**C** cope	**D** resist
5	**A** broken off	**B** wound up	**C** pulled out	**D** packed in
6	**A** stationed	**B** encased	**C** buried	**D** consigned
7	**A** light	**B** shallow	**C** thin	**D** scant
8	**A** stood	**B** revolved	**C** lay	**D** centred

Now check your answers to Part 1 of the test.

PART 2

*For questions **9–16**, read the text below and think of the word which best fits each space. Use only **one** word in each space. There is an example at the beginning (**0**).*

In the exam you will write your answers in CAPITAL LETTERS on a separate answer sheet.

Example: **0**   OF

The Slow Arrival of the Wheel

It is nearly impossible in our post-industrial society to conceive (**0**) .... a world without wheels.

From clocks to huge machinery and from cars to computer discs, (**9**) .... employs cogs, wheels

or other types of cylindrical components that spin on an axis. Yet the wheel took a relatively long time

to be invented and several civilisations reached a relatively high level of technological sophistication

(**10**) .... it. The most likely explanation is (**11**) .... neither terrain nor climate suited the

wheel. Until 10,000 BC, much of the world was (**12**) .... the grip of the last vestiges of the Ice

Age. (**13**) .... was not under ice sheet was covered by desert, jungle or bog – conditions obviously

unsuited for something like the wheel.

Most experts agree that the wheel evolved (**14**) .... the fact that Neolithic man was familiar

with moving heavy objects (**15**) .... putting a roller, such as a tree trunk, under the load.

(**16**) .... techniques were used to move the huge stone blocks to build the pyramids around

2980 BC.

Now check your answers to Part 2 of the test.

PART 3

For questions 17–24, read the text below. Use the word given in capitals at the end of some of the lines to form a word that fits in the space in the same line. There is an example at the beginning (0).

In the exam you will write your answers in CAPITAL LETTERS on a separate answer sheet.

Example: **0** *HEADLINES*

The Word 'Bogus'

For years 'bogus' was a word the British read in newspaper **(0)** HEADLINES **LINE**

but tended not to say. Its popularity among the teenagers of America changed that,

although they didn't use it with its original meaning. It came from the Wild West.

Its first appearance in print, in 1827, was in the *Telegraph* of Painesville, Ohio, where

it meant a machine for making **(17)** .... of coins. Soon, those 'boguses' were **FORGE**

turning out 'bogus money' and the word had **(18)** .... a change from noun to **GO**

adjective.

By the end of the 19th century, it was well-established in Britain, applied to anything

false, spurious or intentionally **(19)** .... But the computer scientists of 1960s **LEAD**

America, to whom we owe so much **(20)** .... innovation, redefined it to mean **LANGUAGE**

'non-functional', 'useless', or 'unbelievable', especially in relation to calculations and

engineering ideas. This was followed by its **(21)** .... among Princeton **EMERGE**

and Yale graduates in the East Coast computer community. But it was the **(22)** .... **ADOPT**

of the word by American teenagers generally, who used it to mean simply 'bad', that

led to it being widely used by their counterparts in Britain.

(23) .... , 'bogus' is one of only about 1,300 English words for which no **INTEREST**

sensible origin has emerged. The *Oxford English Dictionary* suggests a connection with

a New England word, 'tantrobogus', meaning the devil. A rival US account sees it as

a **(24)** .... of the name of a forger, called Borghese or Borges. **CORRUPT**

Now check your answers to Part 3 of the test.

PART 4

*For questions 25–30, complete the second sentence so that it has a similar meaning to the first sentence, using the word given. **Do not change the word given.** You must use between **three** and **eight** words, including the word given.*

Here is an example (0).

0   Robert was offended when he was left out of the team.

exception

Robert .... left out of the team.

0	took exception to being

*In the exam you will write **only** the missing words on a separate answer sheet.*

---

25 The film was so controversial that it was banned in several parts of the world.

caused

Such was .... the film that it was banned in several parts of the world.

26 He had no idea what was going to happen to him when he walked into that room.

store

Little .... him when he walked into that room.

27 You shouldn't let trivial matters worry you so much.

prey

You shouldn't let trivial matters .... extent.

28 He became famous but it cost him his privacy.

expense

His rise .... of his privacy.

29 I helped Ray, with the result that his business became successful.

favour

I .... which his business became successful.

30 I had to wait for the manager for almost an hour before he would see me.

best

The manager kept .... an hour before he would see me.

Before you check your answers to Part 4 of the test, go on to pages 110–111.

WHAT'S TESTED

Part 4 of the Reading and Use of English paper focuses on a mixture of grammar and vocabulary. The answer you write is divided into two distinct parts, each of which is worth one mark. This means that there are really two 'pieces of language' to produce for each answer. In any question, either of the 'pieces' may involve:

- the transformation of one grammatical structure into another, or

- the production of a lexical phrase, such as a fixed phrase, an idiom, a collocation, a phrasal verb, a linking phrase or a phrase with the correct complementation (for explanations of these terms, see the Further Practice and Guidance page for Test 1, Paper 1, Part 1 on page 9, or

- changing a word from one part of speech to another, such as forming a noun from a given adjective.

TIPS

- Remember that you cannot change the form of the word given to you for inclusion in your answer.

- Remember not to exceed the limit of eight words in your answer, or to use fewer than three.

- Remember to copy correctly any words in the sentence you are given which do not change in the answer – carelessness of that kind can unnecessarily cost you a mark.

- Always attempt a complete answer to each question – even if you are unsure that your whole answer is correct, it is possible that one of the two parts will be.

- Always read the words on both sides of the gap carefully, as these provide you with vital information about the nature of the correct answer.

Look at each of the questions in the test again and decide which of the choices A–E in each exercise can correctly fill the first part (1) and then the second part (2) of the gap. More than one of the choices may be correct in each case.

When you have done these exercises, you may wish to change some of your answers to the test.

Question 25	**Question 26**
1	**1**
A caused	**A** he knew
B there caused a	**B** did he know
C the	**C** knew he
D it caused to be	**D** idea he had
E a	**E** did he realise
2	**2**
A the controversy by	**A** what lay in store for
B controversy caused by	**B** what was the store for
C controversially of	**C** what set store by
D controversial for	**D** what the store was for
E controversy by	**E** what was in store for

Question 27

1
A prey on your mind
B be prey to you
C cause you prey
D fall prey to you
E prey on you

2
A to such an
B to great
C by that
D at so great an
E to such a great

Question 28

1
A up in fame
B up to getting fame
C to the fame
D to fame
E in fame

2
A came at the expense
B cost an expense
C meant the expense
D led to expense
E was at the expense

Question 29

1
A did Ray a favour,
B was in Ray's favour,
C found favour with Ray,
D made a favour to Ray,
E did a favour for Ray,

2
A the result of
B the result being
C as a result of
D resulting in
E with the result

Question 30

1
A me that I wait
B the wait on
C me waiting
D me on waiting
E up my waiting

2
A to the best of
B for at best
C at the best of times
D with the best of
E for the best part of

Now check your answers to these exercises and to Part 4 of the test.

PART 5

You are going to read an extract from a book about the history of the US.

For questions 31–36, choose the answer (A, B, C or D) which you think fits best according to the text.

In the exam you will mark your answers on a separate answer sheet.

Progressives in the US

The United States had reached a point, in the closing years of the 19th century, when radical improvements in its political, social and economic arrangements were so plainly necessary that they were actually attempted, and therefore may be called inevitable. Women and men, young and middle-aged, rich, poor and in-between, West, South and North, all acknowledged the necessity and had some hand in shaping the improvements. It was an epoch very much to the American taste, for it seemed a proof that faith in progress, and particularly in the potential for progress in America was justified. The word 'progressive' had long been a favourite in common speech; now it became attached to a political party, a movement, an era. It remains a curiously empty word, but historians will never be able to do without it. And after all due reservations have been made, it would be churlish to deny that the United States did in many respects move forward during this period, did begin to tackle a good many serious problems intelligently. It is a moderately encouraging story.

Big business made itself felt at every stage in the progressive story, and not by any means as a purely reactionary force. All the same, it would be a mistake to suppose that business, however profoundly it had shaped and now coloured the day-to-day operations of American life, was the key to progressivism. Nor could the industrial working class, however active, muster the power necessary to dominate the epoch. That privilege belonged to the new middle class.

This class had emerged as, numerically, the chief beneficiary of the great transformation of American society. America's rapid development under the impact of industrialism and urbanisation implied an equally rapidly developing need for professional services. The need for a new order was generally felt, and implied the recruitment and training of new men, and new women, to administer it. Society was now rich enough to pay for their services. Hence in the last decades of the 19th century there was a mushroom growth among the professions. Doctors and lawyers, of course; but also engineers, dentists, professors, journalists, social workers, architects. This was the age of the expert; he was given a free hand, such as he has seldom enjoyed since. Each new technical marvel – the telephone, the phonograph, the motor-car, the aeroplane – increased the faith that there was a sound technical answer to every problem, even to the problem of government. When a devastating hurricane and flood wrecked the port of Galveston, Texas, in 1901, the local businessmen proclaimed the regular authorities incompetent to handle the task of reconstruction and handed the city's government over to a commission of experts – a pattern that was to be widely followed in the next few years.

This may stand very well for what was happening generally. The new class, conscious of its power and numbers, was anxious to get hold of American society and remake it according to plan. All round were problems that needed solving – crime, disease, bad housing, political corruption – and the new class thought it knew what to do about them. Just as the experts themselves had taken advantage of a society open to the rise of the talented, so they wanted their disadvantaged fellow-citizens to rise also. And this democratic individualistic ideology made it seem perfectly legitimate to bid for political power, that is, for votes: to go down into that arena was simply to carry out one's civic duty. Motives did not need to be examined too closely, since they were self-evidently virtuous. What was new, and important at least to the experts, was the tool-kit they brought to their tasks: their improved spanners, so to speak. The new middle class set out to apply their spanners to such various contraptions as the state and city machines of the old political parties, and the new urban wastelands.

Behind the zeal of these technocrats lay an older tradition, betrayed in the word they used to describe the philanthropic centres they established in the slums, 'settlements': to them the cities were wildernesses, the inhabitants alien savages and the new settlers were bringers both of superior techniques and superior ideas, like the settlers of old. It is thus possible to see in the very approach of these progressives certain limitations, a certain inexperience, which were likely to impede their quest. They were mostly of old American stock, brought up on the old pieties, which their new expertise only veneered. The progressives were too conservative in their instincts, too parochial in their outlook, ever to propose, let alone carry out, fundamental changes in the American system.

31 What does the writer say about the word 'progressive' in the first paragraph?
  A   It should only be used with regard to this period in the US.
  B   No other word has been generally adopted to describe this period in the US.
  C   It was sometimes used inappropriately during this period in the US.
  D   No other word could have united diverse people during this period in the US.

32 What does the writer say about big business during this period?
  A   It ensured that the industrial working class was lacking in power.
  B   It paid too little attention to the importance of the new middle class.
  C   It was beginning to have too great an impact on everyday life in the US.
  D   It played a significant part in the development of progressivism.

33 The writer says that the 'mushroom growth' among the professions
  A   was expected to be only a short-term phenomenon.
  B   resulted from a desire among professionals for greater freedom.
  C   was a natural consequence of other changes at the time.
  D   resulted from fears among Americans about changes in their society.

34 The writer uses events in Galveston to illustrate
  A   the high regard in which specialists were held during that period.
  B   problems which had never been dealt with satisfactorily before.
  C   the speed at which solutions were found during that period.
  D   disagreements caused by the desire for technical solutions.

35 The writer says that when members of the new class tried to get political power,
  A   they sometimes underestimated the social problems of the time.
  B   people made assumptions about their reasons for doing so.
  C   they tended to overestimate the potential of their fellow citizens.
  D   people had realistic expectations of what they could achieve.

36 According to the writer, the use of the word 'settlements' reveals
  A   the insincerity of some of the progressives concerning social problems.
  B   the misunderstandings behind some of the progressives' beliefs.
  C   the confusion that surrounded the progressives' approach to problems.
  D   the similarities between the progressives and previous generations.

Now check your answers to Part 5 of the test.

PART 6

You are going to read a newspaper article. Seven paragraphs have been removed from the extract. Choose from the paragraphs A–H the one which fits each gap (37–43). There is one extra paragraph which you do not need to use.

In the exam you will mark your answers on a separate answer sheet.

Rainmaker with his Head in the Clouds

Critics dismissed Graeme Mather's attempts to make clouds rain. But now recent experiments appear to have vindicated him. Anjana Ahuya reports.

Dr Graeme Mather lived his life with his head in the clouds, as a documentary film to be shown this week shows. Against the advice of almost everybody else in the meteorological community, the Canadian scientist devoted his professional life to trying to make clouds rain.

37	h

Before Dr Mather became involved, the science of weather modification had already claimed many reputations. The idea that clouds could be manipulated first circulated in the 1940s, and efforts gathered pace soon after the Second World War.

38	G

However, the entire discipline fell into disrepute when commercial companies hijacked the idea, took it around the world, and then failed to deliver on their promises. Cloud-seeding, as the process was known, became the preserve of crackpots and charlatans.

39	A

Scientists theorised that if they could inject the cloud with similarly shaped crystals, these imposter crystals would also act as frames around which droplets would clump. The cloud would then be tricked into raining. Silver iodide, whose crystals resemble those of ice, seemed the best bet. Sadly, none of the experiments, including Dr Mather's, which had been going for more than five years, seemed to work. Dr Mather was about to admit defeat when serendipity intervened.

40	C

Dr Mather was convinced that something that the place was spewing into the atmosphere was encouraging the downpour. Subsequent experiments confirmed that hygroscopic salts pouring into the sky from there were responsible. Hydroscopic salts attract water – once in the atmosphere, the particles act as magnets around which raindrops can form.

41	I

He was wary; Dr Mather was known to be a smooth-talking salesman. 'He was charming and charismatic, and many scientists don't trust that,' he says. 'He was also not well-published because he had been working in the commercial sector. Overall, he was regarded as a maverick. On that occasion, he presented results that I was convinced were impossible. Yet the statistical evidence was overwhelming, which I couldn't understand.'

42	e

'If those findings can be reproduced there, it will be the most exciting thing to have happened in the field for 20 years. It will be remarkable because some of the results are not scientifically explainable.' He adds, however, that scientists must exercise caution because cloud-seeding is still mired in controversy. He also points out that, with water being such a precious resource, success will push the research into the political arena.

43	B

Dr Cooper says: 'With the paper mill, he saw something that other people wouldn't have seen. I am still uncomfortable with his idea because it throws up major puzzles in cloud physics. But if Dr Mather was right, it will demonstrate that humans can change clouds in ways that were once thought impossible.'

A Dr Mather refused to be daunted by this image. After all, the principle seemed perfectly plausible. Water droplets are swept up to the top of the clouds on updrafts, where they become supercooled (i.e., although the temperature is below freezing, the water remains liquid). When a supercooled droplet collides with an ice crystal, it freezes on contact and sticks. Successive collisions cause each ice crystal to accumulate more water droplets; the crystals grow until they become too heavy to remain suspended in the atmosphere. As the crystals fall through the cloud, they become raindrops. The ice crystals therefore act as frames to 'grow' raindrops.

B Dr Mather unfortunately will not be involved in the debate about such matters. He died aged 63, shortly before the documentary was completed. It will ensure that this smooth-talking maverick is given the recognition he deserves.

C He and a colleague decided to collect a last batch of data when they flew into a tiny but ferocious storm. That storm, Dr Mather says in the film, changed his life. Huge droplets were spattering on the tiny plane's windscreen. No such storm had been forecast. Back on the ground, they discovered the storm was located directly above a paper mill.

D A trial in Mexico has been running for two years, and the signs are promising. 'We were sufficiently encouraged in the first year to continue the seeding research. But the results are preliminary, because we have only a very small sample of clouds at the moment. We need to work over two more summers to reach a proper conclusion.'

Now check your answers to Part 6 of the test.

E He arranged to fly to South Africa 'with the full intention of explaining what was wrong with the experiment'. Instead, he came back convinced that Dr Mather was on to something. He is now running two experiments, one in Arizona and one in northern Mexico to try to verify the South African results. The experiments use potassium chloride, which is similar to table salt (sodium chloride) and, it is claimed, non-polluting.

F The scientific community remained sniffy in the face of this apparent proof. Foremost among the sceptics was Dr William Cooper, of the United States National Centre for Atmospheric Research (NCAR). Dr Cooper, regarded as one of the world's finest cloud scientists, saw Dr Mather present his astonishing claims at a cloud physics conference in Montreal.

G They involved weather experts firing rockets into clouds to stop them producing hail, which damages crops. The clouds, it was hoped, would dissolve into a harmless shower.

H The desire to do so led him to set up a project in South Africa, which was ultimately to convince him that it was possible. As the programme reveals, experiments around the world appear to prove his faith was justified.

PART 7

*You are going to read an extract from an article about the attitudes of parents towards their children. For questions **44–53**, choose from the sections (**A–F**). The sections may be chosen more than once.*

In the exam you will mark your answers on a separate answer sheet.

In which section are the following mentioned?

a general pattern that emerges from the majority of investigations into favouritism   44 ...B...

the need for parents to be conscious of the way they treat each of their children   45 ...F...

a theory as to why a certain child may be the subject of favouritism   46 ...C...

the extent to which children focus on their parents' attitude towards them   47 ...F...

a feeling that the study of favouritism may not be worthwhile   48 ...D...

evidence of parents' greater tolerance for a certain child   49 ...C...

the large variety of reasons affecting parents' attitudes towards their children   50 ...E...

a factor that could affect the reliability of research into favouritism   51 ...A...

distrust of what some parents say about favouritism in research   52 ...A...

how difficult it is for parents to acknowledge favouritism   53 ...F...

Now check your answers to Part 7 of the test.

Parental Favouritism

A

The American science writer Jeffery Kluger has just published a book in which he argues that, whether we admit it or not, parental favouritism is hard-wired into the human psyche. 'It is my belief that 95% of the parents in the world have a favourite child, and the other 5% are lying,' he declares in *The Sibling Effect: What the Bonds Among Brothers and Sisters Reveal About Us*. That particular figure may be guesswork, but there is plenty of evidence that would seem to back him up. Kluger cites a Californian study of 384 families, who were visited three times a year and videotaped as they 'worked through conflicts'. The study found that 65% of mothers and 70% of fathers exhibited a preference for one child. And those numbers are almost certainly under-representative, since people behave less naturally when they are being watched.

B

Every couple of years, in fact, a new report comes out purporting to lift the lid on parental favouritism. Most often – though by no means always – older siblings seem to come out on top. In 2009 two British professors, David Lawson and Ruth Mace, published a study of 14,000 families in the Bristol area. They found that each successive sibling received 'markedly' less care and attention from their parents than their predecessors. Older siblings were even fed better, as a result of which they were likely to be up to three centimetres taller than their younger siblings. They also had higher IQs, probably because they had the benefit of their parents' undivided attention for the first part of their lives.

C

Anthropologists and evolutionary psychologists argue that there is a sound logic to this. A firstborn automatically absorbs a huge amount of parental time and energy; and once you've invested that much in one child, you might as well keep going – if only to protect the investment. However, a survey of 1,803 British parents with two children claimed to show that younger siblings were given preferential treatment 59% of the time. Parents were more likely to side with a younger child in an argument, lavish them with affection and let them have their own way.

D

It's at this point, I must admit, that I start to feel a bit impatient with the experts. A science that can absorb so many contradictory variables hardly seems like science at all. And if, as the experts all seem to agree, favouritism is so common as to be almost universal, doesn't that make it just – well, normal? Undoubtedly there are families where favouritism is blatant and sustained enough to be seriously destructive. But in most cases, surely, it does not merit such pathologising.

E

When I solicited confessions of favouritism from my fellow parents, I had no luck at all. Lots of people admitted to treating their children differently at different times, according to their needs (and how annoying they're being). But not one felt this reflected any fundamental preference. It is simply part of the warp and weft of family life. The truth is that favouritism is an awfully blunt word for such a complicated subject. How we treat our children is affected by any number of shifting, interlacing factors: birth order, gender, changes in circumstances, our own childhood experiences. Then, too, some characters just hit it off better than others.

F

'I think most of us have short-term favourites, depending on who's going through a "phase",' says Suzanne, a mother of four. 'You can feel immense affection for one child on a Tuesday who then drives you to distraction on Wednesday. But the underlying love is just as intense for all of them. I think long-term favouritism is bookselling nonsense in the majority of cases.' In an anonymous online survey for the website Mumsnet, 16% of mothers admitted to having a favourite child. That's quite a lot – it's a big deal to admit to such parental malpractice, if only to yourself – but it hardly amounts to the psychological pandemic of Kluger's imaginings. On the other hand, things do tend to look different from a child's perspective. Even in the happiest families, siblings instinctively compete for their parents' love. Scrupulous emotional accountants, they are constantly totting up incidents of perceived unfairness. So it makes sense for parents, too, to keep a watchful eye on their own behaviour.

PAPER 2 WRITING 1 hour 30 minutes

PART 1

Read the two texts below.

Write an essay summarising and evaluating the key points from both texts. Use your own words throughout as far as possible, and include your own ideas in your answer.

*Write your answer in **240–280 words**.*

1

Popular Culture and the Profit Motive

Popular culture in industrial societies is contradictory to its core. On the one hand it is industrialised – its commodities produced and distributed by a profit-motivated industry that follows only its own economic interests. But on the other hand, it is of the people, and the people's interests are not those of the industry – as is evidenced by the number of films, records and other products that the people make into expensive failures. To be incorporated into popular culture, a commodity must also bear the interests of the people.

How is Popular Culture Created?

Culture is a living, active process: it can be developed only from within, it cannot be imposed from without or above. A homogeneous, externally produced culture cannot be sold ready-made to the masses: culture simply does not work like that. Nor do the people behave or live like the masses, an aggregation of alienated, one-dimensional persons whose only relationship to the system that enslaves them is one of unwitting dupes. Popular culture is made by the people, not produced by the culture industry. All the culture industries can do is produce a repertoire of cultural resources for the various formations of the people to use or reject in the ongoing process of producing their popular culture.

Write your **essay**.

When you have written your answer, assess it in accordance with the mark scheme.

PART 2

Write an answer to **one** *of the questions* **2–5** *in this part. Write your answer in* **280–320** *words in an appropriate style.*

---

2   You work for a local newspaper, which is considering launching a weekly magazine supplement that would be included in the newspaper. You have been asked to conduct a survey of local people to find out what the supplement should contain. Write a report detailing the findings of the survey and what conclusions can be drawn from it.

Write your **report**.

3   A letter from a reader has recently been published in a newspaper you read, complaining that the newspaper is always full of bad news and never highlights the positive aspects of life. The newspaper has invited readers to write an article entitled *Reasons To Be Cheerful*. Write an article under that title, listing what you believe to be the good things in life, both for you personally and for people in general and giving your reasons for choosing them.

Write your **article**.

4   You have recently visited a city or area as a tourist and found that there are a number of aspects of your visit which you wish to comment on. Write a letter to the head of the tourist office for that area, describing the positive and/or negative aspects of your visit and making any suggestions you feel appropriate.

Write your **letter**. Do not write any postal addresses.

5   Set book questions – a choice from **(a)** or **(b)**.

In the exam you may choose to answer a question on one of the two set books.

Before you write your answer, go on to pages 120–121.

PART 2

For information on What's Tested and Tips see page 59.

To plan your answer for question 2 in Part 2, complete the following notes.

1   Note down as briefly as possible the **topic** of your report.

    ....

2   List as briefly as possible the following:

    • the **main points** in the question which you will have to cover in your report

    • the **comments and opinions** you intend to give with regard to those points

    • any **examples** you wish to give in support or to illustrate these comments/opinions

Main point	Comments/Opinions	Example
Main point	Comments/Opinions	Example
Main point	Comments/Opinions	Example

3   List briefly any additional points you wish to make, which are not mentioned in the question but which you think are relevant to the topic. You may not wish to include any additional points.

Additional point	Comments/Opinions	Example
Additional point	Comments/Opinions	Example

4   Now note briefly how your report will be organised by deciding what each part of it will contain. You may not wish to have as many paragraphs as are listed below.

Opening
Section 1
Section 2
Section 3
Section 4
Section 5
Section 6
Ending

5   Now use these notes to write your report.

When you have written your answer, assess it in accordance with the mark scheme.

SAMPLE ANSWER

Now read this sample answer for question *3* in Part 2 and answer the questions that follow it.

REPORT – WEEKLY MAGAZINE SUPPLEMENT

Research

I prepared a short questionnaire, in which people were asked whether they would be interested in reading a weekly magazine supplement and, if so, what they thought it should include. I listed various categories for sections and articles, and included 'other' for suggestions people might have that I hadn't included. I then spent a week asking people in the streets in the city centre for their views and completing the questionnaires with them. I got the views of 220 people of all ages.

Findings

In general, the people I spoke to were keen on the idea of the supplement, although 15 people said they couldn't see the point and wouldn't have enough time to read one. The idea of a sports section was the most popular, and about 60% of the people I spoke to thought this should have articles about the local clubs and interviews with the players – at the moment, the newspaper only has short match reports. Another popular idea was to have a section for hobbies, with details of clubs that people can join to do them – about 50% liked that idea. Also, about 40% said they would like longer reviews of films, plays and books because the ones in the paper are usually very short. Six people suggested that it would be a good idea to have a restaurant review column, which was not included in my questionnaire. The idea of having a weekly recipe was also quite popular. The most unpopular idea was to include articles about local politics – 80% of the people I spoke to said they didn't want this – and about 70% said they didn't want articles on environmental issues or financial matters.

Conclusions

It would appear that there is enough enthusiasm for the supplement to make it worth doing. However, my survey indicates that people would prefer it to be entertaining and enjoyable rather than having anything serious in it. It should concentrate on people's interests rather than more serious issues and clearly sports, hobbies and reviews should be covered in it.

Content
Are all the main points mentioned in the question covered? Where are these points covered? If any are not covered, which are missing? Are any additional points included? If so, what are they, and are they relevant?

Communicative achievement
Are the style and tone of the report appropriate? How would you describe them? Why are they appropriate or inappropriate? Is the format suitable for a report of this kind? If so, why? If not, why not?

Do you feel that someone reading this report would be clear throughout it what the writer is describing and what their views are? If so, summarise the writer's report briefly. If not, say what you feel is unclear in the report.

Organisation
Is the report well-organised in terms of being divided into sections appropriately? Describe briefly the content of each section. Does the report flow well in terms of the linking of points and ideas within sections and between sections? Give examples of places where the linking is good. If there are occasions when the linking is inadequate or inappropriate, suggest improvements.

Language
Is there a wide range of vocabulary and grammatical structures? If so, give examples. If there are occasions when the vocabulary or grammar is too simple, suggest alternatives.

Are there any mistakes in the use of vocabulary or grammar? Correct any that you find.

Now check your assessment of this sample answer with the assessment.

PAPER 3 LISTENING approximately 40 minutes

PART 1

You will hear three different extracts.

For questions 1–6, choose the answer (A, B or C) which fits best according to what you hear. There are two questions for each extract.

In the exam you will hear each extract twice.

Extract One

You hear a psychologist talking about confidence.

1   What does the speaker say about the word 'confidence'?
   A   Most dictionary definitions of it are inaccurate.
   B   It means a great deal more than simply 'self-assurance'.
   C   It is a hard word to define precisely.

2   What does the speaker say about having confidence?
   A   There is no one who doesn't wish to have it.
   B   It frequently changes into feeling superior.
   C   Some people are incapable of it.

Extract Two

You hear a critic talking about a new book.

3   The speaker says that Goldman's latest book contains
   A   views even more negative than those in his previous book.
   B   confusing comments on actors and directors.
   C   criticism that may be unnecessarily harsh.

4   The speaker believes that Goldman
   A   exaggerates the difficulties of his occupation.
   B   has an unfavourable opinion of his own occupation.
   C   is unaware of how much his work is admired.

Extract Three

You hear a musician talking about American music.

5   What does the speaker say about the James Brown records he mentions?
   A   They conveyed a sense of joy.
   B   They were surprise hits.
   C   They were totally unlike Brown's other records.

6   The speaker says that people growing up in Britain in the 1960s
   A   had only a limited view of what America was like.
   B   had the same view of America as Americans did.
   C   felt that American music was more varied than British music.

Stop the recording when you hear 'That's the end of Part 1'.
Now check your answers to Part 1 of the test.

PART 2

You will hear part of a radio programme about toys, in which the development of a famous toy called Meccano is described.

For questions 7–15, complete the sentences with a word or short phrase.

In the exam you will hear the piece twice.

Frank Hornby worked for a [7   ] .

He was inspired by a book called [8   ] .

The [9   ] he invented did not work properly.

He started to consider the idea of [10   ] parts.

He decided that the parts would need to have a [11   ] in them.

The first parts he made were from a big [12   ] .

The first object that was built with the new system was a [13   ] .

The first name given to the new toy was [14   ] .

Each Meccano set could be made bigger with the use of an [15   ] .

Stop the recording when you hear 'That's the end of Part 2'.

Now check your answers to Part 2 of the test.

PART 3

You will hear an interview with someone whose work is concerned with the design and marketing of products.

For questions 16–20 choose the answer (A, B, C or D) which fits best according to what you hear.

In the exam you will hear the piece twice.

16 David says that the session he has just conducted
    A was longer than most sessions he conducts.
    B illustrates his own beliefs about focus groups.
    C is an example of a new approach to visual planning.
    D concentrated as much on positive as negative attitudes to cleaning.

17 What did David know about cleaning products before the session?
    A Some people could not make up their minds which ones to buy.
    B Manufacturers were concerned about falling sales in them.
    C Some of them looked too dull to appeal to shoppers.
    D People felt that false claims were made about them.

18 One of the comments made during the session referred to
    A regarding the choice of a cleaning product as unimportant.
    B cleaning products all looking the same.
    C the deliberate misleading of shoppers.
    D buying a cleaning product because it is familiar.

19 David says that what the women produced when they were split into groups
    A did not focus on what cleaning products actually do.
    B presented contrasting images.
    C was not what they had expected to produce.
    D was similar to the presentation of other kinds of product.

20 David says that he has concluded from the session that
    A his firm's methods will need to change slightly.
    B he was right to question a certain assumption.
    C cleaning products do not fit into a general pattern.
    D what he had previously thought was not entirely correct.

Stop the recording when you hear 'That's the end of Part 3'.

Now check your answers to Part 3 of the test.

PART 4

You will hear five short extracts in which people are talking about their jobs.

You will hear the recording twice. While you listen, you must complete both tasks.

TASK ONE

*For questions **21–25**, choose from the list (**A–H**) what each speaker likes most about the job.*

A   the atmosphere

B   the challenge

C   the variety

D   the opportunities for promotion

E   the financial benefits

F   the responsibility

G   the lack of supervision

H   the training given

Speaker 1	21
Speaker 2	22
Speaker 3	23
Speaker 4	24
Speaker 5	25

TASK TWO

*For questions **26–30**, choose from the list (**A–H**) what each speaker dislikes about the job.*

A   the premises

B   staff turnover

C   the attitude of management

D   the hours

E   the inefficiency

F   the workload

G   dealing with customers

H   lack of job security

Speaker 1	26
Speaker 2	27
Speaker 3	28
Speaker 4	29
Speaker 5	30

Stop the recording when you hear 'That's the end of Part 4'.

In the exam you will have five minutes at the end of the test to copy your answers onto a separate answer sheet.

Before you check your answers to Part 4 of the test, go on to pages 126–127.

WHAT'S TESTED

Part 4 of the Listening paper tests your ability to understand what speakers say in five short recordings that are connected in terms of general topic, and to match each speaker with the correct choices from two lists of options in two tasks. Each set of options may focus on any of the things listed for Part 1 of the Listening paper: *detail, opinion/attitude, feeling, function, purpose, general gist, topic*, etc (see page 30).

TIPS

- Use the time given to read both tasks carefully before you listen to the recordings. This will show you what the focus of each task is and therefore what you need to identify when you listen to each speaker.

- You will need to concentrate hard in order to answer two questions about each speaker. What each speaker says will last for only approximately 30 seconds and you have to select two correct answers from two lists of eight options.

- Try to get as many answers as possible for both tasks the first time you listen. Use the second time for questions you could not answer the first time and for checking answers you gave the first time you listened.

- Don't choose an option simply because it contains a word or words that a speaker uses – this option may not be the correct answer.

- Speakers will say things that are connected with more than one of the options in each set – you must decide which option in each set exactly matches what a particular speaker says.

- What speakers say may not always follow the same order as the tasks. An answer for the second task may be given by a speaker before the answer for the first task.

The following exercises will help you to answer questions you were unable to answer in the test or to confirm answers that you gave. For each exercise, choose two correct answers.

Questions 21 and 26   *Listen to Speaker 1 again.*
Which of the following does he mention in connection with his job?

A   the interesting nature of his work
B   being treated badly by bosses
C   how likely he is to get a more senior position
D   customers being rude to him
E   how he acquired a certain skill
F   how high his salary is
G   the frequency of errors by others
H   having to do other people's work as well as his own

Questions 22 and 27   *Listen to Speaker 2 again.*
Which of the following does she mention in connection with her job?

A   good relationships with others
B   people leaving because they are upset
C   her own importance
D   not having to justify her actions to people senior to her
E   how often people do their jobs badly
F   problems with customers
G   having to work overtime
H   struggling to complete her work

Questions 23 and 28 *Listen to Speaker 3 again.*

Which of the following does he mention in connection with his job?

A good relationships between colleagues

B the nature of the work done

C how certain people rise to the top

D the behaviour of bosses towards employees

E arguments with customers

F people resigning from their jobs

G the possibility of being sacked for poor work

H the amount of work he has to do

Questions 24 and 29 *Listen to Speaker 4 again.*

Which of the following does she mention in connection with her job?

A receiving an increased salary

B a desire for a more senior role

C wanting to do demanding work

D not doing the same kind of work all the time

E having to work in different parts of the building

F incompetent colleagues

G having to adjust to new colleagues

H fear that she will be dismissed

Questions 25 and 30 *Listen to Speaker 5 again.*

Which of the following does he mention in connection with his job?

A the amount of freedom he has in his work

B the strict application of systems at his place of work

C problems dealing with the approach of managers

D the complex nature of the work he does

E the friendships formed between employees

F the physical surroundings

G how productivity could be increased

H how he feels about the salary he gets

Now check your answers to these exercises. When you have done so, listen again to Part 4 of the test and decide whether you wish to change any of the answers you gave. Then check your answers to Part 4 of the test.

PAPER 4 SPEAKING 16 minutes

PART 1 (2 minutes)   GENERAL AND SOCIAL

Questions that may be addressed to either candidate:

- What kind of things do you do in your free time?
- How long have you been doing them?
- What is it about them that you enjoy particularly?
- Have you taken up any new activities in your free time recently? If so, why?
- Have you given up anything you used to do in your free time? If so, why?

- What countries or other parts of your country have you travelled to?
- What did you like most about these places?
- What did you like least about them?
- How did they compare with your expectations of them?
- Name one place you would not like to go to. What are your impressions of it?

PART 2 (4 minutes)   HISTORY

Discussion between candidates:

Look at the picture on page 137 and discuss which historical period it shows.

(1 minute)

Now look at the picture again.

Imagine that you have been asked to give a presentation about the historical period that you would most like to have lived in.

Discuss the historical periods in the distant past or in more modern times that most interest you. Then decide which historical period will be the subject of your presentation and what aspects of it you will include.

(3 minutes)

PART 3 (10 minutes)   FASHION AND YOUTH

In Part 3 each candidate is given a card and talks alone for two minutes about the topic on the card. After each candidate has spoken, the other candidate is asked a question and the candidate who spoke alone is invited to respond (1 minute).

Prompt Card (a) *(Given to Candidate A, and a copy to Candidate B)*

> Why do so many people follow fashion?
>
> • need to feel up-to-date
>
> • commercial pressures
>
> • how you look matters/has always mattered

One of the following questions for Candidate B:

• Describe a fashion in clothes that you particularly like or liked.

• Describe a fashion in clothes that you particularly dislike or disliked.

• To what extent do you and your friends follow fashion?

One of the following questions for Candidate A:

• What do you think?

• Do you agree?

• How about you?

Prompt Card (b) *(Given to Candidate B, and a copy to Candidate A)*

> Is there too much emphasis on youth in modern life?
>
> • the media/films/music
>
> • what older people have to offer
>
> • attitude in society to young and older people

One of the following questions for Candidate A:

• Do people change as they get older and if so, in what ways?

• How much freedom do young people have in your society?

• Describe an elderly person who you particularly admire.

One of the following questions for Candidate B:

• What do you think?

• Do you agree?

• How about you?

Part 3 finishes with a discussion between the two candidates and the examiner on the general topic (4 minutes).

General questions for both candidates on the topic of fashion and youth:

> • How frequently do fashions in music change in your society?
>
> • Is there anything that is fashionable now that you think you will consider ridiculous when you look back on it when you're older?
>
> • Is anything that was fashionable in the past now fashionable with a different generation in your society?
>
> • Is it possible for older people to be fashionable?
>
> • What is the situation regarding the employment of older people in your society?
>
> • What, if any, restrictions do you think there should be on young people?

DESCRIBING PERSONALITY

In the Speaking paper, you may need to talk about your own or other people's personalities. To check or add to your vocabulary on this subject, look at the adjectives below and group them together under the headings given. Then note down the precise meaning of each one (you may need to consult a dictionary) and describe people you think they apply to, giving examples of their behaviour which justify your description of them.

affable	courteous	intransigent	pig-headed	strong-willed
aloof	crafty	lenient	pompous	stuck-up
arrogant	cunning	mean	pushy	supercilious
assertive	decent	mild-mannered	resolute	surly
big-headed	devious	moody	ruthless	tactful
calculating	generous	narrow-minded	scheming	tenacious
compassionate	genial	obstinate	single-minded	tireless
conceited	hypocritical	patronising	smug	two-faced
condescending	ignorant	persistent	snobbish	vindictive
considerate	indulgent	petulant	spiteful	warm

Kind/Pleasant	Feeling superior	Unkind/ Unpleasant	Determined	Dishonest

Now check your answers to this exercise.

TOPIC VOCABULARY

1 In Part 3 in this test, you are required to talk about the topic of fashion and youth. To check or add to your vocabulary on this subject, complete the words and phrases below.

Fashions/Fashionable	Unfashionable
a cr _ _ _	anti _ _ _ _ _ _
a f _ _	_ _ _ _ _ _ the times
all the r _ _ _	d _ _ _ _
cont _ _ _ _ _ _ _	ob _ _ _ _ _ _
_ _ fashion	old h _ _
in v _ _ _ _	_ _ _ _ _ fashion
_ _ _ _ _ setting	outd _ _ _ _
tr _ _ _ _	outm _ _ _ _

2   Now complete the words and phrases on the left so that they match the definitions on the right.

a h _ _ _ _ _ _ _	a violent young man
a k _ _	a child
a l _ _	a young boy
a l _ _ _	a badly behaved young man
a y _ _	a badly behaved young man
a y _ _ _ _ _ _ _ _	a young person
a y _ _ _ _	a young person
ad _ _ _ _ _ _ _ _ _	period of becoming an adult
ad _ _ _ _ _ _ _ _	young person becoming an adult
ch _ _ _ _ _ _	wrongly behaving like a child
inf _ _ _ _ _ _	behaving like a small child
imm _ _ _ _ _	more like a child than is acceptable
imm _ _ _ _ _ _ _	behaviour that is like a child's
j _ _ _ _ _ _ _	behaving like a foolish child
the y _ _ _ _	young people
y _ _ _ _ _ _ _	like young people

grow _ _	become an adult or start behaving like one
g _ _ _ _ _	like an adult
a g _ _ _ _ _ _	an adult
m _ _ _ _ _	like an adult
m _ _ _ _ _ _ _	behaviour like an adult's
getting _ _	becoming old
m _ _ _ _ _ a _ _ _	no longer young but not yet old
over the h _ _ _	too old to be at your best any longer
p _ _ _ it	too old to be at your best any longer
in your d _ _ _ _ _	very old and weak
an _ _ _ _ _ _	very old
s _ _ _ _ _	very old and suffering from mental weakness
s _ _ _ _ _ c _ _ _ _ _ _	an old or retired person
o _ _ a _ _	the later part of life
an o _ _ a _ _ p _ _ _ _ _ _ _ _ _	an old and retired person
e _ _ _ _ _ _	old (of people)
the e _ _ _ _ _ _	old people

PAPER 4 SPEAKING

PART 2 (4 MINUTES)

Test 1: Careers

PAPER 4 SPEAKING

PART 2 (4 MINUTES)

Test 2: Good and Bad Moods

A

B

C

D

E

PAPER 4 SPEAKING

PART 2 (4 MINUTES)

Test 3: Health and Exercise

A

B

C

D

E

PAPER 4 SPEAKING

PART 2 (4 MINUTES)

Test 4: History

WRITING AND SPEAKING ASSESSMENT

Assessment of Writing

C2	Content	Communicative Achievement	Organisation	Language
5	All content is relevant to the task. Target reader is fully informed.	Demonstrates complete command of the conventions of the communicative task. Communicates complex ideas in an affective and convincing way, holding the target reader's attention with ease, fulfilling all communicative purposes.	Text is organised impressively and coherently using a wide range of cohesive devices and organisational patterns with complete flexibility.	Uses a wide range of vocabulary, including less common lexis, with fluent precision, sophistication and style. Use of grammar is sophisticated, fully controlled and complete natural. Any inaccuracies occur only as slips.
4	*Performance shares features of Bands 3 and 5.*			
3	Minor irrelevances and/or omissions may be present. Target reader is on the whole informed.	Uses the conventions of the communicative task with sufficient flexibility to communicate complex ideas in an effective way, holding the target reader's attention with ease, fulfilling all communicative purposes.	Text is a well-organised, coherent whole, using a variety of cohesive devices and organisational patterns with flexibility.	Uses a range of vocabulary, including less common lexis, effectively and precisely. Uses a wide range of simple and complex grammatical forms with full control, flexibility and sophistication. Errors, if present, are related to less common words and structures, or occur as slips.
2	*Performance shares features of Bands 1 and 3*			
1	Irrelevances and misinterpretation of task may be present. Target reader is minimally informed.	Uses the conventions of the communicative task effectively to hold the target reader's attention and communicate straightforward and complex ideas, as appropriate.	Text is well-organised and coherent, using a variety of cohesive devices and organisational patterns to generally good effect.	Uses a range of vocabulary, including less common lexis, appropriately. Uses a range of simple and complex grammatical forms with control and flexibility. Occasional errors may be present but do not imped communication.
0	Irrelevances and misinterpretation of task may be present. Target reader is minimally informed.		*Performance below Band 1*	

Assessment of Speaking

C2	Grammatical Resource	Lexical Resource	Discourse Management	Pronunciation	Interactive Communication
5	Maintains control of a wide range of grammatical forms and uses them with flexibility.	Uses a wide range of appropriate vocabulary with flexibility to give and exchange views on unfamiliar and abstract topics.	Produces extended stretches of language with flexibility and ease and very little hesitation. Contributions are relevant, coherent, varied and detailed. Makes full and effective use of a wide range of cohesive devices and discourse markers.	Is intelligible. Phonological features are used effectively to convey and enhance meaning.	Interacts with ease by skilfully interweaving his/her contributions into the conversation. Widens the scope of the interaction and develops it fully and effectively towards a negotiated outcome.
4	*Performance shares features of Bands 3 and 5.*				
3	Maintains control of a wide range of grammatical forms.	Uses a range of appropriate vocabulary with flexibility to give and exchange views on unfamiliar and abstract topics.	Produces extended stretches of language with ease and with very little hesitation. Contributions are relevant, coherent and varied. Uses a wide range of cohesive devices and discourse markers.	Is intelligible. Intonation is appropriate. Sentence and word stress is accurately placed. Individual sounds are articulated clearly.	Interacts with ease, linking contributions to those of other speakers. Widens the scope of the interaction and negotiates towards an outcome.
2	*Performance shares features of Bands 1 and 3*				
1	Shows a good degree of control of a range of simple and some complex grammatical forms.	Uses a limited range of appropriate vocabulary to give and exchange views on familiar and unfamiliar topics.	Produces extended stretches of language with very little hesitation. Contributions are relevant and there is clear organisation of ideas. Uses a range of cohesive devices and discourse markers.	Is intelligible. Intonation is generally appropriate. Sentence and word stress is generally accurately placed. Individual sounds are generally articulated clearly.	Initiates and responds appropriately, linking contributions to those of other speakers. Maintains and develops the interaction and negotiates towards an outcome.
0	*Performance below Band 1*				

C2	Global Achievement
5	Handles communication on all topics, including unfamiliar and abstract ones, with very little hesitation. Uses accurate and appropriate linguistic resources with flexibility to express complex ideas and concepts and produce extended and coherent discourse.
4	*Performance shares features of Bands 3 and 5.*
3	Handles communication on a wide range of topics, including unfamiliar and abstract ones, with very little hesitation. Uses accurate and appropriate linguistic resources to express complex ideas and concepts and produce extended and coherent discourse.
2	*Performance shares features of Bands 1 and 3.*
1	Handles communication on a range of familiar and unfamiliar topics, with very little hesitation. Uses accurate and appropriate linguistic resources to express ideas and produce extended discourse that is generally coherent.
0	*Performance below Band 1.*

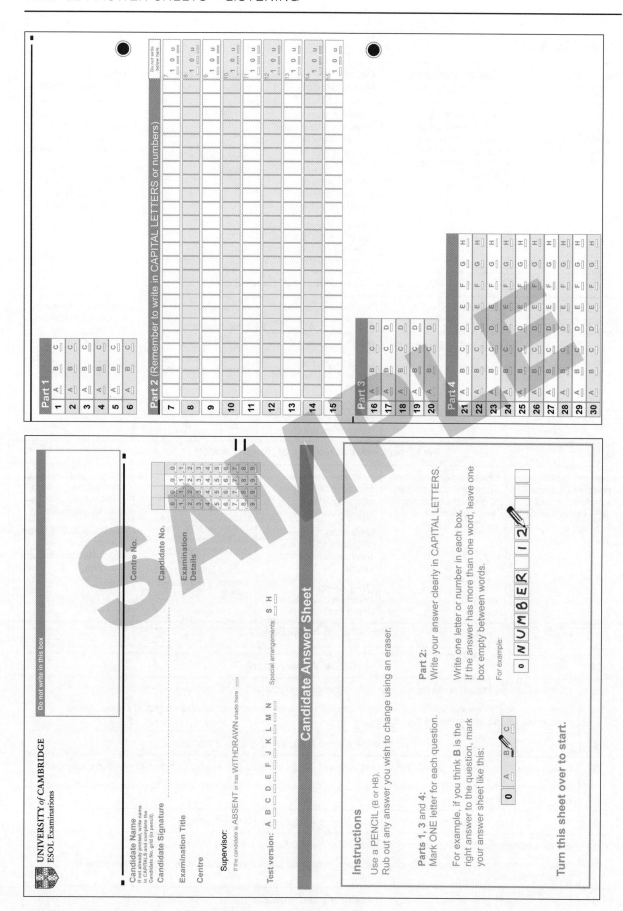

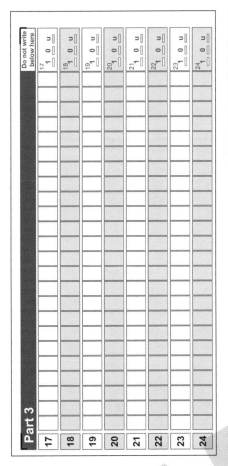

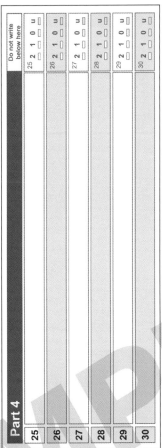

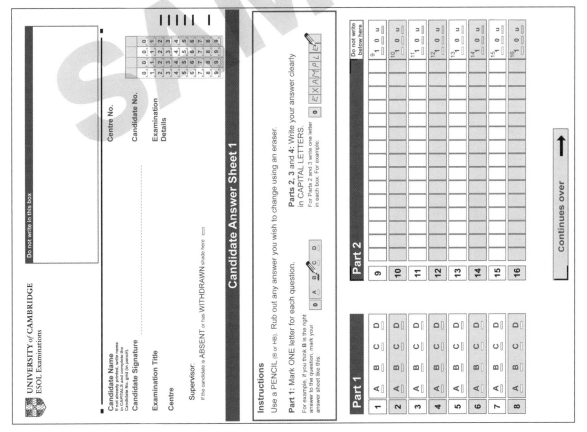

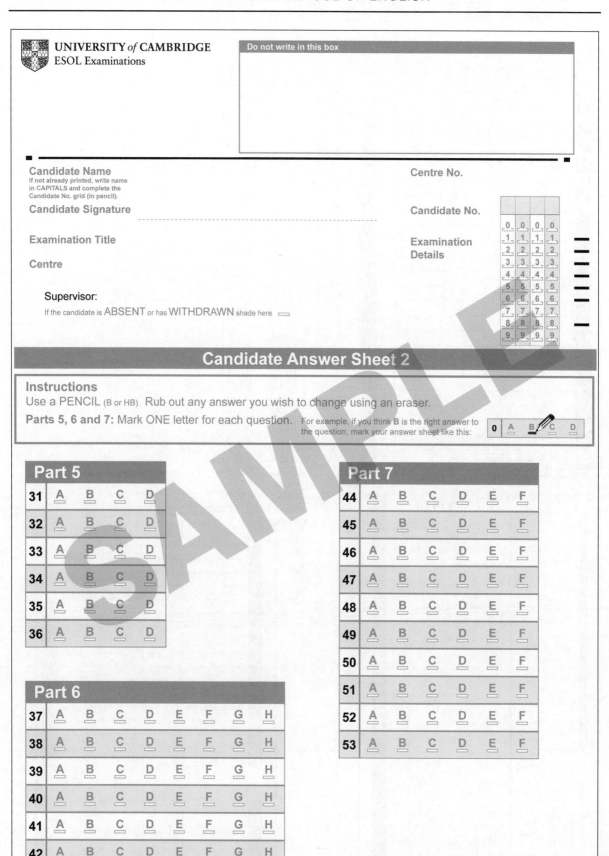

Reproduced by permission of Cambridge ESOL © 2013

LISTENING SCRIPTS

TEST 1, PART 1

You will hear three different extracts. For questions 1–6, choose the answer (A, B or C) which fits best according to what you hear. There are two questions for each extract.

Extract One

Malcolm Gladwell, in his book *The Tipping Point*, has produced a wonderfully off-beat study of that little-understood phenomenon, the social epidemic. His book is organised around the notion of the 'tipping point', the moment when, to put it bluntly, a thing takes off and becomes widespread in a particular society. For fax machines, it happened in 1987; for mobile phones, 1998. Ideas have their tipping points too. The point is that social epidemics usually take us by surprise.

Gladwell makes sense of them by anatomising them, showing how the spread of ideas or behaviour depends on types whom he christens 'connectors' and 'mavens'. Connectors jump-start the epidemic by virtue of the number of people they know – the book provides a test that allows the reader to work out whether they qualify. Mavens are specialists who possess the power of recommendation. Summarised like this, Gladwell's dissection sounds a bit crude. In fact, *The Tipping Point* is a very subtle piece of work, coming out with ideas – not necessarily his own – that make conventional solutions to social problems seem criminally naive.

Extract Two

Why am I up here? 120 metres up the side of this crag, wearing a pair of close-fitting, technicolour climbing-trousers. Only another 25 metres to the top. Only? What am I trying to prove? Why is a man who feels dizzy near the edges of sea cliffs and sweats with fear at the top of towers, why exactly is he spending this warm afternoon, the day after his 46th birthday, dangling over a void attached to a long piece of purple-pink string? There is no answer to such fatuous metaphysical questions. Not when your climbing partner has just disappeared from view, for the first time, somewhere far above your head.

This is it, the proverbial moment. Out on my own. Just me, my vertigo and a pair of borrowed rock boots, which are slightly too small, and a great wrinkled slab of ancient geology and a palpitating, sweat-soaked, miraculously heightened sense of existence. I wouldn't be anywhere else. This is also the moment I realise, with a keen pang of guilt, that I completely forgot to check the small print in my life insurance where it states excluded risks. You know, the awesomely dangerous pursuits that men in their forties are so often drawn to, such as sponsored bungee-jumping and white-water rafting.

Extract Three

Interviewer: Writers rarely admit it, William, but they are in quite a comfortable position when they appear as speakers at events at literary festivals, aren't they? They can read from their work, work already done, needing no more than a light dusting on the train to be in shape for the event. Questions asked on the back of such a sampling are gentle and entirely on the author's terms. Or they can branch out, talk about something which will have some interest because of the writer's own proven involvement with that subject. Questions can be tougher here but writers are used to questions. They ask them of themselves every couple of sentences.

William: Yes, but the main thing is that it's almost invariably a pleasure to meet readers. A writing life is solitary and mute, and often near to that of a depressive in its conditions. I cannot believe there is a writer who has not at times felt that his or her confidence has dropped open underneath like a trapdoor and suddenly there is nothing to build on and they are left dangling there. Meeting those whose equally solitary experience completes the act begun in hope of contact is a relief and an encouragement, as well as a pleasure.

TEST 1, PART 2

You will hear someone called Karen Williams talking about her career. For questions 7–15, complete the sentences with a word or short phrase.

Karen Williams: I left school with an ambition to work in hotels as a manager in England or maybe abroad. My local college offered a two-year Diploma in Hotel Administration and Tourism. The course involved three periods of work experience as well as modules covering hotel front office, restaurant, housekeeping, business studies and languages.

My first work experience was in the housekeeping department of a hotel. It was hard work and I was only there for two weeks. I learnt all about cleaning rooms, what equipment to use, changing beds and, more importantly, about life in a hotel. For the last two days I worked with the floor housekeeper, planning rotas and checking rooms. The second placement was for four months. I went to work in Germany. Although I had studied the language at college, my language skills improved dramatically. Most of the time I worked in the restaurant and housekeeping. The final work experience of five weeks was in the front office of a hotel, where I learnt all about the switchboard, reservations, porter's desk and cashiers.

I decided to carry on studying and do a Higher National Diploma, or HND, in Hospitality Management. During the summer months between one course and another, I worked in a restaurant kitchen. I had never worked in a kitchen before and it was interesting to see how one worked. Although I decided that I didn't want to be a chef, the experience of seeing what goes on was invaluable.

The two-year HND was very interesting. Some students had come straight from school, some from hotel and catering courses and some had got into the course as a result of their age and experience. We studied a range of subjects, including business studies, hotel management, human resource management and operational techniques. There were also some optional subjects and I took conference and leisure facility management, advanced business and languages. The work experience was very useful, and I had to write a detailed report on 'green issues' in hotels. That was probably the thing I found most difficult on the course, although it certainly gave me a different perspective on things. It was interesting – for example, I reviewed give-aways such as soaps and shampoos as part of the report. I became a student member of the HCIMA, the Hotel and Catering International Management Association, when I started the course and I was able to request information from them. Their magazines often have articles of interest that students can use for assignments. My other source of information was *Caterer and Hotelkeeper*, the weekly magazine.

The college was associated with a university, and so after I completed the HND, I was able to go straight onto the third year of a degree in Hotel and Restaurant Management. I completed that course fairly recently and I've just started work as a junior assistant manager at a London hotel. I love the work there, although sometimes the duty management shifts are a bit of a killer. Usually the hotel is overbooked when I am on duty and so I often end up as the one who has to book out guests. We use a nearby hotel of the same standard and provide transport but it is understandable when a guest gets very irate, arriving after a long journey. My aim is to stay here to gain experience before I move on. Possibilities include hotels within the group or maybe abroad, where I can use my languages. One day I'd like to be a General Manager.

TEST 1, PART 3

You will hear an interview with someone who consulted a 'life coach' to improve her life. For questions 16–20, choose the answer (A, B, C or D) which fits best according to what you hear.

Interviewer: My next guest is Brigid McConville, a journalist who decided to get herself a 'life coach'. Brigid, what made you do it and what is a 'life coach'?

Brigid: Well, all was not entirely well with my life. Nothing drastic: I just felt 'stuck' and in need of change,

both on the work front – too much to do, too little time – and at home – ditto. I wasn't miserable enough for therapy or counselling. I simply wanted to get a little more from life. Until recently, the options for someone in my situation would have been extremely limited. Now, however, legions of 'life coaches' are out there, ready and waiting to come to the aid of the frustrated and down-at-heart. For about £40 a session, your personal coach will telephone you once a week, and spend half an hour talking to you in an effort to help you sort your life out.

Interviewer: But isn't this just another self-improvement fad? Like all the self-help books and tapes?

Brigid: Well, I was a bit dubious myself, but I decided to try it. I booked a course with Fiona Harrold, a leading British coach. She identified my anxieties almost immediately. Within half an hour of our first conversation, I found myself agreeing that the first thing I had to tackle was my deeply ambivalent relationship with money. Yes, of course it was rooted in childhood – but what could we actually do about it? Fiona is a passionate advocate of self-belief and, with her characteristic verve, she told me I had to carve out a whole new way of thinking about myself. I must see myself as 'a magnet for money', she said. And she told me: 'Consider yourself someone to whom cash flows effortlessly. Why shouldn't you have an easy life, an abundance of pleasure, leisure and luxury – and all without feeling any guilt?'

Interviewer: How did you react to that?

Brigid: Well, it seemed such a preposterous idea that I laughed out loud down the telephone. But, undeterred by my scepticism, Fiona told me to suspend my disbelief, and gave me a clutch of positive affirmations with which to brainwash myself into readiness for riches. She told me to repeat the following words whenever possible: 'I, Brigid, am now ready to have the ideal life that I deserve.' Doing this, I found, cheered me up no end.

Interviewer: What else did she tell you?

Brigid: Well, subsequent sessions were more practical. First came the mandatory de-cluttering – she told me to throw out as much unnecessary jumble and rubbish as possible, clearing space for all the goodies to come – once the money started to roll in. Then we began trying to cure my personal finance phobia; I dutifully did my sums, and started saving something, however small, every month. My work also came under close scrutiny, too, as I made up my mind to concentrate on jobs that really interested me. Exactly which issues you tackle during coaching is up to you. According to Fiona, most people want to get organised at home and at work, make the most of their abilities and sort out money problems. She reckons that building up confidence is vital. She really does believe that people are capable of doing anything they want to do, and that all that stands in their way is childhood conditioning.

Interviewer: So what did you get out of it all? And would you recommend it?

Brigid: Well, coaching makes you get on and do all those things you've put off for so long, because there is the deadline of the next session. If you don't act in time, your coach probably won't want to speak to you. So coaching is hardly a soft option. But for me, it has provided a great boost. There have been no instant miracles, but things are looking up at work and financially, money and I are definitely on better terms. I still have my doubts about the 'me first' approach – but, then again, it is a healthy counterbalance to the 'me last' way of thinking I am used to.

Interviewer: Thanks, Brigid. Now, if you want to find out more about life coaches …

TEST 1, PART 4

Part 4 consists of two tasks. You will hear five short extracts in which people are talking about cities they have visited. Look at Task 1. For questions 21–25, choose from the list (A–H) why each speaker visited the city. Now look at Task 2. For questions 26–30, choose each speaker's opinion of the city from the list (A–H). While you listen, you must complete both tasks.

Speaker One

Of course, you can't get much of an idea of what a place is like from such a short visit, but I wanted to see if it seemed any different after all these years away from it. I went to a few old familiar haunts but I have to say they didn't give me any great feelings of nostalgia. The cathedral is a magnificent building, for sure, but the rest of it … well, it's not exactly pleasing on the eye. It was busier than I remembered it but all those concrete slabs – what were the designers and architects thinking?

Speaker Two

I spent a couple of days there, because the event ran over two days. So I stayed overnight in a hotel they booked for me and very nice it was too. The event itself was pretty uninspiring – it was one of those where you just get to sit and listen to people going on and on rather than getting involved yourself. But in the evenings I was able to wander around quite a bit and get a reasonable impression of the place. It must be an amazing place to live, so much going on and such a lively atmosphere. No wonder people talk about how glamorous it is.

Speaker Three

I'd seen it on TV quite a bit and I've got friends who tell me that they really like living there. So when the opportunity to move there came up, I decided to go and check it out, find out if it would suit me. It's one thing to go to a place like that as a tourist, but it's totally different to make your home there. I didn't have long but I found out quite a bit about accommodation, transport, entertainment, all that sort of thing. Everyone I spoke to went out of their way to help me and I got the feeling it was a very welcoming place.

Speaker Four

I've been there quite a few times on business trips and I know the place pretty well. A couple of friends of mine had been talking about it, so I thought it would be nice to take them there so that they could see it for themselves. As usual, it was crawling with people, it's on every tourist's must-see list. What with them and all the locals rushing around, it was all a bit much and we were all exhausted by the time we set off home again. There's certainly a lot going on there, but it would take some energy to live there.

Speaker Five

One of the things that came up was whether I'd adapt to such a different lifestyle if I was to be successful and move there. It's a good question. On the one hand, it would be a great opportunity, but a part of me found it rather scary. I've been to the place as a tourist, seen the sights and really liked it, but I'm not used to big city life and the prospect is a pretty daunting one. So even if I do get the offer, I don't think I'm brave enough to take them up on it.

TEST 2, PART 1

You will hear three different extracts. For questions 1–6, choose the answer (A, B or C) which fits best according to what you hear. There are two questions for each extract.

Extract One

Standard strategies for negotiation often leave people dissatisfied, worn out, or alienated – and frequently all three. People find themselves in a dilemma. They see two ways to negotiate – soft or hard. Soft negotiators want to avoid personal conflict and so make concessions readily in order to reach agreement. They want an amicable resolution, yet they often end up exploited and feeling bitter. Hard negotiators see any situation as a contest of wills in which the side that takes the more extreme positions and holds out longer fares better. They want to win, yet often end up producing an equally hard response which exhausts them and their resources and harms their relationship with the other side.

There is a third way to negotiate, a way neither hard nor soft, but rather both hard *and* soft. The method of *principled negotiation* is to decide issues on their merits rather than through a haggling process focused on what each side says it will and won't do. It suggests that you look for mutual gains wherever possible, and that where your interests conflict, you should insist that the result be based on some fair standards independent of the will of either side. The method of *principled negotiation* employs no tricks and no posturing. It shows you how to obtain what you are entitled to and still be decent.

Extract Two

Reporter: Walking into Roly Curtis's clay-processing shed is to rewind to the Industrial Revolution of the early 19th century. An apparition covered in drying clay dust silences the trundling cog wheels and whirring fan belts to greet you in the gloom. Letting in some light, the burly 56-year-old Roly opens the low wooden swing door at the rear of the red-brick building. The tracks of an old narrow-gauge railway slope away into a meadow thick with hawthorn, primroses and teasels. Like his father and grandfather before him, Curtis winches load after load of hand-dug clay from an open cast pit 365 metres away to supply his pottery. I asked him about the history of the pottery.

Roly: It was started in 1831. At first, the company was making simple horticultural containers, such as plant pots. It also made domestic ware: baking bowls glazed in cream on the inside with a brown ring around the top, bread crocks, milk jugs and cream 'settling' pans. But the business began to decline. With the advent of the plastic bowl in the late 1950s – a death blow to potteries countrywide – my father, by then nearing retirement, survived by laying off his remaining four staff and by producing more unusual pots. I worked as an industrial chemist until the lure of the clay proved too strong. I was in my early thirties when I took over here and I've been working alone ever since, making mainly horticultural ware.

Extract Three

If people have one dominant image of the great silent comedian Harold Lloyd, it is probably of a bespectacled figure either dangling from a clock, many storeys above the streets of Los Angeles, in 1923's *Safety Last*, or else clutching girders, in the same town, at similar altitude, as in *Never Weaken*, 1921.

He made his screen debut as an extra in 1912, and the following year he met another extra, Hal Roach. The pair created *Lonesome Luke*, an aggressive figure who, in the year 1916–17, proved a moderate hit. As Lloyd later put it, 'I was quite successful, but not really good.' This changed in 1917, however, when either Lloyd or Roach – history is divided – hit on the idea of making the former don horn-rimmed specs, and reject stylisation in favour of normality. Far more than Charlie Chaplin, or even his

other chief rival Buster Keaton, Lloyd was now someone with whom audiences could readily identify. For the next ten years, Lloyd could do no wrong. Audiences flocked to see his character save the day through his combination of lateral thinking and preternatural physical prowess. But the double onslaught of cinematic sound and the Depression of the 1930s proved fatal to Lloyd's career. His first talkie, *Welcome Danger* (1929), was a hit, but it was to be his last: he was instinctively a visual performer, and his indomitable optimism was now incongruous.

TEST 2, PART 2

You will hear part of a radio programme in which the history of Ty-Phoo Tipps, a brand of tea that is well-known in Britain, is described. For questions 7–15, complete the sentences with a word or short phrase.

In 1820, 24-year-old William Sumner took over an old family grocery and druggist's shop at the top of the Bull Ring in Birmingham. Ten years later, William also had a shop in nearby Coleshill and, in 1835, he is listed as a Grocer and Tea Dealer in the *National Commercial Directory*. All the tea sold at that time came from China.

William brought his elder son, John, into the business in 1845. By 1852, William Sumner and Son were listed as tea and coffee dealers, but it would be many years before they could concentrate solely on tea. William later gave the business to his two sons, but in 1863 they decided to go their separate ways and John took premises at 98 High Street, Birmingham.

In Ceylon (now Sri Lanka) a serious disease affected the coffee industry and tea became a prime crop. By 1875, tea from there was being exported to Britain and this was to be important to the Sumners. John Sumner's son, also called John, joined the business and, due to the construction of a railway tunnel, they had to move to 25 and 26 High Street, Birmingham. At the turn of the 20th century, father and son had a flourishing business which now included wines and spirits, as well as groceries. They had six travellers and 20 horses and a range of vans – life was good.

For a long time, Mary, young John's sister, had suffered from indigestion. One day someone sent her a packet of tea which was different from that sold in the family business. Its particles were very small and, whereas large-leaf teas tended to aggravate her problem, this one promised a cure. She decided to try it and to her delight found that it gave her great relief; she then offered the 'remedy' to other people who suffered from indigestion and they too benefited. Mary told her brother enthusiastically about the tea and asked why Sumner did not sell it.

This was the starting point of a great adventure, although when John told a friend, a wholesale tea merchant, of his intention to buy 30 chests of the tea, he said that the public would not buy tea which looked little better than dust. Nevertheless, John went ahead with his purchase, but instead of selling it loose over the counter, he decided to put it in packets and sell it under a brand name.

John set himself three criteria in choosing the name: it must be distinctive and unlike others; it must be one which tripped off the tongue; and it must be one which could be protected by registration. Finally, he came up with the name 'Ty-Phoo' Tipps – it had an oriental sound, was alliterative with tea, and whilst the name Tipps could not be registered, Ty-Phoo could and was. The double 'p' in Tipps first occurred as a printer's error, but John decided to stick with this spelling.

The first cardboard packets were filled by girls using scoops, who then weighed them before gluing and sealing them. In the first week of production in 1903, they packed 260 kilograms of Ty-Phoo Tipps. To encourage customers to buy his new brand, John offered each purchaser of half a kilo of Ty-Phoo Tipps a generous jar of cream. Soon many customers were drinking the new tea. They discovered that, although it was slightly more expensive, it was more economical and its beneficial digestive qualities gave it great appeal. Other traders also wanted to buy the new brand and John founded a wholesale agency. He took a shop in Corporation Street, Birmingham's most important shopping street, and had a row of girls standing inside the window, packing tea for passers-by to see, whilst inside the shop, tea was served with cream and biscuits.

In 1905, John went to Ceylon and brought back 200 chests of tea, mainly the small-leafed variety known as fannings. He drew attention to the fact that his tea came from the edge of the leaf and did not contain the tannin from the fibrous stalk; he also claimed that the leaf-edge tea could produce 80 more cups per pound of tea than the large-leaf tea. From 1906, John Sumner was having his own special Ty-Phoo teapots made for sale, and during that year he introduced picture cards, similar to cigarette cards, and inserted them in the packets of tea.

In 1932, John Sumner received a knighthood in recognition of his charitable work. When he died in 1934, each of his 346 employees benefited under his will.

TEST 2, PART 3

You will hear an interview with someone whose family spent a year living without television. For questions 16–20, choose the answer (A, B, C or D) which fits best according to what you hear.

Interviewer: Miranda Ingram and her family were avid TV watchers until the day when they found themselves without a television. Miranda, how did that come about?

Miranda: I would love to be able to say that this was because I flung the set through the sitting room window or sold it, but the truth is that circumstances deprived us. We moved to the middle of nowhere, surrounded by mountains, to an ancient cottage, which had never had a TV point. Unbelievably, perhaps, in the 21st century, our options for getting plugged in were remarkably sparse. We could have spent a fortune laying cables to the nearest village and joining their communal aerial, which sent fuzzy pictures every time it rained – and we're talking Wales here, so rain is not a rare occurrence. And any time strong winds or stray animals knocked it out of kilter, the entire system went down for days. Or we could have got satellite television, but when a satellite technician arrived, he looked round at our mountains and saw not breathtaking natural beauty but obstacles. So neither option seemed worth the trouble.

Interviewer: So what was it like to be a family without a television?

Miranda: Well, we trained ourselves not to look at the TV listings so we wouldn't sigh over what we were missing and started to revel in our moral superiority. 'Did you watch ... ?' people would begin, and we would watch their jaws drop as they wondered what on earth we did, half way up a mountain with two small children and no television. At the risk of sounding unbearably smug, we did indeed read more books, listen to more music, and play more board games. And we sat outside and watched the sun set or merely had an early night. Most significant, however, was simply discovering the untold long, pleasant and potentially fulfilling hours there are in an evening.

Interviewer: Surely, there must have been some downside?

Miranda: At times, I must admit, we did feel like cultural oddities. Television enters the language and we didn't know what people meant when they compared someone to an apparently well-known character, or when they used what was presumably a catchphrase from a popular programme. And my husband and I are confirmed news junkies, so we really missed the television when it came to big news events. There are certain stories where television pictures tell more than any amount of radio and newsprint. But like any mild addiction, after an initial withdrawal, before long you hardly give it a second thought.

Interviewer: So why, since you were evidently enjoying life without television, did you get connected again?

Miranda: Mmm, you may well ask. Well, it was my husband who persevered with the satellite option. Not, I'm convinced, because he missed the broadcasts so much. More because he missed playing with the remote control in the way that men love to. Anyway, I went along with it because I'm certainly not one of those anti-TV types that believes the box to be the source of all modern evil: there are lots of interesting and rewarding programmes for both adults and children, and television is a perfectly good ingredient of a well-rounded life. But its insidiousness lies in its being an easy option – like a ready meal – which seduces you into forgetting the rewards that come from putting a bit more into life. So I must say that when the day arrived for our connection, I was apprehensive, terrified that this thing in the corner would dominate our lives.

Interviewer: So how have things turned out? Are you and the children TV addicts again?

Miranda: Well, amazingly, now we have our TV back, the children can take it or leave it. Inadvertently, it seems, our year's abstinence must have coincided with their habit-forming years, so it's a habit they don't have. Occasionally they slump, but often they'll switch on for ten minutes before announcing it's 'boring' and rushing off to do something else. I even find myself proposing half an hour's viewing as an activity, but if they suspect it's because I want to sneak off and do something without them, they are very unlikely to agree. We do watch television again, of course we do, but it is no more than an option among others. We even watch rubbish from time to time, but now it's because it has been one of those days when deciding to vegetate is a deliberate choice, not just a habit.

Interviewer: That's interesting. Thanks, Miranda. After the break, we'll be discussing the subject of television and its impact on our lives with ...

TEST 2, PART 4

Part 4 consists of two tasks. You will hear five short extracts in which people are talking about hearing some unexpected news. Look at Task 1. For questions 21–25, choose from the list (A–H) what the news involved. Now look at Task 2. For questions 26–30, choose from the list (A–H) how each speaker feels with regard to the news. While you listen, you must complete both tasks.

Speaker One

Jack phoned and told me that apparently Helen had taken offence at something I said in the meeting last week. I thought she seemed a bit odd the last time I saw her but she didn't say anything to me. Anyway, it seems that she thought it was so awful that she never wants to speak to me again. Well, to be honest, I couldn't care less, she's always falling out with people, and I can't be bothered even to think about it. I have no desire to spend any time with her if I can avoid it.

Speaker Two

How did I find out? Well, he sent me an email saying that the whole thing was off. No explanation, no reason given, just the simple fact. Fortunately, I haven't lost any money on it because I hadn't got as far as spending any, I was still at the planning stage, but that isn't the point really. I'd had it in the diary for ages, it was all fixed and I was looking forward to it. Ah well, never mind, there's no point getting cross about it and I guess he'll tell me his reasons soon enough. But it's a real shame.

Speaker Three

Well, it was never about the money, because that wouldn't have been any different, it was always about the chance to branch out, do something different for a change. But it wasn't to be. I must say I was taken aback when I heard because I'd been expecting to get it. I'd certainly been given the impression that it was mine if I wanted it. Well, I'd clearly been misinformed and someone else got it instead of me. But maybe it's for the best. I was getting quite nervous about how I'd manage and now I don't have to worry about that, I can just go on as before.

Speaker Four

Michelle phoned me completely out of the blue, saying she was living in some very nice new place now and asking if I'd like to use it while she was away. Well, funnily enough I'd been planning to go over there anyway so it was a very nice coincidence. She's always been very generous to me and done me lots of favours like that over the years. I thanked her and said I'd take her up on it. I'll be very interested to see this new place and there are lots of other things I'd like to find out too, such as what exactly she's doing now and how she's come to be living there.

Speaker Five

It's not every day you get the chance to go to something like that as someone's guest, so I was anxious to grab the opportunity. Apparently, she gets to do that quite often because the company she works for has some kind of involvement in it. I hadn't realised that. I wish I was in that position; she gets to go to these things all the time, lucky her! Of course, I'll have to dress the part, but I imagine I can borrow something. I don't want to let myself down, do I?

TEST 3, PART 1

You will hear three different extracts. For questions 1–6, choose the answer (A, B or C) which fits best according to what you hear. There are two questions for each extract.

Extract One

Pessimism is deeply ingrained in the British psyche. Pessimism is the natural British condition. There is nothing we relish so much as some bad news. Pessimists never expect their holiday plans to run to schedule. When the plane is delayed at the airport, they sigh: 'I *knew* this would happen.' When their bags go missing, they accept the loss with stoicism, reasoning: 'It had to be me.' Our administrators are forever being pressed to disclose their 'contingency plans' and 'Plan B'. Plan A is never expected to succeed.

This national trait starts in childhood with the Christopher Robin stories. Eeyore, the pessimistic donkey who is always certain his tail will fall off, appeals immediately to the young British reader. He connects with our melancholy, phlegmatic side. Irony, on which so much distinctive British humour is based, has pessimism as its prime ingredient. It thinks the worst.

Extract Two

We are all living in the past: the idea of 'now' is an illusion. The discovery, reported by a team of scientists, has the bizarre consequence that your brain is collecting information about the future of an event before it puts together what it thinks it saw at the time of the event. Our brains seem to work in a similar way to the slightly delayed broadcast of live TV shows to provide an opportunity for fast editing changes. The delay with which our brains process visual information has now been measured by scientists, providing new insights into how we use vision to make sense of the world.

Human perception of the outside world seems to be delayed by a minimum of 80 thousandths of a second. This is comparative to live television, which can be broadcast after a delay of about three seconds to allow for editing. 'What you think you're seeing at any given moment is actually influenced by events in the near future,' the scientists say in their report. They used a technique called 'the flash-lag phenomenon', which acts as a visual illusion to the brain. They discovered that human brains seem to develop conscious awareness in an 'after-the-fact fashion', analysing information from both before and after an event before committing to a decision about what happened.

Extract Three

Thomas Edison, the doyen of inventors, said it first: 'No sooner does a fellow succeed in making a good thing, than some other fellows pop up and tell you they did it years ago.' His rueful observation reflects a fact that anyone who has a good idea will run into soon enough: that creativity is such a precious commodity that when even a tiny bit of it appears, people instantly want to lay claim to it. For most of recorded history, having a bright idea was no protection against being ripped off by the unscrupulous. It is not a whole lot better now, but there is something that, in theory at least, makes sure that the credit and the money for the invention go where they are due: patents.

The earliest-known English patent was granted to John of Utynam, a Flemish stained-glass maker in 1449. John received the same privilege as those granted an English patent do to this day: a 20-year monopoly to exploit the fruits of his ingenuity. In return, he was required to teach his process to native Englishmen. That, too, is still part of the philosophy behind the modern patent: that it doesn't just encourage innovation, but also the spread of that innovation. Inventors don't actually have to hold classes to teach everyone else how to make what they have invented, but they do have to disclose how to do it. And what trouble that has caused ever since. For by revealing exactly what you have done and how, you are putting your intellectual jewels right where other people can get them. Not only that, but by stating what is new about your invention, you are revealing your likely marketing strategy.

TEST 3, PART 2

You will hear a radio report about interactive science and technology centres in Britain. For questions 7–15, complete the sentences with a word or short phrase.

'It's more interesting than I expected, I shall come here again,' said nine-year-old James Stimson, who had been enjoying himself at the National Stone Centre in Derbyshire on the day when I went there. He had just seen the fossilised remains of a brachiopod, a prehistoric sea animal that predated the dinosaurs by 120 million years; one of a series of fossils found in a rock face in what, 330 million years ago, was part of the coast of Derbyshire – then comprising tropical lagoons and small islands. The area was part of a huge upland which, from medieval times, has been mined for lead and limestone and now hosts school parties and other groups.

The centre has been created from six worked-out stone quarries. One fascinating fact that visitors to it learn is that we each consume six to seven tonnes of stone a year. James couldn't believe his eyes when he read this on a display board inside the centre's Discovery Building. 'What, we eat stone?' he asked. Well, not exactly. What the display shows is that we use stone in everything from paint to computers to ceiling tiles. Ninety per cent of the stone we use is in construction, in everything from tunnels to tennis courts. But stone is also used in plastics, so you will find it in cars, ships and planes. And as it is also used in producing sugar, flour, pharmaceuticals and poultry feed, we all eat a certain amount of stone.

James and some friends in his party moved on to attempt panning 'gems' from mineral fragments; others followed the site's history, ecology and geography trails. I spoke to James's headmaster, Michael Halls of Turnditch primary school near Derby, who was accompanying the group. He told me that the National Stone Centre is a splendid teaching resource. It helps teachers to teach children all sorts of skills, from observation and looking behind the obvious to hands-on activities, such as dry-stone wall building and making plaster casts of fossils. He told me that it also helps children to appreciate what a changing world we live in. Furthermore, many of the activities there fit perfectly into the National Curriculum, although for the children it's more like an exciting outing than a lesson.

That sums up the philosophy of Britain's 25 or so interactive science and technology centres built on the foundation of Launch Pad, the first interactive gallery at the Science Museum in South Kensington, London, which was opened in 1985. I visited another example. On the site of three disused dry docks in Tiger Bay, Cardiff, Wales, a £7 million pound temple to science and technology called Techniquest has been built. It houses 160 exhibits and science 'interactives'; experiments which people of all ages can try out for themselves. The complex incorporates a 35-seat planetarium, a 100-seater science theatre, a science shop, workshop and galleries. The success of Techniquest has been based on experiments involving liquids that you can cut, bubbles you can walk inside and structures that roll uphill, and a philosophy against the 'don't touch' exhibits of traditional museums. The centre started from the premise that it wanted to change people's attitudes towards science and technology and the idea is that people of all ages have to use all their senses to discover the fun of finding out about science and technology.

At Techniquest, you are as likely to see a granny as an eight-year-old swivelling around, under discreet supervision, in a specially adapted dentist's chair to experience the pull of centrifugal force, or people making odd sounds down a 15-metre-long steel tube to observe how sound waves can clash and distort one another. The favourite exhibition is Puff the Pneumatic Dragon, a huge steel creation in Welsh green and red, whose tongue, wings and claws respond instantly to the fingertip controls of visitors. Puff's 'arteries', the hydraulic tubes and electronic circuits that make him respond, are laid out for all to see. It may not be a formal lesson in control systems, but you cannot fail to learn.

And that is true of all the interactive science and technology centres throughout the country.

TEST 3, PART 3

You will hear an interview with someone who reviews hotels. For questions 16–20, choose the answer (A, B, C or D) which fits best according to the text.

Interviewer: I'm talking to Paddy Burt, who has a weekly hotel review column in a national newspaper and who has just compiled a collection of those reviews for a forthcoming book. Paddy, when you go to a hotel to review it, what's your attitude?

Paddy: I always have high hopes – a 'bet this one's going to be good' feeling. But you never can tell. Hotels that look so idyllic in one of the guides can be a terrible letdown, which is why readers who say they enjoy the column invariably add 'particularly the bad ones'. For example, I recently got this letter from a reader, who says: 'It used to be every other week that you gave some poor hotelier a bashing. Now it's a rare treat to read about one you've been severely critical of, and that's a pity since I love it when you lay into a pretentious but bad one. Of course, it's helpful when you recommend a good hotel, but, for entertainment's sake, do try to find some awful ones, too.'

Interviewer: So are you always aiming to find fault? Are you glad when you find something you can be critical of?

Paddy: I don't have to try. And while I'm always happy to slam into any pretentious hotel that doesn't come up to scratch, it's a different matter when the people are nice and their hotel isn't. I still have to write about it and sometimes it hurts. Hotel-keeping, it has been said, is akin to show business and, in the ones I like best, there is always a leading man or woman who is sometimes so good I think he or she has missed their true vocation. Such hoteliers usually have a sense of humour. They may not like what I have written about them, but will respond in a good-humoured way. They are professionals. Many of them have become friends.

Interviewer: What kind of hotels do you prefer? Is it possible to generalise about that?

Paddy: Well, I admit I have a penchant for owner-run hotels; they are more personal than the chains. With a few exceptions, I like the owners of small hotels. Which is why I've had such fun researching my book of review pieces that have appeared in the newspaper – calling them if they haven't responded to the questionnaire I sent them and either telling them who I am or, if I think they're going to shout at me, pretending to be the assistant I haven't got, Emily. 'She didn't give us a very good review, did she?' some said. Well, no – but maybe they have since made improvements and would like people to know about them? Thus encouraged, the majority of these hoteliers have entered not just into the book but into the spirit and have contributed interesting behind-the-scenes stories.

Interviewer: So some of the hotels you reviewed and wanted to put in the book haven't been included?

Paddy: That's right. There's one, for example, where the owner said – I recorded all the calls – 'After insulting us and lying in her article, there is no way we would help her perpetuate her grievances against the world in a publication.' To specify the lies, he pounced on a remark I had made expressing surprise on being served certain vegetables in his restaurant. 'She doesn't understand proper food,' he said. I was enthusiastic about it, actually, and if he wasn't being so disagreeable, I would have liked to include his hotel in the book. On and on he went. 'Since her visit, we've noticed that a lot of people read her articles and then cross hotels off their potential list as a result of what she's said. They then go to hotels where she's been fawned over and where they probably won't be fawned over. We've also noticed she prefers staying in hotels that are almost empty because that's when they have time to make a fuss of her.' Actually, being fawned over is the last thing that I want.

Interviewer: So your column can provoke quite a reaction, then?

Paddy: Oh, yes. In fact, the same owner also said: 'After she stayed here, we had four hotels asking for her description. They wanted to know what car she was driving and what credit card she had. Unfortunately, we couldn't give a description because she's fairly nondescript.' But the peculiar thing is that when it finally clicked that being in the book wasn't going to cost him a penny, he said he wanted to be included. Maybe it was because he remembered that I had remarked on his resemblance to a much-loved comedian, sadly now dead. I declined his kind offer.

Interviewer: I can see why. Paddy Burt, thanks for talking to me.

TEST 3, PART 4

Part 4 consists of two tasks. You will hear five short extracts in which people are talking about leisure activities they take part in. Look at Task 1. For questions 21–25, choose from the list (A–H) what the leisure activity involves for the speaker. Now look at Task 2. For questions 26–30, choose from the list (A–H) what each speaker particularly enjoys about the leisure activity. While you listen, you must complete both tasks.

Speaker One

The key to it all is that we all get together every week, not just off and on, and that makes it a very nice fixture in my life. It's the social side that matters to me, being with that bunch of people. And we've now been doing that for quite some time, so it's a very established thing. Of course, we have serious discussions, and there are important decisions that we have to agree on as a committee. But it's great fun too and we all go back a long way now. They're some of my very best friends and it's great being with them.

Speaker Two

It started off as just a bit of an interest, but gradually it began to take over and I started doing it instead of other things I used to do. I used to have a range of hobbies that I did from time to time, but all the others went out of the window once I got involved with this. Friends say I've become obsessed but as far as I'm concerned, it's all time well spent and I go into another world when I'm doing it. What I do to earn a living is satisfying but it's also very demanding, and exhausting, and this is a complete antidote to that. I switch off totally when I'm doing it.

Speaker Three

I think it's a very worthwhile cause and I was very keen to get involved once I heard about it from someone at work. The organisation can't function without contributions to keep it going, and that's my part. I haven't got a lot of time to dedicate to it, so it's a question of being organised. I've got a list of people to contact and I work through that bit by bit, sending out a few emails from time to time. It's not the biggest thing in the world to do, but it gives me the nice feeling that I'm making my own contribution to something that needs doing.

Speaker Four

Before I took this up I could never have imagined getting up in public and doing such a thing but now it comes naturally. I had to start from scratch, it was all totally new to me, but I'd always had a secret wish to learn how to do it, and finally I got round to it. I didn't find it all that hard actually, and a bit of regular practice is all I need now. It's a tremendous joy to have got really good at something you haven't done before, and I'm so glad I finally decided to do it.

Speaker Five

Well, I got some of the best equipment – second-hand, otherwise I couldn't have afforded it – and found a good venue. Putting on this kind of thing is easy if you have a clear idea of what you want to achieve. The things I put on aren't massive, they're for a small audience that wants to spend time among like-minded people who enjoy the same kind of thing. So I book good people and do a bit of publicity and so far they've all been successful, and just about viable financially too. The great thing is when people tell me at the end how much they've enjoyed it – that makes it all worthwhile.

TEST 4, PART 1

You will hear four different extracts. For questions 1–6, choose the answer (A, B or C) which fits best according to what you hear. There are two questions for each extract.

Extract One

Most people would admit that they would like to be more confident, more at ease with themselves. So what *is* this elusive thing we call confidence? We all have an idea what we mean when we talk about it. One dictionary describes confidence as 'boldness', but that somehow doesn't seem to be quite right. It isn't boldness we are seeking. Self-assurance seems to be more like it. We want to be able to handle or be comfortable in any situation.

Confidence has a lot to do with our relationships with other people. We don't want to feel inferior to anyone. We don't want to be bullied by anyone. We want to be able to walk into any roomful of people and feel that we *are* just as good as any of them – and know that we *are* just as good as any of them. Perhaps this is all very obvious. Of course we all want these things. Yet wanting and having it is very different. And if not all of us have confidence, if we haven't been born with an abundance of it, we must set about obtaining more.

Extract Two

William Goldman, winner of two Oscars for his screenplays, is also widely known for *Adventures in the Screen Trade*, his splenetic observations on the movie business. His latest book, *Which Lie Did I Tell?*, covers his professional heartaches since the last book. Goldman's attitude to Hollywood and his principal grouch remain the same: the screenwriter takes the rap, the director takes the credit, the stars take the awards. Actors' egos come in for stick, and even when they are being modest, Goldman's insincerity detector is working away, perhaps too industriously. For an idea of Goldman's view on directors, you have only to refer to the index, where under 'directors' there are entries for 'fear of', 'as lacking vision', 'media attention to' and 'as screwing things up'.

I would have liked more about Goldman's real, as opposed to film, life. With the glimpses he allows – a lonely child weeping inconsolably on a visit to the theatre, a desk-bound adult in awe of men of action – he suggests that he nurtures his insecurities as a resource. 'I think I have a way with pain,' he writes. 'When I come to that kind of sequence I have a certain confidence ...'. Perhaps he really likes the pain of the business, even the dismaying fact that no one knows who writes the movies. He can suffer anonymously in a trade in which his words might belong in anyone's mouth.

Extract Three

At the height of his powers in the 1960s, James Brown, the 'Godfather of Soul', styled himself the hardest-working man in show business. Brown, it was claimed, worked 364 days a year, criss-crossing America from gig to gig by bus and train. On a number called *Night Train*, Brown played the role of conductor, shouting out the stops along the way: Miami, Florida; Atlanta, Georgia; Raleigh, North Carolina; Washington DC, 'oh, and Richmond, Virginia, too'. The song was so successful that he followed it with *Mashed Potatoes USA*, repeating the trick with a new set of names – New York City, Boston, Buffalo, 'going straight down the road, gonna stop at Cleveland, Ohio ...'. Listening to these songs as a teenager, I was enthralled. More than just arbitrary lists of places, they were celebrations of America.

For anyone growing up in Britain in the 1960s, America was an object of romance forged in song, a place where the girls were prettier, the skies bluer, the cars bigger, the action harder and faster and more intoxicating. These songs described a vista of possibilities that found no equivalent in British music. They hinted at a vastness, a variegated landscape and a range of experiences that demanded to be celebrated. Even to the Americans, it seemed, America was exotic. They believed its own mythology, they got excited about just being there, and if they were excited by it, how could I fail to be so?

TEST 4, PART 2

You will hear part of a radio programme about toys, in which the development of a famous toy called Meccano is described. For questions 7–15, complete the sentences with a word or short phrase.

Frank Hornby, creator of Meccano, was born in Liverpool in 1863. He was one of the seven children of provision dealer John Hornby and his wife, Martha. He married Clara Godefroy in 1887 and they had three children, two boys and a girl. Although Frank worked as a book-keeper and cashier for a meat importer, and became chief managing clerk, he spent much of his spare time inventing things, a hobby stemming from childhood.

One of the books Frank had been given when a young boy, *Self-Help*, by Samuel Smiles, told the stories of famous inventors, and outlined the difficulties they faced before they reached success. It had a lasting influence on him. The story that fascinated him most was of Plaissy, who invented a white glaze for earthenware, but had many failures on the way. Deciding to be an inventor was one thing; how to set about it was another. He thought he might develop a machine to solve the problem of perpetual motion. Through experiments and study of the principles of mechanics, he learned many skills, but had to abandon the project and turn to other ideas, such as a submarine which, when placed on the water submerged itself, was propelled for some distance under water, but then, alas, failed to re-emerge. He lacked adequate tools in his small workshop, but was never discouraged.

As he gradually accumulated more tools, his ideas turned to interchangeable parts which could be used for a variety of purposes – here was the germ of the Meccano system. After he and his wife Clara had boys of their own, he delighted in making mechanical toys for them. One Christmas Eve, during a long train journey, he thought of his workshop and the problem he had in getting small parts for a crane they were constructing. Later he wrote, 'I felt that what was required were parts that could be applied in different ways to many different models, and that could be adjusted to give a variety of movements by alteration of position, etc. In order to do this, it was necessary to devise some standard method of fitting one part to any other part; gradually there came to me the conception of parts all perforated with a series of holes of the same size and at the same distance apart. Such parts I realised could be bolted up to a model in different positions and at different angles, and having done their work in one model could be unbolted and applied to another.'

Gradually his ideas clarified, but little did he think that they would change the rest of his life, and result in a hobby that would give hours of pleasure to boys of all ages, in all parts of the world. Enthusiastically, he started to put his ideas into practice, first making strips from a large piece of copper, which was soft and easy to work. He decided that all the strips would be one and a quarter centimetres wide, with equal-sized holes along the centre at one and a quarter centimetre intervals. At first he made a strip six and a half centimetres long, then a 14 centimetre strip and so on, up to 32 centimetres, which seemed to him an enormous part. The measurements have never been changed since. Similarly, he had to make his own nuts and bolts, and his own angle brackets, axles and wheels – it was a long job, but it was a great day for Frank and his boys when they assembled their first Meccano crane. He was so sure his system was good that he consulted a patent agent and obtained an English patent on 9th January 1901. Foreign patents followed.

His invention was originally called 'Mechanics Made Easy' and was marketed by Hornby and his employer, D.H. Elliott, trading as Elliott and Hornby. The trademark Meccano was registered in 1907 and Elliott and Hornby was sold to Meccano Ltd in 1908, Hornby becoming a director. In 1914, Meccano Ltd moved to a purpose-built factory in Liverpool, the company's home until 1979. Over the years, different Meccano sets were introduced, each set converting by means of an Extension Pack into the next larger-sized set. Eventually, there were over 300 individual Meccano parts.

Hornby Clockwork trains arrived in 1920, electric ones in 1925. Other products followed, including speedboats, aeroplane and car constructor outfits and Dinky Toys, which were launched in 1933. When he died in September 1936, aged 73, Frank Hornby was a millionaire.

TEST 4, PART 3

You will hear an interview with someone whose work is concerned with the design and marketing of products. For questions 16–20, choose the answer (A, B, C or D) which fits best according to what you hear.

Interviewer: Welcome to the world of visual planning. I'm in the offices of a London design firm, where design consultant David Muir has just finished conducting a session with a group of women on the subject of cleaning products. David, tell me exactly what it is that you've been doing.

David: Yes, well, visual planning usually unites a designer with a manufacturer to construct an appropriate image for a product. But in the age of the focus group, when garnering opinions from members of the public at sessions with small groups is almost an industry in itself, the process has been short-circuited. Today, shoppers are being asked to design the perfect product themselves. In the three-hour brainstorming session I've just done, a dozen housewives and working mothers were asked to unleash their cleaning foibles, hates and woes, and possibly change the way such products are packaged and sold.

Interviewer: Is there anything about cleaning products that poses particular problems when it comes to selling them?

David: Research has exposed the world of soaps, bleaches and powders to be a confusing mass, a 'many-headed monster', so cluttered with scientific jargon and swathed in lurid packaging as to be often unintelligible. Despite enormous annual advertising budgets, the congested market is failing to bloom as healthily as manufacturers might wish. To arrest the crisis, my firm has been called in. Firstly, we filmed shoppers dithering in supermarkets over washing powders. Stage two was the focus group I've just run.

Interviewer: Tell me about what kind of things you did in this session.

David: Well, for example, at the back of the room, scores of products were on display. The women were asked to put them into groups – what we call a 'brand-mapping' exercise – and select any favourites. Many of the brands elicited complaints that they are ugly and confusing. I noted comments like: 'The products don't say clearly what they do', and 'I don't want all this science', and 'I spend quite some time down that aisle'. Then 'I just grab what I know', and 'I don't understand the difference between concentrated and non-concentrated products, or biological and non-biological.'

Interviewer: So, having got their views, what was the next step?

David: Then I asked them to imagine how they would want a cleaning product to make them feel. I split the women into three groups and got them to tear up magazines and fabric samples, forming giant collages on boards to represent the colours, textures and images of their ideal cleaning goods. And the finished boards – a mass of soft lilacs and mauves, fruit and flowers and images of homely comfort – represented a dramatic shift from the way these goods are normally presented. There are no 'germ-busting' explosions.

Interviewer: So what have you concluded?

David: I've concluded that, as I suspected, the missing ingredient when it comes to the marketing of cleaning goods is emotion. Research already shows that it is not an enjoyable sector for shoppers. The accepted belief is that when people buy detergents, there is low emotional involvement, that they are on automatic pilot. But our research shows they want to have more fun, they want products to be about their lifestyle. It's my belief that the visual dimension is vital. Research shows that 73% of purchase decisions are made in the store. But no one is really considering the consumer's emotional needs. That's why in this session, I asked them to express what they feel in a visual sense and create three perfect brands. There's an opportunity for genuine innovation here, to respond to consumers' emotional side. People don't want all this industrial language any more. What we're doing here is extremely radical.

Interviewer: So, a successful session then?

David: Very much so.

Interviewer: OK, now I'd like to move on to another aspect of your work. When it comes to …

TEST 4, PART 4

Part 4 consists of two tasks. You will hear five short extracts in which people are talking about their jobs. Look at Task 1. For questions 21–25, choose from the list (A–H) what each speaker likes most about the job. Now look at Task 2. For questions 26–30, choose from the list (A–H) what each speaker dislikes about the job. While you listen, you must complete both tasks.

Speaker One

Well, some people would probably regard it as rather dull, but it suits me fine. I'm happy just to go in every day and do as I'm told; I don't have any great ambitions to rise up the chain or anything like that. I sort out customers' problems all day long, and you have to be pretty patient to do that, but I am. I have a pretty high level of skill at that particular thing and I get very well-rewarded for it, which is the main thing for me. The place is very poorly run, which can be very irritating as it leads to all sorts of mistakes, but basically I just get on with sorting them out.

Speaker Two

When you're in charge of anything, you're bound to upset some people, it goes with the territory, but it's a position that comes naturally to me. I like the fact that my decisions matter and I like to think I'm good at running things. If something goes wrong, I try to make sure I do something about it myself, not just blame other people. The downside, though, is that I tend to take on too much. Some days are a nightmare as I rush around trying to get everything done.

Speaker Three

Well, we all get along very well in the department, which is just as well because otherwise we'd all be pretty fed up every day. The people at the top think that it's their role to hand out orders and tell people off all the time, so we're under a fair bit of pressure from that direction. They have no idea how to treat people, to be honest. If we talked to the customers like that, the place would soon go bust! We have a laugh actually, and that's what makes going to work enjoyable. We don't let the pressure get us down, we have fun.

Speaker Four

I took the job because I felt I wasn't being stretched in my previous place. I wanted to realise my potential, do something that enabled me to show what I was capable of. And that aspect is the thing that makes me stay there, because I like having to get to grips with things I haven't tackled before. This often means working late, trying to find a solution. What I'm not so keen on though is the constant changes of personnel. One day I'm working with one set of people and the next day they've all gone and been replaced by a whole new bunch.

Speaker Five

What's really good is not having someone looking over your shoulder all the time. Lots of places are obsessed with their systems and rules and regulations but that's not the case here. Instead, we're all left to our own devices and we can just get on with the real work that needs doing. It's all pretty formal, though, and people don't have much to do with each other. What really gets me down, though, is how shabby the place is. They should spend some money on doing it up.

KEY AND EXPLANATION

TEST 1

p8–10 PAPER 1, PART 1

FURTHER PRACTICE AND GUIDANCE (p9–10)

For explanations, see the explanations to the questions in the test, which follow.

1 **A** distant   **B** faint
   C secluded   **D** far-away

2 **A** quick   **B** impulsive
   C abrupt   **D** prompt

3 **A** like   **B** type
   C own   **D** self

4 **A** weighed up   **B** made up for
   C set against **D** settled up with

5 **A** advantageous **B** indulgent
   C privileged   **D** gainful

6 **A** dense   **B** filled
   C inundated   **D** plentiful

7 **A** sorely   **B** utterly
   C fully   **D** appreciably

8 **A** length   **B** phase
   C while   **D** course

p8 PAPER 1, PART 1 (TEST)

Note: all explanations in this part refer to the meaning or use of each option most closely related to the question, not necessarily to the only meaning or use of each option.

1 mark per question (Total: 8)

Meeting Marvin Gaye

1 **A:** If someone is **distant**, they are not friendly or communicative. The writer is saying that although he found it exciting to work with Ray Charles, he did not find him a very friendly person.

   B: If something is *faint*, it is not clear or detailed.

   C: If something is *secluded*, it is away from other people and very private.

   D: If someone is *far-away*, they are physically a long distance away.

   All the options are connected with the idea of distance or being apart from others, but only A can be used to describe a person's personality.

2 **D:** If you are **quick to do something**, you do it quickly, especially in response to something. The writer is saying that Marvin Gaye had a good sense of humour and laughed a lot.

   A: If you are *prompt in doing something*, you do something that you are supposed to do without delay.

   B: If you are *impulsive* or do something that is *impulsive*, you act or form a judgment suddenly or because of a sudden desire, rather than thinking carefully first.

   C: If someone is *abrupt*, they say things quickly and then say nothing more, in a way that is considered rude.

   All the options refer to speed, but only D is both appropriate in the context and fits grammatically. (A might fit the meaning but it does not fit grammatically.)

3 **D:** If something has **something all of its own**, it has a quality that is unique to it. The writer is saying that Marvin Gaye spoke in an almost poetic way that was unique to him.

   A: Someone or something *of a certain type* belongs to a certain category and is typical of it.

   B: A person's *self* is their normal personality and behaviour, what they are normally like.

   C: *The like of something* is something similar to or comparable with it.

   All the options refer to the nature of something, but only D completes the required fixed phrase.

4 **C:** If something **makes up for something**, it compensates for it so that something negative is balanced by something positive. The writer is saying that a positive aspect of Marvin Gaye's personality – his *disarming* (making people feel friendly towards him) *sincerity* – was much more important than an aspect of Marvin Gaye's personality he didn't like (his *affectations* – behaviour that is not natural and is intended to impress).

   A: If you *set something against something else*, you judge something by comparing a positive aspect of it with a negative aspect or a negative aspect with a positive aspect.

   B: If you *weigh up something*, you consider it carefully by looking at different aspects of it.

   D: If you *settle up with someone*, you pay them the money that you owe them.

   All the options are phrasal verbs connected with the idea of balancing things, but only C fits the meaning in the context.

5 B: If you feel **privileged**, you feel that something that has happened to you or been given to you is an honour and you are grateful for it and proud that you have been chosen for it. The writer is saying that he felt this way because he admired Marvin Gaye.

A: If something is *advantageous to you*, it benefits you or is useful to you.

C: If someone is *indulgent* towards someone, they have so much affection for them that they allow them to have or do anything they want.

D: If you find *gainful employment*, you do something which is profitable or earns you an acceptable amount of money.

All the options are connected with the idea of something benefiting someone, but only B can be used to describe a feeling.

6 B: If something is **filled with** something, it contains a lot of it or consists entirely of it. The writer is saying that there were a lot of contradictions and contrasts in Marvin Gaye's personal life.

A: If someone is *inundated with* something, they receive a lot of something, for example offers or requests.

C: If something is *plentiful*, there is a lot of it, it exists or is available in large quantities.

D: If something is *dense*, it contains a lot of something and is complicated.

All the options are connected with the idea of having or containing a lot of something, but only B can be used with the preposition 'with' and has the correct meaning in the context.

7 C: utterly means 'completely', 'totally' or 'absolutely' and can be used for emphasis with adjectives that convey both positive and negative ideas. The writer is saying that Marvin Gaye's work was done in a totally professional, highly efficient and highly organised way.

A: *appreciably* means 'considerably' or 'much' and is used with comparative adjectives.

B: *fully* means 'completely' or 'entirely', so that nothing could be added or so that the feeling described is as strong as it could be.

D: *sorely* means 'very badly' or 'very much' and is used with this meaning in a few phrases such as 'sorely missed', 'sorely tempted' and 'sorely needed'.

All the options can be used with the meaning 'very' or 'very much', but only C can be used to form a correct collocation.

8 A: a while means 'a period of time'. If something *takes a while*, a period of time is required before it happens or is complete. The writer is saying that he had known Marvin Gaye for a period of time before he realised that he was experiencing major problems in his life.

B: *a phase* is a stage or period of time during the development or progress of something.

C: *a length of time* is a period of time

D: The word *course* is used to refer to a period of time in phrases such as *during the course of* and *over the course of*.

All the options refer to a period of time, but only A has the correct meaning in the context and can form a phrase with the verb 'take'.

p11 PAPER 1, PART 2

1 mark per question (Total: 8)

Laughing is Good for You – Seriously

9 by: *By* is used to describe the amount by which something is greater or less than something else. The writer is comparing the number of times children laugh with the number of times adults laugh and saying that adults laugh a couple of hundred times a day less than children do. Obviously, this is an enormous difference, and the figure is introduced by the phrase *as much as* to emphasise how great the difference is.

10 look: If you *take a look at someone/something*, you look at them. The writer is talking here about what you see if you look at people's faces. *Look* is the only noun that fits the meaning here and correctly forms a collocation with *take*.

11 alone: *Let alone* is a linking phrase meaning 'and therefore certainly/probably not', when the result of the first thing being the case is that the second thing certainly or probably isn't the case. The writer is saying that, since you might not see someone smiling, you're very unlikely to see anyone laughing.

12 view: The linking phrase *in view of* means 'considering', 'taking into consideration' or 'because of'. The writer is saying that it's a pity people don't laugh more because it has been proved that doing so is good for you.

13 and: The writer is giving two ways in which laughing is good for you – it *counters* (acts against) stress and *enhances* (improves, makes more effective) the immune system, which is the body's natural reaction against disease.

14 reasons: *Reason* is followed by *why*, not *because* in the structure *There is a/The reason* + *why* + *subject, verb, etc.* The writer is introducing an explanation of the causes of adults laughing much less than children.

15 let: If you *let something show*, you reveal it, rather than trying to keep it hidden. The word *let* is the only word that can complete this phrase so that it both has the right meaning in the context and is correct grammatically – *let* is followed by the infinitive without *to* and there is no *to* before *show*.

16 out: If you *grow out of something*, you become too old, mature or big for it. The writer is saying that when people become adults they stop reacting in the *spontaneous* (natural, without first thinking or planning carefully) way that children do. No other word can complete the phrasal verb with this meaning.

p12 PAPER 1, PART 3

1 mark per question (Total: 8)

Tube Inspired a Book

17 budding: If someone is described as *a budding something*, it means that they are beginning to become one and would like to be a good one. The writer is saying that Preethi Nair would like to be a successful author.

18 enthusiastically: If you are *enthusiastic about something*, you are very interested in or excited about it. The verb is *enthuse (about)* and the noun is *enthusiasm*. The writer is saying that Preethi Nair talks to her in an excited way.

19 innermost: Someone's *innermost thoughts/feelings*, etc are their deepest and most private thoughts or feelings. The writer is saying that the book tells the reader the private thoughts of the characters in it.

20 consultant: *A consultant* is someone whose profession involves giving expert advice to companies. A *management consultant* is a consultant who advises companies on management methods and the training of managers. The writer says that people who do this job are under a lot of pressure.

21 pursuit: If you are *in pursuit of something*, you are trying to achieve or obtain it. We are told that Preethi Nair gave up her job so that she could try to achieve her ambition to be a writer.

22 contentment/contentedness: If you feel *contentment*, you are satisfied with the situation you are in or with life in general. The adjective is *content (with)* or *contented*. The verb is *content yourself with something*, meaning 'be satisfied with something because it is the best you can have, even though it is not exactly what you want'. The word *contentedness*, which has the same meaning, is not often used. Preethi Nair is saying that giving up her job made her happier.

23 lasting: If something is *lasting* (adjective), it continues for a long time or has an effect that continues for a long time. The writer is saying that having two very different cultures in her background had a big effect on Preethi Nair.

24 far(-)away/far-off: A *far(-)away place* is one which is a long distance from another place or from the place where you are. The writer is saying that India is a long way from London.

p13 PAPER 1, PART 4

2 marks per question (Total: 12)

25 positioned himself by the door (1 mark)

so (1 mark)

If you *position yourself somewhere*, you move to a particular place or put yourself in a particular physical position, usually because you have a reason for doing so. The linking structure *so as to do something* means 'in order to do something' or 'with the intention of doing something'.

26 nothing short of (1 mark)

miraculous/a miracle (1 mark)

If something is described as *nothing short of + adjective/noun*, this means that it is absolutely equal to being that thing and not less than it. A *miracle* is something wonderful that happens and is completely unexpected because there is no reason to believe that it will happen. The adjective is *miraculous*.

27 did everything in my power (1 mark)

to prevent/stop (1 mark)

If you *do everything in your power to do something*, you try as hard as you possibly can in order to do it. If you make sure that something doesn't happen, you *prevent/stop something (from) happening*.

28 were justified in (1 mark)

making such a (1 mark)

If you are *justified in doing something*, it is reasonable for you to do it and there are good reasons which mean that you are right to do it. If you *make a fuss (about something)*, you become more agitated than is necessary about something that concerns someone else too and this causes them problems or annoys them. The phrase *complain so much* has to be transformed into the phrase *make such a fuss* to convey the extent of the complaining.

29 a lot of problems to (1 mark)

contend with (1 mark)

The structure *was faced with + noun* can be transformed into the structure *had + noun + to face*. If you have to *contend with something*, you have to face it or deal with it and it is a difficult thing to overcome or solve.

30 of a sudden (1 mark)

there was loud applause (1 mark)

The phrase *all of a sudden* means 'suddenly' or 'quickly and unexpectedly'. The phrase *they started to applaud loudly* has to be transformed into the phrase *there was loud applause from them* – the verb *applaud* has to become the noun *applause* and the adverb *loudly* has to become the adjective *loud* to describe the applause. *There* has to be used as the subject, instead of *audience*.

p14–19 PAPER 1, PART 5

FURTHER PRACTICE AND GUIDANCE (p16–19)

For explanations, see the explanations to the questions in the test, which follow.

Question 31

1 Yes. He says that there are familiar stereotypes of professors, lawyers, detectives and reporters in the fifth sentence.

2 No. He lists what other people think comedians are like but does not mention how comedians feel about this.

3 absent-minded – G   arrogant – C

venal – F   introspective – N

gloomy – H   insecure – A

cynical – L   smug – D

parsimonious – K   autocratic – E

vulgar – I   amoral – J

shallow – B   selfish – M

Question 32

1 Yes, in the final sentence of the second paragraph.

2 A

3 No, he gives his own opinions on them only.

4 Yes, in the last but one sentence of the second paragraph.

Question 33

1 C

2 humour and jokes

3 No

4 No, only that they don't want it to be known that they wrote it.

5 *meek, quiet, bashful, discreet, modest, unassuming*

6 No

Question 34

1 B

2 *ginger* and *snap*

3 B

4 C

Question 35

1 B

2 No

3 Yes. He says that some of them are wits, that there are *Jokes and jokers* at the top of society and that *Some of our rulers do make us laugh.*

4 No

5 B

6 B

Question 36

1 *funnymen, comics, funsters* and *jesters*

2 Yes, he says they *administer relief.*

3 C

4 B

5 C

p14–15 PAPER 1, PART 5 (TEST)

Note: the numbers in brackets after each explanation refer to the relevant question in the Further Practice and Guidance pages.

2 marks per question (Total: 12)

Comedians

31 B: In most of the first paragraph, the writer is asking questions rather than making statements – he is therefore mostly raising possibilities rather than directly stating his own views. With regard to comedians, he wonders what *corny* (repeated so often as to be completely unoriginal) *characteristics ... we attribute to* (people regard as belonging to) them. He then lists a large number of characteristics, all of which are regarded as negative and used when describing people in a disapproving way. **(3)**

A: The writer talks about the familiar *stereotypes* (generalisations commonly made by people concerning the characteristics of other groups of people) of professors, lawyers, detectives and reporters. In each case, the adjective applied to them reflects a negative view of them and is used for expressing disapproval of someone. He therefore believes that these people have a negative image, as do comedians, and does not suggest that they have a better image than comedians. **(1, 3)**

C: The writer says that people generalise both about comedians and about people in other professions. He says that the stereotypes of people in other professions are *cheaply laughable examples from the world of travesty* (are easy to make, ridiculous descriptions that misrepresent in an exaggerated and unfair way). He also says that the characteristics commonly associated with comedians are true if you read their *superficial stories* (stories that have no depth and do not attempt to present anything serious or thorough) *in the tabloids* (popular newspapers in Britain that are commonly associated with sensational stories and gossip about famous people rather than serious articles). Both of these statements suggest that he may not believe that the characteristics commonly associated with people in certain professions and with comedians are accurate. However, he does not suggest that it's easier to generalise about people in other professions than it is to do so about comedians – he does not make a comparison concerning this, he merely says that generalisations are made about all of them, which may not be accurate. **(1)**

D: The writer does refer to negative judgements being made about comedians. In the first sentence he wonders why anyone would want to *put themselves up for* (willingly present themselves as a candidate for) *disparagement* (being treated as useless, stupid or of little value). He also lists the enormous number of negative characteristics he believes are commonly associated with comedians. However, at no point in the first paragraph does he refer to the feelings of comedians concerning what their image is and how they are commonly regarded. (2, 3)

32 B: The writer says that people who prefer or *are drawn to* (attracted to) *anonymity* (being unknown to almost everyone else, not attracting attention) are on an *emotional and intellectual course* (feel and think in a particular way) that is *easily observed but not easily deflected* (easy to see but not easy to change the direction of). The writer is therefore saying that such people have a certain way of thinking which they seldom change from. (2)

A: In the final sentence of the paragraph, the writer says that, for people who wear uniforms and prefer anonymity, the idea of performing to an audience and *craving* (wanting very much) attention is *abhorrent* (disgusting, something intensely disliked). He is therefore saying that they think it is a terrible thing and certainly wouldn't want to do it themselves. However, he does not say that they actually criticise other people who do do it. (1)

C: The writer suggests that he thinks people who want a life of anonymity and wear uniforms have *inadequacies* (weaknesses of character) in his general tone in the paragraph. However, he does not refer to their opinions of themselves or imply that they realise they have weaknesses. (3)

D: The writer says that if *their egos ache for* (if their idea of themselves means that they have a strong desire for) *recognition and praise*, this desire is something that has to be *contained* (not expressed), *frustrated or satisfied within the rut they occupy* (the boring, routine life they lead). The last phrase here indicates that the writer believes their need for recognition and praise can be satisfied within the life they lead, which includes their working life, since he has already told us that he is talking about people who wear uniforms or *livery* (uniforms with designs that are unique to the particular company they represent). (4)

33 A: The writer says in the first line of the paragraph that *comics* (people who perform comedy, comedians) are not to be found among shy people such as *doormats* (people who allow others to treat them badly), *doormice* (extremely shy people), people who are *meek* (timid and willing to let others dominate them), *bashful* (shy) *scholars* (academics), *hermits, anchorites and recluses* (people who live quiet, simple lives, completely apart from all other people, perhaps

for religious reasons), people who are *discreet* (not wishing to draw attention to themselves), people who are *modest* (not talking about their own qualities or abilities) and people who choose to live a life of *obscurity* (not being well-known at all) and *seclusion* (being apart from everyone else). However, he says that in this *stratum of society* (among shy people), there is *humour* (the ability to amuse others or to appreciate things that are amusing) and there are *jokes* (formally constructed little stories with endings that are meant to make people laugh). He then gives the example of two people who have an *unassuming* (not wishing to draw attention to yourself) *existence* who write comedy for radio and TV shows. His point therefore is that shy people can't perform comedy but they can write it. (1, 2, 5)

B: The writer says that shy people are capable of humour and jokes, because humour can exist in any circumstances, like *lichen* (a plant that grows on rocks, trees or walls) *in Antarctica*. However, he does not refer to how humorous such people think they are and does not say that they are better at humour than they think they are. (2, 5)

C: The writer mentions the two *lesser-known comedy writers* as examples of shy people who are capable of humour and jokes but he does not say that they are worried that others may not share their sense of humour. Indeed, they send their material to radio and TV shows, which indicates that they hope that others will find it funny. (3, 5, 6)

D: The writer says that the two writers he mentions send *topical jokes* (jokes about matters that are of interest or in the news at the present time) to TV and radio shows and that when they do so, it is *on condition that their real names are not revealed*. This means that they use false names when sending in their material and make it clear to those they send the material to that they do not want their real names to be used. Therefore, they choose not to get any recognition for their material, even if it is considered good enough for inclusion in the TV and radio shows they send it to. (4, 5, 6)

34 D: The writer says that the material written by the writers he has mentioned is based on *wordplay, puns and similar equivoques* (all types of humour that involve the clever use of words) and not *aggressive comic observation of life*. He believes that this is because people who live in the *self-effacement* (modesty, not trying to impress) of a *humble life* (people who are not important in society, do not wish to draw attention to themselves and do not talk about their qualities or abilities) also live a life of *sterility* (in this context, lacking imagination or excitement). As a result, it seems *feasible* (possible) to him that before they even begin to decide what is funny, and therefore to write it, their idea of what is funny has been *emasculated* (considerably weakened) because of the life they lead. They have no *ginger and* *snap* (vigour, liveliness, spirit) in their *daily round* (everyday life) and so their humour is limited to *juggling with language* (rearranging it, in this context in order to use combinations of words in a humorous way). The writer clearly feels that their humour lacks something, from his general tone in describing it, and what it lacks is *spirit* (energy, liveliness, vigour, aggression) because it is a reflection of the kind of lives they lead and the kind of people they are. **(1, 2, 3, 4)**

A: The writer does not criticise their humour for being similar to or copied from other people's humour, nor does he refer to it being a kind of humour that is very common. **(3C, 4B)**

B: The writer does not say that it is a kind of humour that does not make sense or may not be easily understood by people, even though he does say that it is based on the clever use of words. **(1A, 3A)**

C: The writer does not say that the humour is too simple or not subtle enough – indeed, the fact that it is based on the clever use of words suggests that it may be sophisticated, and it is the fact that it is based entirely on the clever use of words and not on strong emotions or observation of life which he dislikes about it. **(1C)**

35 D: The writer says that in the top *echelons* (levels) of society there is humour, and *wits* (people who say things that are both clever and funny) and that jokes and *jokers* (people who say or do amusing things or play tricks on people) *circulate* (can be found all over) the *loftiest* (highest) level of every advanced society. However, such people feel no *compulsion* (strong urge) to amuse the *hoi-polloi* (ordinary people, as opposed to those at the top of society). Some of them, he says, do make us laugh (in this context, *us* must mean ordinary people) but they don't have to do that for a living. Their comedy is *constricted* (limited and narrow) because they live a constricted life (presumably meaning that they only know people from their own level of society) and so they only amuse each other and do not have *the common touch* (the ability to get on well with, and in this context presumably amuse, people from lower levels of society). He is therefore saying that some people from the top of society are capable of comedy but that their comedy is of such a narrow kind that ordinary people would not find it funny and so they could not earn a living as comedians. **(1, 3, 5, 6)**

A: The writer says that people at the top of society do not have a sense of humour that is in common with those from other levels of society, but he does not refer to their opinion of the humour of people at the lower levels of society or suggest that they have a low opinion of those people or their sense of humour. **(1, 2, 6)**

B: Both *wits and jokers* are people who deliberately try to amuse others and the writer says that these exist at the top of society. **(3)**

C: The writer says that some people at the top of society *do make us laugh* although he does not make it clear whether he thinks that when they make ordinary people laugh this is intentional or not. He therefore does not directly state that they do not know that other people laugh at them. **(1, 4)**

36 C: The writer wonders whether comics are *called to their vocation* (whether they take up the occupation because they see it as the natural and most suitable thing for them to do). He wonders whether the need of the *mirthless masses* (people who have nothing to laugh about) tends to *summon forth* (bring out or call for) comedians, who are ready to *administer* (provide) *relief as their sole raison d'être* (their only or most important reason for existing). He wonders whether the phrase *a born comedian* (someone who is bound to become a comedian because of their natural ability and qualities) will *do for* (applies to) all comedians or even to most of them. And he wonders whether they are, as people like to think, *inescapably driven to expression* (whether they feel an irresistible urge to express themselves through comedy). He therefore wonders whether it is true that even most comedians become comedians because that is the natural thing for them to become, whether comedians feel that comedy is their vocation and the reason why they exist, and whether they feel an urge they cannot resist to become comedians. **(1, 2, 4B, 5C)**

A: The writer says that people need comedians because they provide them with relief and that they like to think that comedians become comedians because of some powerful urge they cannot resist, but he does not say that people expect too much of comedians. **(1, 2, 4A)**

B: The writer says that perhaps people like to think that great comedians are like great painters and composers in the sense that all of them feel a strong urge to become what they become, but he does not compare these people in terms of whether they can be considered great or not. **(1, 3, 5D)**

D: The writer says that comedians are important to the *masses* because they provide them with relief and does imply that they feel it is their role to provide this relief, but he does not refer to wondering whether or not comedians are aware of how important doing so is. **(1, 2, 4C, 5A)**

p20–21 PAPER 1, PART 6

2 marks per question (Total: 14)

Husband and Wife

37 F: In the opening paragraph we learn that Thanet is happy, and why.

In F, *And so* refers back to the fact that he was a happy man. Because of that, he relaxed in his armchair and *reflected* (thought about) how satisfied he was with his life. However, he was *blissfully unaware* (happy and unaware of a reason to be unhappy) that he was about to have a shock.

In the paragraph after the gap, he is still unware of the shock to come, continues to relax, and he and his wife briefly talk about whether to watch the news on television or not.

38 C: In the paragraph before the gap, they talk briefly about watching the news.

In C, they have stopped talking about that and Joan is reading her book again, while he reads a newspaper. He becomes aware that she is not concentrating on her book but is *restless* (unable to sit still because of feeling anxious) and this is very unusual because she usually concentrates fully when she is reading.

In the paragraph after the gap, she makes a number of nervous movements, which continue the description of her in C as 'restless'. She *fidgeted* (moved around in her seat in a nervous manner), put one leg on top of the other and then reversed that, *fiddled with* (kept touching and re-arranging) her hair and chewed the edge of her thumb.

39 H: In the paragraph before the gap, he asks her if something is the matter and when she hesitates to reply he says '*Out with it*', which means 'Tell me' or 'Say what you are thinking'.

In H, she still does not reply, he begins to feel the first *faint stirrings of alarm* (feelings of slight anxiety) and she eventually says that she thinks he isn't going to like the thing that she is *trying to pluck up* (gain or accumulate) *the courage* to tell him.

The paragraph after the gap begins with him replying to what she says at the end of H '*Oh?*' in a way that is described as *warily* (suspiciously, cautiously). He replies in this way because in H he has begun to feel alarmed and she has told him that she needs courage to tell him what she is going to tell him. She then tells him that she has to start thinking about whether, as they have already agreed, she is going to return to work or not when *Ben starts school* (this presumably means that when one of their children starts school she will not have to stay at home to look after him and will be able to start work again).

40 G: In the paragraph before the gap, she says that she knew he wouldn't like the idea of her returning to work. He says that is not true but that it will take him some time to get used to the idea. She says that he is just pretending to approve and that in reality he is *dead against it* (completely opposed to it).

In G, we are told that *she was right* because *he was*, which refers back to the end of the preceding paragraph and means that he was completely against the idea of her going back to work. We are then told that throughout the eight years they had been married, she had been *the good little wife* (this phrase is used to indicate a feeling that she had done what was expected of her without argument but implies that she would have had a right not to behave like this) who had not had a job and had brought up the children, looked after the home and made sure that everything *was geared to* (arranged in order to suit) *Thanet's convenience*. She was different from his colleagues' wives because she never *nagged* (continuously criticised or complained to someone, in this case her husband).

In the paragraph after the gap, we are told that now, *in a flash* (suddenly, very quickly), he *saw all of that changing*. The phrase *all of that* refers back to the whole situation concerning their arrangements that is described in G. He imagines that there will be problems if she returns to work.

41 B: In the paragraph before the gap, he has thought about how different theory and practice are – in the context this means that when the idea of her returning to work was just an idea, it had been something he could *contemplate with equanimity* (think about in a calm manner), but now that it was a real possibility, he didn't like it at all.

In B, he begins by saying that it is not true that he is against the idea. The first thing he says, beginning *Nonsense*, refers back to what she says to him before the previous gap (gap 40) and he is denying the accusation she makes immediately before that gap. This reference back to something earlier in the text is logical because there is no conversation after the paragraph before gap 40 and this point in the text, so the next piece of dialogue continues the conversation from where it was left earlier. In B, she says that despite what he says, she thinks he is against the idea, and he then says that he thought she had decided to do an art course, not get a job.

In the paragraph after gap 41, *it* in her phrase *consider it seriously* refers to the art course he mentions at the end of B and she says that she was interested in doing such a course *at one time*.

42 E: In the paragraph before the gap, she says that she wants to do something less *self-indulgent* (only for her own enjoyment) and more useful and wonders whether saying this sounds *horribly priggish* (that indicates a belief that you are morally superior in a way that is very unappealing to others).

In E, he replies *To be honest, yes*, which refers back to what she says at the end of the paragraph before the gap and means that he thinks what she has said does sound *horribly priggish*. He says that, however, he understands what she means, and she then asks him to confirm that he doesn't think she is being stupid in wanting to do something useful.

In the paragraph after the gap, he does confirm this – *Not in the least* refers back to what she asks at the end of E and means that he doesn't think she is being stupid at all. He then asks her what she is thinking of doing and she says that she doesn't know but feels she might need to do a course or some training.

43 D: In the paragraph before the gap, she says that she can arrange something for her to do by September and he asks whether she has *gone into* (investigated, made enquiries about) *it* (getting a job or doing a course or some training) *yet*.

In D, her reply refers back to what he says at the end of the paragraph before the gap – when she says she wanted to speak to him about it *first*, she means she wanted to discuss it (the subject of her going back to work, doing a course or doing some training) before *going into it*. She then asks if he is sure he doesn't mind and he says that he doesn't, lying *valiantly* (bravely) that he had been expecting this to happen *sooner or later* (at some point in the near or distant future, eventually).

In the final paragraph, the opening phrase refers back to the end of D, and means that he had been hoping that this would happen – that she would go back to work – *very much later* (a lot further in the future). *And preferably not at all* means that in fact he had hoped that it would never happen.

The paragraph which does not fit into any of the gaps is A.

p22–23 PAPER 1, PART 7

1 mark per question (Total: 10)

Kents Cavern: Inside the Cave of Stone-Age Secrets

44 D: At the time of Father MacEnery's discovery in the south of England, scientists were *barely coming to grips with* (were still finding it difficult to accept and adapt to) the discovery of evidence in the north of England that animals that could only be found in tropical countries had once existed there. There was therefore widespread surprise that such animals had existed in the south as well as the north.

45 F: The writer says that today Kents Cavern is *one of the most important archaeological and palaeontological sites in Britain* and it *is still producing wonders* (amazing discoveries). These *astonishing* discoveries *may again revolutionise our understanding of our origins*.

46 B: After finding the fossil teeth, Father MacEnery *continued his search in silence* because he was worried that, if the other members of the party knew about it, they would become so excited and so keen to take fossils away with them that his discoveries *would be damaged*. Therefore he kept them a secret.

47 D: Until the 1820s, nothing was known about *humanity's origins* or *what Britain was like millennia ago*.

48 E: Father MacEnery felt *intellectual shock*, and was *electrified* by the realisation that his discovery of both fossil teeth and tools in the same place meant that *man and extinct beasts* had existed at the same time.

49 C: In 2011, it was established that a human jaw found in the cave is in fact *7,000 years older than was thought* and it is therefore part of *the oldest Homo sapiens in northwest Europe*.

50 A: One man in the group wanted to discover *an ancient Roman temple*, whereas the priest (Father MacEnery) wanted to find *fossils*.

51 F: The idea that the Earth was only 6,000 years old *was fatally undermined* (was destroyed by evidence, was shown to be definitely incorrect) in the 19th century. Geologists at that time *were revealing the great antiquity of our world* (were showing how old it really is).

52 B: Father MacEnery found places in the cave *where the ground had already been disturbed* before the visit of his party.

53 A: The writer describes the cave as a *strange world of darkness* that contained *vast chambers, narrow fissures and magical stalactites that formed crystalline chandeliers and pillars*.

PAPER 1	
PART 1	8 marks
PART 2	8 marks
PART 3	8 marks
PART 4	12 marks
PART 5	12 marks
PART 6	14 marks
PART 7	10 marks
TOTAL	72 marks

To be converted into a score out of 50 marks.

p24–27 PAPER 2, PART 1

Each answer is given marks out of 20

FURTHER PRACTICE AND GUIDANCE (p25–27)

1　C, D

2　A, D

MARK SCHEME

Content

The essay should include a summary of these **four key points**:

Text 1 (a) people worry about crime despite any statistics indicating that it is falling

(b) people get their fears about crime from a variety of sources

Text 2 (a) people don't trust crime statistics and think they are deliberately inaccurate

(b) people's main concern is whether they will be personally affected by crime

Communicative achievement

This is an essay and so the register should be neutral or formal. The reader should be clear both as to what the key points in each text are and the candidate's own opinions and responses to those points.

Organisation

The essay should be coherently organised in paragraphs, with clear linking between the summaries of the key points and the candidate's own views. An introduction and conclusion are not essential.

Language

The essay should contain an appropriate level of accurate grammar and vocabulary. Vocabulary connected with the topics of crime and feelings should be correctly used, as should grammatical structures for describing and comparing points of view/information, presenting and supporting opinions, and linking points in complex sentences.

ASSESSMENT OF SAMPLE ANSWER (p27)

Content

The four key points are all covered in the second paragraph in a way that shows full understanding of those points as expressed in the texts. The answer discusses both texts together, rather than one after the other and this approach works well here. There are no irrelevant points. The writer's own opinions are given in the last paragraph.

Communicative achievement

The register is suitably neutral/formal. The answer rephrases the key points from the text in a very coherent way, and the opinions expressed in the third paragraph

are completely clear. The opinions also make logical sense in relation to the key points from the texts.

Organisation

The essay is well-organised and divided into paragraphs in a simple and effective way. The essay opens with a sentence summarising the topic, the second section summarises the texts and the third section presents opinions linked to the issues raised in the texts. The points made and opinions expressed all link together so that the essay flows well from start to finish.

Language

A good range of grammatical structures is used, including accurate use of the passive, past modal (*may have been*), and the present participle (*falling, resulting, covering*). There are a number of complex sentences that demonstrate good control of grammar, with coherent linking. Good and appropriate vocabulary is used throughout, both single words (*faked, reassure, misconduct*) and phrases (*word of mouth, in the spotlight, a great deal of, losing the authority to*).

There are a few mistakes: *the society* should be 'society' without 'the'; *doesn't exist* should be 'isn't'; a *concern* can't be *true* – this should be 'justified'; *the youth crime* should be 'youth crime' without 'the'; and *Does it take to be* should be 'Do you have to be' or 'Is it a matter/question of being'. However, these mistakes do not seriously affect understanding of the points being made.

Mark

Band 4 (13–16 marks out of 20). This is a good essay, which fully meets the requirements of the task. There are some errors but the general level of fluency demonstrated is quite high.

p28 PAPER 2, PART 2

MARK SCHEMES

Question 2

Content

The report should include:

- description of the organisation's structure and comments on it
- evaluation of strengths and weakness of the organisation
- description and evaluation of performance and attitude of those in charge
- description and evaluation of performance and attitude of those working/studying in the organisation

Communicative achievement

Register appropriate for report done as part of a course – formal or neutral. Report format – clear and brief introduction, followed by separate sections, probably with headings, dealing with each separate aspect required for the assignment, and perhaps a brief conclusion. The reader should understand fully and clearly the structure of the organisation and the writer's opinions on the organisation.

Organisation

The report should be well-structured, with description and comment appropriately linked.

Language

Language of analysing, evaluating and describing, as well as language for expressing and supporting opinions.

Question 3

Content

The letter should describe one or more common national stereotypes and comment on them, and should describe a stereotype of the writer's nationality and comment on the accuracy or otherwise of that.

Communicative achievement

The register must be appropriate for a reader writing to a magazine – could be formal, informal or neutral and perhaps even a mixture of these. Standard letter format. The reader should understand what the writer has described and the writer's views on that.

Organisation

Clear introduction stating why the reader has decided to write the letter – to agree with the unflattering views expressed in the magazine article, disagree with them, or both. Clear organisation of points made: clear description of stereotypes and clear expression of views on them, with appropriate linking between stereotypes and comments on them. Clear paragraphing and appropriate linking between paragraphs. Clear, although probably brief, conclusion.

Language

Language of describing and analysing and language for expressing and supporting opinions.

Question 4

Content

The review should inform the writer as to the content of the exhibition or museum and what makes it special or particularly poor.

Communicative achievement

Register could be informal, formal or neutral – the writer may wish to make the review amusing, serious or purely objective. The format should be appropriate to a review: description followed by comment in each paragraph or in separate paragraphs. The reader would be informed as to the content of, and other relevant points concerning, the exhibition or museum and able to decide whether they would be interested in visiting it or not. The reader would also find the review entertaining, because the competition asks for 'the most interesting review'.

Organisation

Clear development of points of view, with appropriate linking between description and comment and between different aspects of the exhibition or museum.

Language

Language of narrating (to describe writer's visit), describing (exhibition or museum) and evaluating (writer's views).

PAPER 2

PART 1	20 marks
PART 2	20 marks
TOTAL	40 marks

To be converted into a score out of 50 marks.

p29–32 PAPER 3, PART 1

FURTHER PRACTICE AND GUIDANCE (p30–32)

For explanations, see the explanations to the questions in the test, which follow.

Question 1 A, B, F
Question 2 A, C, D, E, F
Question 3 A, B, C, D, E, F
Question 4 A, B, C, D, E
Question 5 A, B, D, E
Question 6 D, F

p29 PAPER 3, PART 1 (TEST)

Note: the letters in brackets after each explanation refer to the relevant options in the questions in the Further Practice and Guidance pages.

1 mark per question (Total: 6)

1 **B:** The speaker says that the title, which is *The Tipping Point*, is a *notion* around which the book is organised and that it describes *the moment when, to put it bluntly* (to phrase it in a direct, unsophisticated way), *a thing takes off* (suddenly becomes very popular or successful) *and becomes widespread in a particular society*. Since this is the central notion of the book, and the speaker has said that the book is a *wonderfully off-beat* (unconventional, unusual) *study of that little-understood social phenomenon, the social epidemic*, the speaker clearly means that the definition of a 'social epidemic' is 'something that becomes widespread in a particular society'. **(A, B)**

A: The speaker says that the title describes the point when something becomes widespread, but she does not say that this is the point at which they are at their most widespread, or imply that after that they become less widespread. **(C)**

164

C: The speaker gives examples of things that have *tipping points* – two of the examples are of inventions (fax machines and mobile phones) and the speaker says that *ideas* also have *tipping points*. She goes on to say that *the point is* (the important matter is) that social epidemics *usually take us by surprise*. Therefore, she is saying that whatever form the social epidemics take, they usually happen unexpectedly. This is not the same as saying that they worry people at the point when they first happen. **(D, E, F)**

2 **A:** The speaker describes the book's writer as *coming out with ideas* (expressing ideas) – *not necessarily his own* (which may not be his own, original ideas) – *that make conventional solutions to social problems seem criminally naive* (so foolish and lacking in knowledge of the reality of something that they are disgraceful and totally unacceptable). The speaker is therefore saying that the writer, having studied social epidemics, comes to some unconventional conclusions about how to solve social problems, which disagree with and are far better than the ideas people normally have on that matter. **(D, E, F)**

B: The speaker says that Gladwell *makes sense of them* (social epidemics) by *anatomising them* (examining them in enormous detail) and that he shows that they are heavily influenced by *connectors and mavens*. The speaker says that *Summarised like this* (If the book is summarised as simply an account of what 'connectors' and 'mavens' do), the writer's *dissection* (highly detailed examination) *sounds a bit crude* (seems rather simple and lacking in the required complexity). However, the speaker says, the book is *a very subtle piece of work* (it is clever, complex and not as straightforward as it may at first appear). **(A, C)**

C: The speaker refers to the writer's use of the terms 'connectors' and 'mavens'. She says that the writer defines 'connectors' as people who *jump-start the epidemic* (cause it to start suddenly, as when a car engine starts as a result of the car being pushed) *by virtue of* (because of) *the people they know* – in other words, they know influential people and by telling them about something they can cause it to become a social epidemic. She says that there is a test in the book that lets readers find out whether *they qualify* (whether they can consider themselves 'connectors'). She says that 'mavens' are defined in the book as *specialists who possess the power of recommendation* (people who are experts in a particular field and whose recommendation of something to the public can make it become popular and widespread). She therefore explains what the terminology she mentions means but she does not say that readers will have difficulty understanding the terms. **(B)**

3 **C:** The speaker wonders *Why am I up here?* (Why am I high up this crag – a steep, rough mass of rock – ?) He wonders *What am I trying to prove?* (What do I want to show as a result of climbing the

crag?) He wonders *why exactly* (the precise reason why) a man of his age (he implies that at the age of 46 he is quite old for such an activity) is *dangling over a void* (hanging or swinging over a large empty space below him). He says that there is no answer to *such fatuous* (stupid, foolish) *metaphysical questions* (philosophical questions concerning the meaning of life). He is therefore asking himself why he is doing this, what the point of it is. **(B, D)**

A: The speaker says that he is someone who feels *dizzy* (the uncomfortable feeling that everything is spinning round that some people have when ill or in high places) *near the edges of sea cliffs* (steep rocks on coasts) and *sweats* (produces liquid through the skin) *with fear at the top of towers* and implies that it is therefore strange for him to climb to the top of a rock. We know that he is high up and near the top because he says *Only 80 feet to the top*, indicating that he is only a short distance from the top. Feeling bad in high places is a common experience for him and so he doesn't wonder why he feels bad in the high place he is now. **(A, C)**

B: The speaker says that it is impossible to answer the questions he is asking himself when *your climbing partner has just disappeared from view* and is *somewhere far above your head* – clearly, his climbing partner has disappeared and he knows that he is a long way above him. He therefore doesn't wonder where his partner is, he has an idea where that person is. **(E, F)**

4 **B:** The speaker says that this is *the proverbial moment* (the moment that is well-known and talked about by a lot of people – he means that people who have done similar things talk afterwards about this moment during the experience). He says that he is on a *great wrinkled slab of ancient geology* (a huge old rock that has lines in it rather than being smooth) and that, at this moment, he has a *palpitating* (with the heart beating very fast), *sweat-soaked* (very wet as a result of sweating), *miraculously* (very remarkably and unexpectedly) *heightened* (made very intense) *sense of existence* (feeling of being alive) and that he *wouldn't be anywhere else* (would not wish to be in any other place). He is therefore saying that he is experiencing a good feeling of great excitement and that he is very glad to be where he is. **(A, B, C)**

A: The speaker says that at this moment he realises *with a keen pang of guilt* (with a strong and uncomfortable feeling of guilt) that he had forgotten to check *the small print* (the details in a legal document that are often printed in small type and which you might fail to notice or read but which may be very important) where it *states excluded risks* (where the document says which risks a person might take which the insurance policy will not cover). He is therefore saying that he did not look carefully at his life insurance policy to find out what the insurance company would refuse to pay money for if he had an accident as a result of taking a risk that is mentioned in the document. He does care about failing to do this; he says he feels guilty about it. **(D)**

C: The speaker says that the things mentioned in life insurance documents as activities that are not covered by the policy are the *awesomely* (enormously and very challengingly) *dangerous pursuits* (activities) *that men in their forties are so often drawn* (attracted) *to*. He is saying that men of his age (he is 46) are often attracted to dangerous sports of a kind excluded from insurance policies, but he is not saying that at this moment he feels that age does not matter when it comes to doing such activities. **(E, F)**

5 **B:** The interviewer says that writers who speak at literary festivals are *in quite a comfortable position* (do not have to worry and are not faced with difficulty) although they *rarely admit it* (they seldom say that this is the case, the implication being that perhaps they want people to feel that such appearances are hard work for them). She says that if they read from their own work, the only preparation they have to do is to give this work a *light dusting* (literally, to clean it a bit; in this context, to prepare something that has not been looked at or used for a while) when they are travelling to the event so that it is *in shape* (in good or suitable condition) for the event. Questions asked by the audience *on the back of* (in response to, as a result of) *such a sampling* (a small part of something bigger that is tried as an example) are gentle and *entirely on the author's own terms* (the questions are all questions that the author is willing and happy to answer). If writers *branch out* (move away from their normal area, in this case their own work), and into a different subject which they have a *proven* (known, established) involvement with, they may be asked *tougher* (more difficult) questions. She is therefore saying that the questions asked if writers read from their own work are easier than the ones asked if they talk about something else. **(A, B, D, E)**

A: The interviewer says that questions about subjects writers are involved with may be *tougher* but she adds that *writers are used to questions* because they *ask them of themselves every couple of sentences* – she is therefore saying that because they ask themselves questions all the time when they are writing, they are able to deal with being asked difficult questions by audiences and she does not imply that they dislike this, as it is something they are accustomed to. **(C, E, F)**

C: The interviewer talks about how little preparation may be required of writers before they appear at literary festivals but there is no implied criticism here, and she is not saying that they should prepare more thoroughly. In fact, she is saying that little preparation is required if they are going to read from their own work. When she says that writers rarely admit this, she is suggesting that they do not want people to

know that little preparation is required, but she is not saying that this is because they know they should do more preparation. **(A, B)**

6 **A:** William says that it is *almost invariably* (nearly always) a pleasure to meet readers because *meeting those whose equally solitary experience* (this refers to readers, and William is saying that the experience of reading is as solitary – done alone – as the experience of writing) *completes the act begun in hope of contact* (makes writers feel that the act of writing, which they began with the hope that readers would read what they wrote and that in this way they would make contact with readers, has been successfully carried out). In other words, he is saying that when writers meet people who have read their books, they feel that they have made contact with people through their writing, which was their aim when they started writing. He adds that the feeling that they have done this makes them feel relieved and encouraged, as well as pleased. **(D, F)**

B: William says that the existence of a writer is solitary and *mute* (silent, they don't speak to anyone when they are writing) and that this is like the life of someone suffering from the illness of depression. He says that all writers sometimes lose all confidence, as if a *trapdoor* (a door in a floor) has opened beneath them and they fall through it so that they are left *dangling* (hanging or swinging) above the empty space below it. He therefore talks about what writers really feel like when they are writing but he does not say that they are keen for readers to realise that this is what it is like to be a writer. **(A, B, E)**

C: William says that writers often lose all confidence and that they gain *relief and encouragement* from meeting readers but he does not say that readers supply them with ideas they can use in the future. Instead, he is saying that readers make them feel good about what they have already written. **(C, F)**

p33 PAPER 3, PART 2

1 mark per question (Total: 9)

7 **planning rotas:** A *housekeeper* in a hotel is responsible for the good condition of the rooms, particularly with regard to the cleaning of them. The *floor housekeeper* is responsible for the rooms on one particular floor or storey of the hotel. A *rota* is a timetable or schedule concerning when duties have to be carried out and who will carry them out at these times. In this case the rotas concerned the cleaning of rooms.

8 **front office:** The *front office* she refers to is clearly the reception area of the hotel, where staff deal with guests, rather than other offices in other parts of the hotel which guests do not go to.

9 **H(h)ospitality M(m)anagement:** In general terms, *hospitality* is the entertainment and treatment of guests. As a subject for study, it concerns hotels, restaurants, etc, and the management of them with regard to guests.

10 **operational techniques:** This means methods for carrying out activities and practices, in this case in a hotel. She also studied *human resource management*, which means the management of staff and is also known as *personnel management*.

11 **green issues:** This means 'environmental matters' or 'matters which concern doing things which are good for or do not damage the environment'.

12 **give-aways:** A *give-away* is a free gift, something which is given to people that they do not have to pay for. She mentions soaps and shampoos as examples of things that hotels give to guests.

13 **HCIMA:** The full name of the organisation she joined was the *Hotel and Catering International Management Association*.

14 **Caterer and Hotelkeeper:** This is clearly a trade paper or trade journal (a newspaper or magazine produced for and distributed among people working in a particular kind or area of business). A *caterer* is someone whose job involves providing food and drink for social events, companies, etc and a *hotelkeeper* is the manager or owner of a hotel.

15 **overbooked:** If a hotel is *overbooked*, an administrative mistake has been made and more people have booked rooms than there are rooms in the hotel, so it is impossible to accommodate all the people for whom bookings have been taken. The same verb is used with regard to an aircraft flight, when the number of passengers who have booked seats is greater than the number of seats on the aircraft.

p34 PAPER 3, PART 3

1 mark per question (Total: 5)

16 **D:** Brigid says that *all was not entirely well* with her life (not everything in her life was all right) but that there was *Nothing drastic* (nothing very seriously wrong). She simply felt *stuck* (as if she was not making progress) both in her working life and her personal life because she had too much to do and too little time in which to do it – when she says *ditto*, she means that that was her situation at home as well as at work. However, she wasn't *miserable enough to get therapy or counselling* (her situation wasn't bad enough for her to go to a psychiatrist or psychologist or to a counsellor – someone who gives professional advice about personal problems) and all she wanted to do was *get a little more from life* (enjoy life a bit more). She says that until recently, there would not have been many options for someone in her situation

but now there are life coaches, who are suited to someone in her situation.

A: She says that there are now *legions* (lots of) life coaches *out there* (in existence in a place) and that they help people who are frustrated and *down-at-heart* (unhappy), and she mentions what they do and how much they charge, but she does not say that she got this information from reading about them or that reading about them caused her to consult one.

B: She says that she had a small problem both in her working life and her personal life and that the problem in both of them was the same (she felt *stuck and in need of change*), but she does not say that her situation was getting worse.

C: She says that she didn't feel that therapy or counselling were appropriate in her situation but she does not say that she had already tried them. She says that the options for someone in her situation were limited, but she does not say that she had tried any of these options.

17 **A:** Brigid's coach told her that she should consider herself a *magnet for* (someone or something which powerfully attracts) *money* and someone *to whom cash* (money that can be spent) *flows effortlessly* (without her having to make any effort).

B: She says that she agreed with her coach that her attitude to money was *rooted in childhood* (began and became established when she was a child) and she says that her coach told her that she had to *carve out* (create through effort) a completely new attitude, but she does not say that she was told that her attitude to money was untypical of her personality or that it differed from her attitude to other things.

C: She agreed with her coach that she had to do something about her *deeply ambivalent relationship with money*. This means that she had mixed feelings about money rather than a clear single attitude towards it, not that she gave it more importance than she should.

D: Her coach told her what her individual attitude to money should be but she does not say that her coach generalised about people's attitudes to money or said that most people have the wrong attitude to it.

18 **C:** Her coach advised her to repeat that she was ready to have the perfect life she deserved and she says that when she did this, it *cheered me up no end* (it made me feel very much happier).

A: What she had to repeat was one of *a clutch of* (a small group of) *positive affirmations* (statements expressing a positive attitude) *with which to brainwash myself into* (force myself to accept the idea of) *readiness for riches* (being ready to be rich), and so the idea was that by repeating the words she would convince herself that she was going to be rich. She says that she did repeat the words and it made her feel better but she does not say that she felt that repeating them was a silly thing to do while she was doing it, even though it is possible that this was the case.

B: When her coach told her that she would be rich, have a wonderful life and not feel guilty about it, she thought that this was a *preposterous* (totally ridiculous and unreasonable) idea and she *laughed out loud down the telephone*. She therefore did not conceal her feelings, she made them clear and expressed them openly.

D: She says that her coach was *undeterred* (not discouraged) by her *scepticism* (doubtful response to what someone claims) and told her to *suspend my disbelief* (decide to believe temporarily that something you know not be true is true). Her point is therefore not that her initial feeling was one of confusion but that she didn't believe what she was told and was then persuaded to accept it.

19 A: Brigid says that she was told that most people have the same aims with regard to their personal and working lives, their abilities and money and that the only thing that *stands in their way* (is an obstacle that prevents them from achieving their aims) *is childhood conditioning* (attitudes that were forced on them by other people and became their established attitudes when they were children). She was therefore told that most people's problems with regard to organising their lives, *making the most of* (taking the greatest advantage possible of) their abilities, and money resulted from their experiences during childhood.

B: She says that her work *came under close scrutiny* (was carefully analysed, presumably by both herself and her coach) and that she decided to concentrate on jobs that interested her. This means that she decided to direct her attention towards jobs that interested her rather than jobs that did not, but she does not say that she became able to *concentrate* (use her mind intensely) better.

C: She mentions several things that she was told to do. Firstly there was *the mandatory* (compulsory – presumably she means that people are always told to do this) *de-cluttering* (making things no longer in a state of disorder, tidying something which is untidy), which involved her throwing away useless things she had so that she would have room for all the *goodies* (desirable items) she would have when she was rich. Then she dealt with her financial situation and started saving money, and made changes in her working life. However, she does not say that she had more difficulty doing any one of these things than doing any of the others.

D: Her coach told her that her situation, like most people's, resulted from childhood, but she does not say that she herself began to wonder what had caused her to be in the situation she was in – she was told what the cause was.

20 B: Brigid says that she is still unsure about the *'me first' approach* but thinks that it is *a healthy counterbalance to the 'me last'* attitude she used to have. What she means by this is that coaching has given her the attitude that she should be more selfish and see her interests and wishes as more important than those of others, and she is not completely comfortable with that idea. However, she thinks that it balances in a good way her previous attitude, which was to consider other people's interests and wishes more important than her own and to think of herself as the least important person. She therefore feels that her previous attitude was wrong and that it is right for her to be more selfish now.

A: She says that coaching *is hardly a soft option* (cannot be regarded as an easy choice requiring little effort) but that for her it provided *a great boost* (it had a very positive effect on her, gave her a great deal of help and encouragement). What she is saying is that coaching requires a lot of effort on the part of the person having it and that she put that effort in and got good results. She is not saying that it hasn't been worth it because there has been too much effort on her part and too few benefits for her in return for this effort.

C: She says that there have been *no instant miracles* (coaching has not had immediate wonderful results) but *things are looking up* (her situation is improving). However, she does not say that she began to expect that her coach would make miracles happen in her life; she simply says that miracles have not happened.

D: She says that if you have a coach, you have to deal with things that you have *put off* (delayed dealing with) because you have *the deadline* (point in time by which something must be done that has been fixed or imposed by someone else) *of the next session* (the next time you speak to your coach). If you haven't taken the appropriate action by that time, your coach will not wish to speak to you. What she is saying is that if you haven't done what you are supposed to do by a certain time, your coach may decide there is no point in having a session, and so this may limit the number of sessions you have. However, this is something the coach and not you would decide, so she is not saying that it's a good idea to have only a limited number of sessions.

p35 PAPER 3, PART 4

1 mark per question (Total: 10)

21 F: The speaker went there because he *wanted to see if it seemed any different after all these years away from it*. He visited some *old familiar haunts* – places he used to go to regularly when he lived there – and wanted to see if he felt any *nostalgia* (fond feelings about the past) when he was there again. So the speaker had lived there in the past and wanted to see the place again.

22 D: The speaker went there to attend an event that lasted for two days. At the event she had to *listen to people going on and on* (talking too much) and there was not a chance for participants to get involved. So she clearly attended a conference that she did not enjoy.

23 H: The speaker had been given an *opportunity to move there* – the chance to go and live in the city – and so he decided to go to the place and *check it out* – find out about it, do some research into it. He got information about things such as accommodation during his visit, and the purpose of his trip was to get information about living in the city.

24 E: Friends of the speaker *had been talking about* the city and the speaker *thought it would be nice to take them there so that they could see it for themselves*. She knew the place *pretty well*, having visited it a few times, and went there in order to show her friends what the place was like.

25 A: The speaker refers to something that *came up* (became a topic during a conversation). This concerned whether he would be able to adapt to a different lifestyle if he was *successful* – this must mean that he is talking about a job interview. Later he says that if he *gets the offer* (if they offer him the job) he doesn't think he will accept it.

26 B: The speaker says that although the cathedral is *magnificent*, the rest of the city is not *pleasing on the eye* (not nice to look at). He says there are lots of *concrete slabs* (big, ugly buildings made of concrete) and suggests that the city's *designers and architects* have produced a city that looks horrible.

27 C: The speaker says that the impression she got of the city from her visit there was that it is *an amazing place* with a *lively atmosphere* and she can fully understand (*No wonder* means it is not at all surprising) that other people describe it as a *glamorous* city. So she can understand why people say that it is an exciting city.

28 A: The speaker says that everyone she spoke to during her visit *went out of their way to help me* (made a special effort in order to help her) and she *got the feeling it was very welcoming place* (a place where people are friendly to strangers).

29 D: The speaker says that the place was *crawling with people* (very crowded), particularly because it's a place that all tourists want to see. She says that it was full of people *rushing around* (moving around quickly) and it was *all a bit much* (difficult for them to deal with). They became *exhausted* because there were too many people there and the place was so busy.

30 G: The speaker says that the idea of living in the city is *daunting* (frightening) because of being a very big challenge. He says that he would not be *brave enough* to do that. He is *not used to big city life* and the prospect of it scares him.

PAPER 3
PART 1   6 marks
PART 2   9 marks
PART 3   5 marks
PART 4   10 marks
TOTAL   30 marks
To be converted into a score out of 50 marks.

p36–40 PAPER 4

Marks out of 25 are given for performance in the speaking paper.
To be converted into a score out of 50 marks.

TEST 2

p41 PAPER 1, PART 1

Note: all explanations in this part refer to the meaning or use of each option most closely related to the question, not necessarily to the only meaning or use of each option.

1 mark per question (Total: 8)

A Message for Lisa

1 A: If information is **confidential**, it is secret in the sense that it cannot be made known to anyone other than the specified people who are allowed to have it. The writer is saying that the teacher told Lisa he was not allowed to tell her what was in the message for her, which seemed ridiculous to her.

B: *Intimate details* are those which are private and personal to someone. (*I didn't want to tell a complete stranger all the intimate details of my life.*) If two people are *intimate*, their relationship is a very close one and they know each other's private and personal details. (*I know her quite well but I'm not an intimate friend of hers.*)

C: *Clandestine* behaviour is done secretly, so that other people, who would disapprove, will not know about it. (*She had clandestine meetings with her lover.*)

D: Something that is *undercover* is done secretly because it may be regarded as breaking rules (*The company was accused of making undercover payments to people in exchange for information on their rivals.*) *Undercover* work is work done by a spy or police officer to get information about people who do not know who they really are (*Two officers went undercover to find out about the drug dealers in the area.*)

All the options mean 'secret' in some way, but only A fits the precise meaning in the context.

2 A: If someone **pleads**, they ask in a desperate way or urgent way, because they really want something or really want someone to do something. Lisa really wanted Pete to give her information about the message and asked him to do so in a very strong and emotional way.

B: If someone *asserts* something, they state it in a very strong way because they are certain that it is true. (*She asserted that her version of events was the correct one.*)

C: If someone *craves* something, they desperately want it. (*After a hard week at work, he craved some peace and quiet.*)

D: If someone *pledges to do* something, they promise to do it in a very serious way. (*The new government pledged to improve the lives of the people.*)

All the options are connected with the idea of wanting something very much or saying something very strongly, but only A describes the way in which someone asks for something.

3 B: If you **obey rules**, you act according to what the rules state, you do what is required by the rules. Pete refused to give Lisa any information about the message because according to college rules, he was not allowed to do that.

A: If you *fulfil* requirements, you do or have what is required. (*She didn't get an interview for the job, because she didn't fulfil all the criteria for selection.*)

C: If you *conform to/with* something, you do what is required according to a rule or an expectation. (*All students must conform to the standards of behaviour listed below.*)

D: If you *comply with* a rule or law, you do what it requires you to do, you do not break the rule or law. (*All businesses must comply with the laws concerning Health and Safety.*)

All the options mean 'do what is required', but only B is used both with 'rules' and without a preposition.

4 C: If you are **wary of somebody/something**, you are suspicious of them or cautious with regard to them, because you fear that they could cause you problems or do you harm. The writer is saying that Lisa had been taught as a child not to trust people who believed in rules.

A: If you speak or react in a *guarded* way, you do so cautiously. (*My comments were guarded because I didn't want to offend anyone./Reactions to news of this latest development have been guarded in government circles.*)

B: If you are or feel *uneasy (about something)*, you are anxious or worried about it. (*Joe is a rather aggressive person and he makes me feel uneasy.*)

D: If someone is *edgy*, they are nervous or agitated and likely to get upset or angry at any moment. (*George has got a lot on his mind and this has made him rather edgy.*)

All the options mean 'cautious' or 'nervous', but only C can be followed by 'of'.

5 C: If something **brings** something, it causes it to exist, results in it or is followed by it. The writer is saying that as Lisa walked towards the office to collect the message she became more and more optimistic that it would result in her and Quentin being together again.

A: If something *leads* to something, it results in it or causes it. (*What was it that led to this problem?*) If you *lead someone to a place*, they follow you there. (*The hotel owner led me to my room.*)

B: If something *arises*, it occurs or appears. (*Whenever a serious problem arises, Helen panics.*) If something *arises from/out of something*, it happens or follows as a result of it. (*My interest in the theatre arose from/out of a visit to a play when I was very young.*)

D: If something *puts someone in mind of something*, it causes them to think about or remember it. (*This situation puts me in mind of something that happened to me many years ago.*)

All the options are connected with the idea of 'causing something', but only C fits grammatically.

6 B: If something **occurs to someone**, it comes into their mind or they realise it. The writer is saying that Lisa realised just before she reached the office that Quentin didn't know she was at college.

A: If something *strikes someone*, it comes into their mind suddenly or they suddenly become aware of it. (*It strikes me that there is a very simple solution to this.*)

C: If something *dawns on someone*, it becomes clear or obvious to them after a period of time. (*Gradually it dawned on me that he had been telling me lies.*)

D: If something *springs to mind*, it comes into someone's mind quickly or they suddenly think of it. (*I've been trying to come up with some new ideas but unfortunately nothing springs to mind at the moment.*)

All the options are connected with the idea of a thought coming into someone's mind, but only B fits grammatically.

7 D: If you **have no way of doing something**, it is impossible for you to do it. The writer is saying that Quentin couldn't have known that Lisa was at college.

A: If you *have no access to something*, you do not have the chance to have or use it, it is not available to you (*people with no access to a good education*).

B: *The route to something* is the way in which it is achieved or the process through which it is reached (*a book which claims to teach you the route to success in business*).

C: *Scope for something* is the opportunity for something to exist. (*In this job, there is scope for innovation.*)

All the options are connected with the idea of the ability to do or have something, but only D fits both in terms of the precise meaning in the context and grammatically.

8 D: If something **takes your breath away**, it surprises, pleases or excites you very much. The writer is saying that Lisa's mood changed so much and so quickly when the head of the department spoke to her that she was extremely surprised by this change.

A: If you *catch your breath*, you stop breathing for a moment because of a sudden feeling of fear or shock. (*When the figure suddenly appeared out of the darkness, I caught my breath.*)

B: If you *draw breath*, you breathe in after a period of not doing so. (*He spoke at great length, hardly drawing breath the whole time.*)

C: If you *hold your breath*, you deliberately stop breathing for a short time, perhaps because of fear or excitement. (*hold your breath underwater/The competitors held their breath as the name of the winner was about to be announced.*)

All the options can be used in phrases with 'breath', but only D completes the required idiom.

p42–43 PAPER 1, PART 2

FURTHER PRACTICE AND GUIDANCE (p43)

For explanations, see the explanations to the questions in the test, which follow.

9	B	11	B	13	D	15	D
10	C	12	A	14	A	16	A

p42 PAPER 1, PART 2 (TEST)

1 mark per question (Total: 8)

Advertising in Britain

9 out: If you *set out to do something*, you start taking action with the intention of achieving a particular aim. *Establish* here means 'discover and prove'. Clearly the newspaper in question asked readers to vote for their favourite adverts or to complete a survey or questionnaire.

10 many: The phrase *as many as* followed by a number is used for emphasising that a number is considered high. In the next sentence, the writer says that British people admire television adverts and so it is clearly logical that a lot of them would have responded to the newspaper's attempt to find out what the best ones were.

11 in: If something abstract *lies in* something else, it exists or can be found there. The writer is saying that the reason why so many people responded is that British people admire television adverts.

12 own: If something exists *in its own right*, it exists separately from others with which it could be associated and has its own distinct identity. The writer is saying that television adverts have become a distinct art form, separate from other art forms.

13 up: If you *end up doing something*, you do it, or something happens, at the end of a series of events or a period of time. The writer is saying that it seemed impossible in 1955 that people would later think that TV commercials were as sophisticated and innovative as programmes.

14 them: This refers back to the *ads* (adverts/commercials) mentioned earlier in the sentence. The writer is saying that the programmes during which the ads appeared were considered sophisticated and innovative, but when adverts first appeared they were not.

15 their: This phrase means 'the making of them', 'them' being commercials. In this phrase *making* is a noun, and it needs to be preceded by the plural possessive *their*, since it refers to *commercials*. The writer is talking about how much money is spent and how much thought is given to produce each second of a TV commercial.

16 is: If something *is the case for something*, it is true of something. The writer is comparing television commercials and movies, opera, etc in terms both of what is involved in making them and the profits made from them and is saying that the amount is greater for commercials than for movies, etc. The verb *is* must be singular because the subject of it is *the case*.

p44 PAPER 1, PART 3

1 mark per question (Total: 8)

Captain Webb

17 undoing: *Someone's undoing* is the thing that ruins their life or causes them to fail completely. The writer is saying that the fact that Webb refused to give up swimming was disastrous for him in the end.

18 obscurity: If you live *in obscurity*, you are not at all famous or well-known. The writer is saying that nobody had heard of Webb until he swam the Channel.

19 **exhaustion:** If you are suffering from *exhaustion*, you are extremely tired and have no strength or energy left. The writer is saying that Webb was extremely tired when he finally arrived on the other side of the Channel.

20 **stardom:** *Stardom* is the situation or status of being very famous as a performer. The writer is saying that being very famous had an enormous effect on Webb, and caused him to make a terrible mistake.

21 **applause:** *Applause* is approval expressed by a crowd or audience by clapping (hitting their hands together). If you *crave something*, you want it desperately. The writer is saying that Webb was extremely keen to receive the praise and admiration of others.

22 **endurance:** *Endurance* is the ability to continue doing or surviving something difficult or unpleasant for a long time without giving up. An *endurance event/ contest*, etc is a sports event in which the competitors have to do something (swim, run, cycle, etc) for a very long time. The writer is saying that Webb took part in a swimming event that lasted for six days.

23 **punishing:** If something such as a timetable, schedule, workload, etc is *punishing*, it requires an enormous amount of effort and energy on the part of the person doing it because they have to do a great many things, and it may make the person doing it extremely tired or ill. The writer is saying that Webb's timetable when he went to America was full and that he did too much while he was there.

24 **regardless:** The linking phrase *regardless of* means 'paying no attention to' or 'in spite of'. The writer is saying that Webb ignored advice not to try to swim the Niagara river.

p45 PAPER 1, PART 4

2 marks per question (Total: 12)

25 **was instrumental in** (1 mark)

the drafting (1 mark)

If someone/something *is instrumental in something/ doing something*, they are the cause of it or the most important reason why it happens. The verb *drafted* has to be transformed into the noun phrase *the drafting of*, meaning 'the process of drafting'.

26 **you stuck to/by** (1 mark)

what we originally (1 mark)

The third conditional structure *If + subject + had + past participle* can be transformed into the structure *Had + subject + past participle*. If you *stick to/ by something*, you do not change it after you have agreed to it or decided on it. The verb *agreed* has to be given the subject *What* and the phrase *our original agreement* changed to *what we originally agreed* – *original* has to become an adverb to describe the verb *agreed* rather than an adjective describing the noun *agreement*.

27 **spare a thought for** (1 mark)

those/(the) people whose (1 mark)

If you *spare a thought for someone*, you give them some consideration because they are in an unfortunate situation, rather than thinking in a selfish way. The relative pronoun *who* comes before a verb or subject and has to be replaced by the structure *whose + noun* because *lives* is a noun.

28 **to admit defeat** (1 mark)

while there was still/while there remained (1 mark)

If you are *loath to do something*, you are reluctant or unwilling to do it. If you *admit defeat*, you accept that you are not going to succeed and stop trying. The phrase *noun + to remain* has to be transformed into the structure *there + to be + still + noun* or, more formally, *there + to remain + noun*.

29 **rose/(were) lifted** (1 mark)

when I caught sight (1 mark)

If *your spirits rise/lift/are lifted*, you become happier or more cheerful after being unhappy, usually because of something that happens to cause this. If you *catch sight of something*, you see it suddenly or for a moment.

30 **do wonders for** (1mark)

the way you look (1 mark)

If something *does wonders for something/someone*, it is extremely beneficial for them because it changes them in a very positive way. The phrase *the way someone looks at something* has the same meaning as the phrase *someone's attitude to something*.

p46–48 PAPER 1, PART 5

2 marks per question (Total: 12)
Piper and Buxxy

31 **C:** Piper is said to have looked *relaxed and dependable* and there are two references to his *conservative* (respectable, traditional) style of dress. When he spoke, his *outward reserve* (the fact that he seemed like someone who tended not to express feelings or opinions) is mentioned and the fact that he *let some of his excitement for the project show through* indicates that he was so excited about the project that he could not conceal this excitement even though he was generally reserved when making his speech. The narrator says that he provided the audience with *reassurance* (the confident feeling that there is nothing to worry or have doubts about when someone is worrying or having doubts) and made them feel that *Despite appearances* (Although it did not appear to be the case), *the Tahiti must be a respectable, conservative* (without involving much risk) *investment* – if it was not, *why would someone like Irwin Piper be involved with it?* In other words, the Tahiti did not look like a good thing for them to invest in and Piper seemed like a calm, quiet and

respectable person who would not normally get involved with a casino. The fact that such a person was involved with it made them feel that it might be a suitable thing for them to get involved with too.

A: We learn that this was a *big moment* (a very important one) for both of them because they had to get their audience to invest $200 million. Piper tells them in a *reasonable, persuasive voice* that the Tahiti is a *remarkable financial opportunity* for them. He talked about *numbers, strategy, competitive analysis* (presumably, how the Tahiti could compete for customers). There is no mention of him talking about anything other than the business aspects of the Tahiti and so it must have been clear to the audience that his main purpose in his speech was to get them to invest money in the Tahiti.

B: He talked about the financial opportunity *in abstract terms* (in a general way, without going into detail) and he only talked about numbers, strategy and competitive analysis to the extent that the audience would be made to feel that the Tahiti was *in safe hands* (being efficiently run by trustworthy people), but he did not keep talking about these matters to the extent that the audience would get bored. We are therefore told that the audience felt that he spoke more in general terms and did not give much detail because he did not want to bore them, not because he was less comfortable when giving details.

D: He gave the audience the impression that they would be wise to invest in the project but he is not said to have mentioned whether anyone had already expressed an interest in investing in it. The phrase *competitive analysis* does not indicate that there was competition among people to invest; it is a term relating to the financial details of the project.

32 B: The narrator says that Buxxy's *abrasive* (direct, rather aggressive), *rough-edged* (unsophisticated) *manner jolted* (caused a sudden reaction in, resulting from shock) *his audience after the smooth* (sophisticated, charming but perhaps not sincere) *Piper*. In other words, Buxxy's manner was so different from and so much more energetic than Piper's, that the audience were intially shocked when he started to speak.

A: The narrator says that on the rare occasions when Buxxy was still during his speech, the fact that he stopped moving around was *for a melodramatic* (dramatic in an exaggerated way) *pause, to let the full consequence* (significance, importance) *of what he had just said sink in* (be absorbed or fully understood by the audience). It is therefore clear that the narrator believes that Buxxy put in these pauses deliberately, with a particular intention.

C: Although the audience were *bewitched* and *captivated* (both these words mean 'greatly attracted')

by Buxxy and he paused to allow people to absorb the significance of things he had said, we are not told that the audience's reaction to him resulted from the first points he made or that he started off with his most important points.

D: His face and hair are described but the descriptions are factual rather than intended to convey any opinion of him, and the narrator does not say or imply that his manner came as a surprise because he looked like someone who would have a different manner of speaking.

33 B: The narrator says that *Seen through Buxxy's eyes* (As described by Buxxy), *the tackiness* (poor taste and poor quality) *and loneliness of a big casino disappeared* (they didn't notice it, it did not seem to them to exist) and they saw instead *the glamour, the glitter* (the excitement associated with the world of entertainment), *the amazing technological effects*. In other words, although the casino could have looked like a tacky and lonely place, they saw it as a glamorous, exciting place as a result of the way that Buxxy described it to them.

A: Most of the audience were obviously impressed by the tour because by the end of it they were ready to invest money in the casino immediately, but the narrator does not say that they were so impressed because it was the first time they had ever been inside a casino.

C: They were shown the private rooms where the *high-rollers* (people who gamble large sums of money) played and they saw the *amazing technological effects*, but the narrator does not say that the fact these things exist was unexpected or that they indicated that the project was nearer to completion than the audience had thought.

D: They were shown the rooms where the high-rollers played and the high-rollers are described as *wallowing in* (taking enormous, selfish pleasure in) *sophistication, power and money*. The audience are not described as doing so, and although it is likely that they were so impressed by this that they were willing to invest immediately because they imagined themselves playing in those rooms, the narrator does not say that Buxxy encouraged them to imagine themselves in those rooms.

34 D: The narrator says that when he sat down after asking his questions, some faces in the audience *bore* (had expressions of) *disapproval* and he thinks this was because they regarded him as a *spoil-sport* (someone who ruins the pleasure of others) who had taken *cheap shots at* (made unpleasant, unintelligent and unjustified comments about) the *great guys* (the wonderful men – Buxxy and Piper) and their casino. In other words, he felt that they looked as if they were angry with him and thought that he was not justified in asking the questions he asked.

A: He says that his English accent *jarred in the glitzy* (glamorous) *Las Vegas surroundings*, which means that it sounded strange and out of place there but he does not say or imply that he thought this meant people would not take him seriously.

B: When the narrator stood up, Piper's face showed the *barest trace of* (a very faint sign of) *a frown* (an expression of annoyance, worry or confusion), which shows that he was slightly concerned as to what the narrator would say. After the narrator's first question, Piper *stiffened* (his body became tense), which again indicates that he was concerned. If he had been expecting the narrator's questions, he would not have made either of these reactions.

C: The narrator says that nobody asked any difficult questions about Piper's background, or any *tedious* (dull, boring) questions about technical matters connected with the casino and that even *the most cynical* (negative in attitude, seeing only bad aspects) investor was *under the spell of* (had been completely charmed by, as if by magic) what they obviously thought was *the greatest casino on earth* – clearly the audience seemed to have faith in the project. However, this was not why he asked his questions. He had obviously been planning to ask them anyway because he says that he *had thought through this moment carefully*. He had therefore gone to the casino with the intention of asking these questions and the audience's attitude did not influence or cause that.

35 C: The narrator says that, although Piper had not answered his questions properly and that *if anyone pursued him on this* (if anyone asked him further questions about these matters), *doubts might creep in* (people might start to have doubts about him), he wasn't going to *push it* (it wasn't his intention to proceed with the matter or put pressure on him) *any further*. This was because he had achieved his *objective* (aim) which was that Piper would realise that he knew something (presumably something bad about Piper) and that Piper would realise that he would tell others about it.

A: When Piper had answered the questions, he *looked around the audience quickly*, presumably to see what their reaction was. It was *a dangerous moment* for him because before then the audience had been *eating out of his hand* (under his control, believing everything he said), but now *doubts might creep in* because he hadn't answered the questions properly. He was therefore worried that they might not find his answers convincing and he knew he had not answered the questions properly, but the narrator does not say or imply that the audience realised that he had not answered them properly or that they had not found his answers convincing.

B: Piper said that he was happy to answer the questions. To the first question he replies that all applications for gambling licences are checked out

(this means the same as *scrutinised* in the narrator's question – checked or inspected thoroughly). To the second, he says that he has a lot of investments and doesn't have details of all of them *at my fingertips* (in a place close enough for him to get them immediately). In neither of these replies does he dismiss the questions as concerning only very minor matters and he seems to take them seriously.

D: The narrator says that when Piper *rose to his feet*, he was as *unruffled* (calm) *and urbane* (sophisticated) *as ever*. He therefore did not appear to the audience to be feeling uncomfortable, even though he probably was.

36 A: When the *bellboy* (a young man in a uniform who works in a hotel carrying bags, giving messages, etc, especially in the US) told the narrator that Piper would like to see him and he then made his way to Piper's suite, he thought *That didn't take him long*, which means that he was expecting Piper to ask for him at some point, although he had not expected it to happen so quickly.

B: After Piper had expressed his anger with the narrator and threatened to *sue* him (take him to court in a legal case in order to get money from him), the narrator felt that Piper had put him *on the defensive* (in a position in which he was under attack and could be defeated) for a moment. This was because he wondered whether he had made a mistake in upsetting such a powerful man – presumably because someone so powerful could do damage to him, particularly financially. He was therefore briefly concerned that he might regret upsetting Piper because of what Piper could do to him, not because he had begun to feel that he might have been mistaken in thinking that Piper was dishonest.

C: In Piper's first speech to him, he said that he wasn't a *two-bit* (unimportant, minor) *bondsman* (a kind of financial trader) who the narrator *could play games with* (not take seriously, treat dishonestly) and that if he were to even *allude to* (refer indirectly to) a certain place again, he would sue him for so much money that he would not be able to pay off the debts in his lifetime. The fact that all this put the narrator *on the defensive* indicates that he had not been expecting him to say these things; if he had been expecting it, he would have been able to respond immediately.

D: Piper suggests that the narrator is treating him like a *two-bit bond salesman* and tells him that he is in fact rich and powerful and has lawyers he could use to hurt the narrator. He therefore does accuse the narrator of underestimating him. However, he does not refer to other people who have done this or to what he did to them as a result.

p49–54 PAPER 1, PART 6

FURTHER PRACTICE AND GUIDANCE (p51–54)

For explanations, see the explanations to the questions in the test, which follow.

Question 37	Question 41
1 A and C	1 A and D
2 A and C	2 A and B
3 A and C	3 B and C

Question 38	Question 42
1 C and D	1 A and D
2 B and C	2 A and D
3 B and D	3 A and D

Question 39	Question 43
1 A and D	1 A and C
2 A and D	2 B and C
3 B and C	3 C and D

Question 40

1 B and D
2 C and D
3 A and B

p49–50 PAPER 1, PART 6 (TEST)

Note: the numbers in brackets after each explanation refer to the relevant question in the Further Practice and Guidance pages.

2 marks per question (Total: 14)

The Perils of Pizza Making

37 F: In the opening paragraph, the writer says that his first pizza was *cremated* (burnt to ashes, as is done with dead bodies in a ceremony at funerals) and that he hadn't even got to the stage of putting toppings on it. We therefore know that it was thrown away because it was useless. He then tells us that pizza dough should be made into *perfect circles*. Obviously he had failed to do that with his pizza (**1A**) and Francesco had looked at his *sorry effort* (poor attempt) and *sighed* (presumably with disappointment or disapproval) (**1A**).

In the first sentence of F, *it* refers to the pizza the writer had prepared. His pizza *wasn't so much a circle* (this refers back to the requirement that pizzas be prepared as perfect circles in the first paragraph) *as an early map of the world* (presumably something without a regular shape) (**3C**). Francesco then picked it up on his *paddle* (an implement on which pizzas are placed and then put into the oven) and threw it *disdainfully* (with contempt or great disapproval) into the oven to destroy it (**3A**). The reference to it

burning on a *funeral pyre* (a pile of wood on which dead bodies are burnt as part of funeral ceremonies in certain religions) echoes the reference to it being *cremated* in the first paragraph.

In the paragraph after the gap, the writer goes on to talk about the art of pizza-making. He says that pizzas have to be prepared in the correct shape (**2A**) and says that doing this was causing him *grief* (a lot of trouble) (**2C**).

38 D: In the paragraph before the gap, the writer has told us that pizza-making is *an art* (something requiring skill and special ability) and that there is a *procedure* for shaping pizzas before they are cooked (**1C**), which was causing him trouble (**1D**).

In the first sentence of D, *it* refers to the procedure. The writer then describes Francesco carrying out the procedure to show the writer how to do it (**3D**), beginning with what has already been prepared and put into the fridge, and then going on to the first thing that is done with this (**3B**).

The paragraph after the gap continues the description of Francesco carrying out the procedure to show the writer what to do (**2B**). *From here* means 'after this stage of the procedure' (after it was *mixed with a small handful of polenta*). The writer then describes each stage of the procedure for preparing the dough for a pizza (**2C**).

39 H: In the paragraph before the gap, Francesco completed the preparation of a pizza from the dough with the right shape – *a perfect circle* (**1D**) – and the writer describes how he did this (**1A**).

At the beginning of H, the writer says that it was now his turn to try to achieve *the same result* that Francesco had achieved (**3C**) – a pizza with the right shape. The rest of H describes the writer beginning to attempt to do the same as Francesco had done (**3B**) and problems he encountered doing so.

In the paragraph after the gap, the writer continues his description of his own effort to do what Francesco had done. He explains what you are supposed to do to create a pizza with the right shape (**2D**), how you can easily go wrong by pressing too much (**2A**) and what happened as a result of him making this mistake.

40 A: In the paragraph before the gap, we have been told that, while trying to prepare the dough into the right shape, the writer could not resist the temptation to press *everything in sight* (**1B**) and that pressing in the wrong places resulted in *thick edges and a thin centre* (**1D**).

The first phrase in A *To put those things right* refers back to the two things that were wrong with what the writer produced – it had thick edges and it had a thin centre (**3A**). At the end of A, the writer says that he *did some twirling* (twisted or turned the dough around and around) and that as a result *flour showered everywhere* (flour flew around in the air and onto the ground) – something which might well have made the writer look foolish (**3B**).

After the gap, we learn that the writer attracted the attention of some customers, which means that obviously the preparation and cooking of pizzas in this restaurant was carried out in a place where the customers could see it being done (**2D**). The writer realised this to his *horror*, which means that he was not at all happy that people could see him doing badly (**2C**).

41 E: In the paragraph before the gap, we have been told that the writer became the focus of some customers' attention (**1A**) and that he didn't like this because he reacted with *horror* when he realised that they were watching him prepare a pizza (**1D**).

The first sentence of E (*Clearly, the stage was all mine.*) refers to the fact that the writer realised that people were watching him and that he was the centre of attention as he tried to do the right thing but failed (**3C**). E continues with a description of his attempt to make a pizza properly. The reference to feeling *more and more eyes on him* means that he felt that more people were now watching him in addition to those he mentions in the paragraph before the gap. In the last sentence, the writer says that something terrible then happened (**3B**).

In the paragraph after the gap, we learn what the *worst thing* was – a hole appeared in the writer's pizza – and that he felt *crestfallen* (extremely disappointed) and defeated as a result (**2A**). We also learn that this pizza was then destroyed by Francesco in the same way that his first one had been (**2B**).

42 G: In the paragraph before the gap, we have been told that the writer's second attempt was also a disaster (**1A**) and that it had to be destroyed like the first one (**1D**).

In G, *as it did so* in the first sentence refers back to *go up in flames* immediately before the gap and means 'as it went up in flames' or 'as it burnt'. The writer was naturally *baffled and embarrassed* by his second attempt having to be destroyed (**3D**). However, he felt that he was *onto something* (making some progress) and his next attempt was more successful. He realised *where I had gone wrong* before and so was very careful when he reached that stage again. His efforts now to prepare the pizza correctly *began to work* (**3A**).

At the beginning of the paragraph after the gap, Francesco noticed that what he was doing was beginning to work – that he was doing it properly – and that is why he *applauded* (expressed approval by clapping his hands together) (**2D**). The writer was so pleased by his comparative success that he wanted to tell the little girl that he could make pizzas. Francesco

then decided that the writer's pizza was good enough for them to put toppings on (**2A**).

43 C: In the paragraph before the gap, we have been told that the writer had made a pizza base that was good enough for toppings to be put on (**1A**), that he was pleased about this (**1C**) and that they then put the toppings on.

In C, *Having done that* means 'having *put on a thin smear* (a layer, roughly applied) *of tomato sauce and some mozzarella*' and *it* in *it was time to get it on to the paddle* is the pizza, now ready to be cooked. The writer then *headed for* (went towards) the oven (**3D**) to put the pizza in to cook it (**3C**).

After the gap, *When I got there* means 'When I reached the oven' (*there* refers back to the oven at the end of C). The writer reached the oven and Francesco told him whereabouts in the oven is the best place to cook a pizza (**2B**). He then put the pizza he had made into it, and watched it cooking so that it could be eaten rather than being burnt because it was no good, which is what had happened to his previous efforts (**2C**).

The paragraph which does not fit into any of the gaps is B.

p55–56 PAPER 1, PART 7

1 mark per question (Total: 10)

A Wander through Britain's Woodlands

44 B: The place has both *recently planted* trees in its heathland and *ancient* forest, so it has both new and very old trees in different parts of it.

45 D: The writer says that the people who run the place *claim* that it has the tallest tree in Britain – the implied meaning is that they say it but it may not be true. The writer then says that if someone is *sceptical* (very doubtful) about this claim, they could measure the tree to see if it is the tallest in Britain or not.

46 D: In the 19th century, *trees from overseas* were added to the native species that were already there. These trees were found by people in different countries at a time when *plant hunting* (looking for new plants) was *all the rage* (a very popular and fashionable activity).

47 A: The writer says that the place has a lot of *fair-weather friends* (people who only go there when the conditions are pleasant for them) and conditions later in the year *deter* them (make them not want to go there). There are a lot of people who only like the place when it's *warm and sunny* and they make it *too crowded* during the parts of the year when the weather is like this. It is *at its best later in the year*, when these people don't go there because of the weather and so it is not crowded.

48 B: The writer says that action taken there by local people *stirred the beginnings of the modern conservation movement* (was the origin of today's widespread conservation action in many places). All the trees were cut down and removed and local people reacted to this *devastation* (massive destruction) by saving and restoring the place. The writer says that this was when the whole idea of people taking part in conservation of natural places began.

49 A: The writer says that it is called a *heath* (an area of open land with wild grass and plants), but in fact it contains many other things as well as a heath, and lists those elements (*parkland*, *hedgerow*, *paths*, *hillside* and *thickets*). Although it has the word *heath* in its name, it is not just a heath and so the name doesn't describe exactly what it is.

50 C: The writer describes a *challenging* walk that is worth the effort because *the views are spectacular*. This walk is for *enthusiastic* hill walkers, and it is *certainly not a gentle stroll*. It involves an *arduous* journey (a difficult and tiring one). So, people who enjoy an energetic walk can do one that they will enjoy very much.

51 D: Because of its *sheltered location, high rainfall and warm temperatures*, there is *spectacular* (extremely impressive, fantastic) *tree growth* in the place.

52 A: The writer says that the organisation that runs the place has made a lot of rules and regulations in order to make it a very organised place. He says that they *fuss* (take unnecessary action, worry unnecessarily) about many things. However, despite their efforts, the place *still feels quite wild*. It is a wild place and the rules and regulations have not really changed that.

53 B: The trees were cut down and removed *within weeks* of a law being passed that authorised this action. The writer is saying that this action happened very soon after official approval for it was given.

PAPER 1

PART 1	8 marks
PART 2	8 marks
PART 3	8 marks
PART 4	12 marks
PART 5	12 marks
PART 6	14 marks
PART 7	10 marks
TOTAL	72 marks

To be converted into a score out of 50 marks.

p57 PAPER 2, PART 1

Each answer is given marks out of 20

MARK SCHEME
Content

The essay should include a summary of these **four key points**:

Text 1 (a) aeroplane not generally chosen as most important invention of last hundred years

       (b) may be most important invention because of its effect on tourism and emigration

Text 2 (a) aeroplane changed from a wonderful thing to something causing terrible damage

       (b) air travel now normal for the majority rather than a small minority

Communicative achievement

This is an essay and so the register should be neutral or formal. The reader should be clear both as to what the key points in each text are and the candidate's own opinions and responses to those points.

Organisation

The essay should be coherently organised in paragraphs, with clear linking between the summaries of the key points and the candidate's own views. An introduction and conclusion are not essential.

Language

The essay should contain an appropriate level of accurate grammar and vocabulary. Vocabulary connected with the topics of inventions and attitudes should be correctly used, as should grammatical structures for describing and comparing points of view/information, presenting and supporting opinions, and linking points in complex sentences.

p58–63 PAPER 2, PART 2

MARK SCHEMES

Question 2

Content
The report should include:

- reasons for setting up the group
- how the group should be set up, including personnel
- issues the group could deal with
- advantages of having the group

Communicative achievement

The register should be appropriate for the relationship between student/employee writing the report and authority/employer who has requested it and will read it – formal or neutral. Report format of clearly separate sections, probably with section headings. The reader would understand precisely what the writer is recommending and why.

Organisation

The report should be organised into sections, each of which deal with each aspect mentioned in the input. Clear and brief introduction and conclusion. Appropriate linking within sections and perhaps also between sections.

Language

Language of describing, hypothesising and recommending, including expressing and supporting opinions.

Question 3

Content

The review should inform the reader about the TV channel or radio station, evaluate it in terms of what it broadcasts, describe the nature of its viewers or listeners and compare it with others.

Communicative achievement

The register could be informal, formal or neutral but should be consistent throughout. The format should be appropriate for a review – description followed by comment within paragraphs or in separate paragraphs. The reader would be informed about the TV channel or radio station and be able to decide whether it would appeal to them, or whether their views on it match those of the writer.

Organisation

Clear development from description to comment and then to comparison, with paragraphing and linking – both within and between paragraphs – appropriate to this.

Language

Language of describing, evaluating, analysing and comparing.

ASSESSMENT OF SAMPLE ANSWER (p61)

Content

The review covers all the aspects mentioned in the question. The writer describes and comments on what the radio station broadcasts, explains who its listeners are and why, and compares it with bigger radio stations in general terms.

Communicative achievement

The register is neutral throughout, with an informal final sentence, which is appropriate in the context. The format is appropriate, with each paragraph on different aspects of the radio station. The opening paragraph is not really part of the review, it is more of a note to the magazine itself, and perhaps this should not have been included.

The reader would learn a great deal about a radio station that it is assumed they had not previously heard of, and would be in a position to decide whether it would appeal to them or not.

Organisation

The review is very well-organised, with description of the various aspects of the radio station combined with comment on these in each paragraph. The second paragraph describes the radio station in general terms, the third paragraph talks about its listeners, the fourth paragraph talks about what it broadcasts and the fifth paragraph compares it in terms of bigger stations. There is some good linking throughout, for example the use of *but* after the negative verb in the second sentence of the third paragraph, *Nevertheless* (third paragraph), *Concerning* (fourth paragraph), *Though* (fifth paragraph) and *To my mind* (fifth paragraph).

Language

There is some very good use of vocabulary and structure, for example *on air* and *run by* (second paragraph), *even if they don't have to* and *the middle of the night* (third paragraph), *colourful* and *easy going* (fourth paragraph), *compete against*, *broad range* and *filled a gap in the market* (fifth paragraph) and *tune in to* (last sentence). The final sentence provides a lively and effective way of ending the review.
There are no real mistakes in this review.

Mark

Band 4 (13–16 marks out of 20). A very good review, with a good level of general fluency and no errors.

Question 4

Content

The article should cover the points raised in the input article, i.e. whether children and young people are given too much and think life is easy.

Communicative achievement

The register could be informal, formal or neutral as the input article seems neutral. Article format – clearly divided, possibly short paragraphs. Article could have appropriate sub-headings. The reader would understand the writer's point of view fully and clearly.

Organisation

Clear development of argument, with each point expanded and probably exemplified. Clear and relatively brief introduction and conclusion. Appropriate paragraphing and linking.

Language

Language for expressing and supporting opinions.

178

ASSESSMENT OF SAMPLE ANSWER (p63)

Content

The main points are fully covered and the article is directly relevant to them throughout. It focuses on the issue of whether young people are given too much by their parents and the consequences of this.

Communicative achievement

The register of the article is suitably neutral, with a serious approach to the topic. Some of the piece involves short, sharp, sentences and this is entirely suited to an article, in terms of impact on the reader. The format is fine, with clearly divided paragraphs making and expanding separate points. There hasn't been an attempt to present the piece as clearly an article, with sub-headings, but this is not at all essential.

The writer's point of view is entirely clear and the reader would have no trouble in understanding that the writer is saying that parents spoil children, perhaps because they feel guilty about not giving them enough attention, that this can result in them being unable to deal with challenges later in life and that therefore their upbringing should involve preparation for adult life as well.

Organisation

The article is very well-organised. The first paragraph is an effective introduction in which the writer's main point is presented briefly; the second deals with the causes of the main point. The third paragraph deals with the results of it and the final paragraph is an effective conclusion, which makes a suggestion rather than merely repeating any points made before. There is some excellent linking, for example *On the one hand ... but on the other hand* (third paragraph) and *All in all* (last paragraph).

Language

There is some good use of vocabulary and structure, for example *depends mainly on* (first paragraph), *I hold the view* and *bad conscience* (second paragraph), the ending of a sentence with a preposition in *big challenges they have to deal with* (third paragraph), and the use of *proper*, meaning 'appropriate' or 'correct' in the final paragraph. In general, the article is relatively simple in terms of vocabulary and structure, but not too much so. There are a couple of relatively minor mistakes. In the first sentence it should say *generalise on* or *about*; in the first sentence of the third paragraph it should say *making* not *make*, to go together with the previous structure *by giving*. These errors do not affect understanding of the points being made.

Mark

Band 4 (13–16 marks out of 20). A good, competent answer that flows well, fully addresses the question and demonstrates a good level of fluency.

PAPER 2

PART 1   20 marks
PART 2   20 marks
TOTAL   40 marks
To be converted into a score out of 50 marks.

p64 PAPER 3, PART 1

1 mark per question (Total: 6)

1 **B:** The speaker says that soft negotiators want *an amicable* (friendly) *resolution* and make concessions (agree to let the other side have some things they are asking for), but that they *often end up exploited and feeling bitter* (the outcome is often that they feel someone has taken advantage of them and they feel annoyed that something has been unfair to them). Hard negotiators think that negotiation is *a contest of wills* (a struggle between people who are each determined to get what they want) and that the side that *holds out longer* (refuses to surrender or give in for the longest time) will be the side that *fares better* (gets the best result). However, they discover that their attitude has produced *an equally hard* (in this context, determined, tough) *response* from those they are negotiating with and this experience *exhausts them* (makes them very tired, uses all their energy) and damages their relationship with the other side. The speaker is therefore saying that both types of negotiator have certain expectations regarding what the results of their method of negotiating will be, but that both types find that the results are different from and worse than the results they had expected.

A: The speaker is not saying that it is better in some circumstances to be a soft negotiator and in others to be a hard negotiator, he is saying that both methods have disadvantages.

C: Although the speaker is saying that both methods can result in the negotiator feeling bad, he is not saying that they are not sure they will succeed during the time when they are negotiating. In fact, he suggests that they are confident then, because they expect their method to succeed.

2 **C:** The speaker says that through principled negotiation people *decide issues on their merits* (individually and objectively, rather than as part of a general theory or being influenced by personal feelings) and that the results of this method are *based on some fair standards independent of the will of either side* (they are reached according to generally accepted ideas of what is fair, which are not influenced by the personal wishes of the people involved in the negotiations).

A: The speaker says that people should *look for mutual gains* (try to gain things which are to the advantage of both of them) but that when their interests conflict they should reach an agreement that is objectively fair and that enables them both

179

to *obtain what you are entitled to and still be decent* (honourable, behaving in a morally acceptable way). He is therefore saying that through principled negotiation people can get what is rightfully theirs, and so they will not feel that the outcome has been unfair to them.

B: The speaker says that principled negotiating does not involve *haggling* (bargaining, arguing involving both sides trying to get what they want) and that it also does not involve *tricks or posturing* (insincere or unnatural behaviour in order to create a certain impression or achieve a certain effect). Instead, it involves reaching an agreement that both sides can consider fair. The speaker does not say that this requires greater or less effort on the part of the negotiators than other methods of negotiating.

3 **C:** The reporter says that if you go to the shed, it is as if you *rewind* (this is what you do to make a recording go back to an earlier part or to the beginning, here it means 'go back') *to the Industrial Revolution* in the 19th century. She also says that Roly gets clay from the pit in a way that is *Like his father and grandfather before him* (the same as previous generations of his family did). The speaker therefore mentions twice the relationship between the pottery now and periods a long time in the past.

A: The speaker says that an old railway track is near to the pottery and that it leads to a *meadow* (a field) *thick with* bushes, plants and flowers and so it sounds as if the pottery is in an isolated place that few people go to apart from Roly, but the speaker does not say this or emphasise that it is a lonely place that people rarely visit.

B: The speaker talks about the *gloom* (darkness) of the place and mentions the door to the building and the colour of the building. However, she does not say that if you go inside the pottery, you are surprised to find that it contrasts with its external appearance.

4 **A:** Roly says that the pottery began to *decline* (do badly) as a result of *the advent* (arrival) *of the plastic bowl* (which was manufactured in factories rather than made individually in potteries) and that in the 1950s this was *a death blow to potteries countrywide* (something which caused potteries throughout the country to go out of business because they could not survive it).

B: He says that the pottery used to make *horticultural* (connected with gardening) *containers* and *domestic ware* (goods for use in the house), but that developments in the 1950s had a bad effect on it. He does not say that it was a mistake to make the kind of things it used to make or that any mistake was made with regard to developments in the 1950s, which he seems to see as having an inevitable result.

C: He says that his father was able to continue in business but that doing so involved *laying off* (making unemployed because there was no work for them to do) the last four people still working there and producing pots that were more unusual. He probably does support what his father did but he does not say so or defend or justify his father's actions.

5 **B:** The first character mentioned is Lonesome Luke, who was *aggressive* and *a moderate hit* (quite but not very popular). Lloyd then decided to reject stylisation in *favour of normality* (to portray a character that seemed like a real person rather than one that was clearly unrealistic and created just for film). The character he then created was someone that audiences could *readily* (easily) *identify* with (someone they felt was like them). This character was very successful and for ten years, while he was playing that character in films, Lloyd *could do no wrong* (everything he did was very successful and popular) and audiences *flocked* (went in very large numbers) to his films.

A: It is not clear whether the idea for the new character came from Lloyd or his friend Roach. The speaker says that *history is divided* on this matter (some people who have done research, written books, etc on the subject say it was Lloyd and others say it was Roach). The speaker is therefore saying that it is not clear who *hit on* (thought of) the idea of the new character, and so she is not saying that it was definitely Lloyd's friend Roach's suggestion.

C: The speaker says that Lloyd felt that he was *not really good* when playing the character of Lonesome Luke and that he then played a character that was much more popular than Lonesome Luke. However, she does not say that this was a result of his ambition increasing, and he may well have been extremely ambitious from the very start of his career.

6 **A:** The speaker says that there were two reasons why Lloyd's career suffered – the *double onslaught* (two things attacking) that *proved fatal to Lloyd's career* (that were disastrous for his career and caused it to end) were the invention of films with sound and the Depression of the 1930s in the US (this was a period of high unemployment during which a great many people were very poor). As a result of the latter, *his indomitable optimism was now incongruous* (his character's constant belief that everything would be all right despite the problems he was faced with didn't seem appropriate). The speaker is therefore saying that the attitude of Lloyd's character did not fit in with the general unhappy mood of the period and this was one of the two reasons why his career suffered.

B: Lloyd made one *talkie* (a film with sound rather than a silent film) and it was a *hit* (popular, a success) but he didn't make any more. The speaker says that this was because he was *instinctively a visual performer* (he was suited to doing things that were entertaining to watch rather than to dialogue). The speaker does not say or imply that Lloyd didn't want to make any more films with sound or that he was not keen to make the one that he did make. He may well have wanted to make other films with sound in order to continue his career but his style wasn't suited to films with sound and that is the other reason why his career came to an end.

C: The speaker says that Lloyd's highly successful character combined *lateral thinking* (a way of solving problems by means of ideas that may not seem logical) and *preternatural physical prowess* (physical strength that seemed to go beyond what is natural or normal) in order to *save the day* (prevent disaster when it seems certain to happen). She also says that the character's optimism didn't suit the times during the 1930s. However, there is nothing that the speaker says which suggests that Lloyd himself began to lose confidence or that that was why his career suffered. His career suffered because of the arrival of films with sound and because of the Depression, not because he lost confidence in himself as a performer.

p65–67 PAPER 3, PART 2

FURTHER PRACTICE AND GUIDANCE (p66–67)

For explanations, see the explanations to the questions in the test, which follow.

Question 7 B	Question 10 C	Question 13 A
Question 8 A	Question 11 B	Question 14 B
Question 9 A	Question 12 C	Question 15 B

p65 PAPER 3, PART 2 (TEST)

1 mark per question (Total: 9)

7 **National Commercial Directory:** A *directory* is a reference book listing information such as names, addesses, telephone numbers, etc, usually in alphabetical order. In this case, clearly, the names, addresses, etc of businesses throughout the country were listed under various categories. William Sumner was listed under the category Grocers and Tea Dealers.

8 **wines; spirits:** We are told that *at the turn of the 20th century* (at the beginning of it), William and his son John's business included *wines and spirits* (strong alcoholic drinks served in small quantities, such as whisky, vodka and gin) as well as groceries.

9 **indigestion:** Mary *suffered from indigestion* (a painful stomach complaint that usually lasts for a short time, resulting from problems when food passes into the stomach). She found that tea consisting of large leaves *aggravated her problem* (made it worse, more severe) but when she was sent some tea that consisted of small particles, she found that this *gave her great relief* (made the problem much better) and so she offered it to other people who had the

same problem as a *'remedy'* (something that cures a medical problem).

10 **dust:** When John Sumner told his friend that he was going to buy 30 *chests* (large, strong boxes in which tea was transported) of the tea Mary had discovered, the friend, who was a *wholesale tea merchant* (someone who traded in tea, in this case, selling it in large quantities to shopkeepers for sale to the public) told him that people would not want to buy it because it *looked little better than* (not much better than) *dust* (small particles of powder or dirt).

11 **oriental:** John wanted a name which *tripped off the tongue* (was easy and pleasant to say) and the name he *came up with* (produced, thought of) was *alliterative with tea* (both words in the name began with the same letter as *tea*) and had an *oriental sound* (sounded like a word from a language of the East, especially eastern Asia, for example, Chinese or Japanese).

12 **printer's error:** The word 'Tipps' with two 'ps' does not exist in English and presumably it was intended that the word would be 'Tips' (as in 'the ends or edges of something', in this context, the leaves of the tea plants). The double 'p', we are told, first happened *as a printer's error* (was the result of a mistake made by a printer, presumably when printing labels or something similar for the tea). Clearly, John Sumner decided not to change the spelling once that mistake had been made.

13 **jar of cream:** To encourage people to buy the tea, John offered anyone buying a certain quantity of it *a generous* (in the context of the size of something, this means 'large') *jar* (glass container in which certain kinds of food are sold or kept) *of cream*.

14 **edge of the leaf:** John brought back a kind of tea called fannings, and he *drew attention to* (tried to make people notice and realise, presumably in his advertising) the fact that this type of tea was taken from the edge of the leaf of a tea plant, and not from the *fibrous stalk* (the stem at the base of the plant, consisting of fibres), which contained the chemical tannin (which presumably people did not want in their tea).

15 **charitable work:** John received a *knighthood* (a high honour given by the British Queen or King for services to the country – the person awarded this is given the title 'Sir') *in recognition of* (as a sign of official praise for and approval of) *his charitable work* (his acts of charity, for example giving money or other help to the less fortunate people in society, or helping or setting up organisations to provide such things). It was after his death that he helped his employees, all of whom *benefited under his will* (were left money by him in the legal document in which people say what will happen to their possessions and money after they die).

p68 PAPER 3, PART 3

1 mark per question (Total: 5)

16 A: Miranda says that the *communal aerial* (rod or tower that transmits TV signals) *sent fuzzy* (unclear, blurred) *pictures* every time it rained and that in Wales rain is not a *rare occurrence* (it happens regularly). In other words, the reception from the aerial was poor whenever it rained, and so the reception was often poor.

B: When the satellite technician came to see them, he *saw not breathtaking natural beauty but obstacles* (he wasn't interested in how beautiful the place was, he only noticed the problems he would face if he tried to install satellite TV there). The point is not that they doubted his ability to install satellite TV, it is that he thought it would be very difficult or impossible to do so.

C: She doesn't say that it would be hard to link up with the communal aerial. She says that it would have been expensive to do so – they *could have spent a fortune laying cables to the nearest village* – and that the results would not have been good, because the reception was poor from the communal aerial and the entire system *went down* (stopped working completely) if *strong winds or stray animals* (animals that had wandered from the place where they should be) *knocked it out of kilter* (hit it so that it went out of its correct position).

D: She says that she *would love to be able to say* that they lived without TV by choice – that she threw the TV away or sold it – but that in fact *circumstances deprived us* (the situation they found themselves in meant that they couldn't have TV). She does say that they were living in a place of *breathtaking natural beauty* but that was not why they had no TV.

17 C: Miranda says that they started to *revel in our moral superiority* (to enjoy enormously the feeling that they were morally superior to people who had TV). When people started to ask them if they had watched a particular programme, Miranda *would watch their jaws drop* (their mouths open wide as an expression of astonishment) when they realised she had no TV, and they would wonder *what on earth* (an emphatic expression of surprise, indicating that it is extremely hard to know what the answer could be) the family did instead of watching TV. Clearly, therefore, she enjoyed seeing how surprised people were when they realised she and her family had no TV.

A: She says *At the risk of sounding unbearably smug*, which means 'I know that this might sound as if I am very pleased with myself in a way that others won't like', they did read more books, listen to more music and play more games. However, this is what she says to the interviewer, not what she said to people who found out that she didn't have a TV. She does not say that she told other people that they did these things

instead, that she enjoyed doing so, or that she might have sounded self-satisfied when talking to them.

B: She says that they read more books, listened to more music and played more board games than before but this is not the same as saying that these were hobbies they had had and then stopped before moving to the cottage. It seems that in fact they did these things before, but when they moved to Wales they did them more.

D: She says that one enjoyable outcome was that they discovered the *untold* (very many), *long, pleasant and potentially fulfilling hours there are in an evening* – that evenings seemed a great deal longer and that it seemed that there was much more time in which to do things that make you feel happy and satisfied. She does not, however, say that these were energetic things or that they felt more energetic, and in fact implies that they felt more relaxed. In addition, she says that sometimes they *merely had an early night* (simply went to bed earlier than usual), which suggests they were more relaxed or tired rather than energetic.

18 D: Miranda says that they felt like *cultural oddities* (people who were not normal in terms of being part of the culture) because they did not understand when other people referred to well-known characters on TV or used a *catchphrase* (a phrase used often by a performer or in a programme that is associated with that person or programme by the public) from a popular TV programme. She therefore felt that it was a disadvantage that they were no longer informed about some of the things people talked about as a result of not having a TV, because this made them feel they were in some way strange.

A: She talks about programmes that were popular but that they didn't know about because they did not have a TV, and these may have been series, but she does not say that they had previously liked particular series and were unhappy about not being able to follow them any more. She does say that they wished they could watch *big news events* on TV but these are not series.

B: She says that she and her husband were *confirmed news junkies* (people who were established in the habit of being addicted to watching the news – *junkie* usually means 'person addicted to drugs') and that therefore they really missed watching the news on TV. However, she says that their addiction was only *mild* (not strong), and that after an *initial withdrawal* (an initial period of suffering because of the absence of something you are addicted to), *you hardly give it a second thought* (you hardly think about it at all). Their desire to watch the news was therefore not constant, it went away after a short period of time.

C: She says that they were in the habit of watching the news on TV and that a major disadvantage of not having a TV was that they couldn't do that, but she does not say that they normally discussed what was in the news and now couldn't. She says that other people talked about popular TV programmes and that they didn't know what these people were talking about because they hadn't watched them, but she does not say that previously they had discussed programmes they watched on TV.

19 A: Miranda says that she *went along with* (agreed to, accepted) having a TV installed because she is *certainly not one of those anti-TV types who that believes the box* (an informal word for 'television set') *to be the source of all modern evil* (the cause of everything that is bad in the modern world). She says that she thinks there are lots of programmes on TV that are *interesting and rewarding* (worthwhile) *for both adults and children* and that television can be part of a *well-rounded* (appropriately balanced and varied) *life*. She is therefore saying that people of all ages – which in this context must include her, her husband and their children – benefit from having TV, and that was one of the reasons why she agreed to have a TV again.

B: She does not say that her attitude changed, it seems to have always been the same. She agreed because she thinks that TV is worth having and also because her husband wanted to have one, although she thinks this was because he wanted to play with the remote control device, not because he wanted to watch certain programmes. She doesn't say that she agreed because she had previously disapproved of TV and then approved of it.

C: She says that her husband *persevered with the satellite option* (continued to investigate the possibility of them having satellite TV installed) and says why she thinks he was so keen to have a TV again, but she does not refer to any disagreement between them about having a TV again.

D: Although she is in favour of TV, she says that *its insidiousness* (its ability to become powerful in a harmful way without people noticing that this has happened) *lies in its being an easy option* (results from the fact that it is an easy thing for people to do) because, like a *ready meal* (a meal you don't have to prepare yourself because it has already been prepared when you buy it), it *seduces you into forgetting the rewards that come from putting a bit more into life* (it persuades you by being attractive to forget that you can gain a great deal more satisfaction out of life if you put more effort into living your life). The point she is making is that TV can make people lazy or that watching it can be a result of their laziness, but she does not say that this was why her own family got a TV again. She was *apprehensive* (anxious) that it would dominate their lives and so she felt that it might make them lazy but she doesn't say that they got it because they were lazy – they got it because her husband wanted it and she thought that it was a good idea, despite the disadvantages of TV that she talks about.

20 B: She says that she sometimes finds herself *proposing half an hour's viewing as an activity* to her children, but that they tend to refuse to do it if they think she is suggesting it because she wants to *sneak off* (go somewhere else quietly and secretly) and *do something without them* while they are watching TV.

A: She says that they *even watch rubbish from time to time* but not that the children now have a clearer idea of what programmes are rubbish and what programmes are worth watching. She also says that often, after ten minutes of watching TV, they decide that it's boring and switch it off, but she does not say that this is because they decide that some programmes are rubbish and others are not.

C: She says that they never had the habit of watching it, not that they have decided not to return to that habit. She says that their *year's abstinence must have coincided with their habit-forming years, so it's a habit they don't have* (the year they spent without a TV happened by chance during the same period in which their habits were beginning to form, so that in fact they formed the habit of not watching TV and never got into the habit of watching it).

D: She says that the children occasionally *slump* (sit in a tired or lazy way) and watch TV and that sometimes the whole family decide *to vegetate* (do nothing at all, be totally inactive) in front of the TV, which means that sometimes they do watch it because they are feeling lazy. She adds that to do this now is a deliberate choice rather than a habit.

p69 PAPER 3, PART 4

1 mark per question (total 10)

21 G: The speaker says that someone (Jack) told him that another person (Helen) *had taken offence at* something the speaker said the previous week in a meeting. This means that Helen was angry about what the speaker had said and regarded it as rude and unpleasant. She is so angry about it that she does not want to talk to the speaker again.

22 D: The speaker was told that *the whole thing was off* (cancelled). This was an arrangement that had been fixed some time ago for a particular date – the speaker had *had it in the diary for ages*.

23 B: The speaker was *taken aback* (surprised) when he heard that the news. He had expected to *get it* and had been *given the impression that it was mine if I wanted it*. This was clearly a job because the speaker talks about the issue of money and *the chance to branch out, do something different for a change*. However, someone else *got it* (the job), and the speaker is taking about an unsuccessful job application.

24 F: The speaker's friend offered her the opportunity to *use* the place she was living in *while she was away* (to live in her home for a period of time when she would not be there). The speaker wanted to go there and says that she told her friend she would *take her up on it* (accept her offer).

25 H: The speaker has been given the chance to *go to something* (attend it) as someone's *guest* (he has been invited to accompany someone who has been invited to the event). The company that person works for has some involvement in the event. The speaker says he will have to *dress the part* (wear something appropriate for such an event).

26 B: The speaker says that he *couldn't care less* (is not at all interested, is not at all worried) about the situation with Helen. He *can't be bothered even to think about it* (he does not want to use any energy thinking about it). He obviously dislikes Helen and has no interest in the fact that she is angry with him.

27 D: The speaker says that the situation is *a real shame* – she is very disappointed about it. She *was looking forward to it* but it is not going to happen now. She says there is *no point getting cross* (angry) but she is disappointed because something she wanted to happen is not going to happen.

28 E: Although the speaker was surprised by the news and the fact that he did not get something he had expected to get, he is not disappointed and thinks that *maybe it's for the best* (perhaps it's a good thing). Before hearing the news, he was *getting quite nervous about how I'd manage* but now he does not have to worry because the situation is not going to happen. He is therefore relieved that something that made him feel nervous is not going to happen.

29 C: The speaker says that she is not only interested in seeing the friend's new home, but she also wants to find out *lots of other things* about her friend's new life. So she wants to find out things about her friend that she has been wondering about.

30 F: The speaker thinks that his friend is *lucky* because she *gets to go to these things all the time* (frequently attends events like this one). He says that he wishes he was in that position, so he is envious of her because of the fact that she goes to events like this and he would like to go to them often too.

PAPER 3

PART 1	6 marks
PART 2	9 marks
PART 3	5 marks
PART 4	10 marks
TOTAL	30 marks

To be converted into a score out of 50 marks.

p70–73 PAPER 4

Marks out of 25 are given for performance in the speaking paper.
To be converted into a score out of 50 marks.

FURTHER PRACTICE AND GUIDANCE (p72–73)

DESCRIBING FEELINGS

SADNESS

dejected: sad and depressed, and not feeling hopeful about the future

despondent: without hope and therefore extremely unhappy

devastated: extremely unhappy and upset because of something terrible that has happened that affects you personally

dismayed: fairly unhappy because of something unexpected that has happened

dispirited: discouraged or depressed because something bad has happened and as a result, something you hope for seems unlikely to happen

distraught: extremely unhappy and upset because of something terrible that has happened, especially when showing this by crying, etc.

distressed: very unhappy and suffering a great deal emotionally as a reaction to something

downcast: sad and depressed, especially in comparison with previously feeling happy or not feeling unhappy

ANGER

cross: fairly angry (this word is often used by adults talking to children)

enraged: caused to feel or show that you feel very angry

infuriated: extremely annoyed

irate: very angry (this word is used especially to describe other people, rather than yourself)

mad: angry, in phrases such as *go mad* or be *mad at/ with someone*

resentful: annoyed for a long period after something that you consider unfair has happened

touchy: easily offended or upset; sensitive and likely to get angry suddenly

ANXIETY

agitated: nervous and worried, especially when having previously been calm

apprehensive: nervous and anxious about something that is going to happen in the future because you think it is going to be unpleasant for you

bothered: worried

concerned: worried

edgy: nervous and therefore easily annoyed or upset

harassed: feeling stressed and anxious because of pressure, having too many things to do, etc.

petrified: extremely frightened

tense: anxious and worried, especially when also silent

unnerved: nervous after previously having been confident or relaxed, because something has happened to make you lose confidence or courage

worked up: having got into a very worried or nervous state because of something that has happened

wound up: having got into a very anxious or stressed state because of something that has happened

SHOCK

appalled: very shocked because of something you consider totally unacceptable or disgusting

astounded: extremely surprised or shocked

flabbergasted: completely amazed or astonished

outraged: very shocked, and possibly also upset or angry, because of something that you consider morally wrong

speechless: so surprised and shocked, and possibly also angry, that you are unable to speak

staggered: extremely surprised or shocked

stunned: amazed; so surprised or shocked that you are unable to think clearly

taken aback: greatly surprised by something that is said or happens and therefore unable to respond immediately

CONFUSION

baffled: very confused and totally unable to understand, solve or answer something

bemused: confused and unable to think clearly

bewildered: very or totally confused

flustered: confused and nervous because of trying to do too many things at the same time or because of not knowing what to do next

perplexed: confused and worried, especially because you cannot understand why something has happened

thrown: confused or disturbed by something that has happened, so that you are unable to respond to it quickly or to continue what you were doing

TOPIC VOCABULARY

CONFLICT

acrimonious: (adjective) If something is *acrimonious*, it involves angry and bitter feelings and people being nasty to each other.

altercation: (noun) An *altercation* is an argument or disagreement involving people shouting at or fighting each other.

animosity: (noun) If you feel *animosity towards* someone, you strongly dislike them or have feelings of aggression towards them.

antagonise: (verb) If someone *antagonises someone*, they make them respond in an aggressive way by doing or saying something that makes them angry.

antipathy: (noun) If someone has *antipathy towards* someone or there is *antipathy between* people, they strongly dislike that person or each other.

bad blood: (idiom) If there is *bad blood between* people, they dislike each other intensely, often as a result of particular things that have happened in the past.

bicker: (verb) If people *bicker* with each other, they argue about unimportant things, often in a way that is considered childish.

bone of contention: (idiom) If something is a *bone of contention between* people, it is matter that they disagree about very strongly.

enmity: (noun) *Enmity towards someone/between people* is when people feel that someone is their enemy and therefore have aggressive and very unfriendly feelings towards them.

fall out: (phrasal verb) If people *fall out with* each other, they have an argument or disagreement as a result of which they are no longer friendly with each other.

feud: (noun) If there is a *feud between people*, they have a disagreement that lasts for a long time and that involves them saying and doing nasty things to each other.

friction: (noun) If there is *friction between* people, they disagree with and dislike each other.

hostility: (noun) If you feel *hostility towards* someone, you feel aggressive towards them, as if you would like them to be harmed in some way.

incompatible: (adjective) If people are *incompatible with* each other, they can't live or work together in a reasonable way because they are so different from each other that they cannot have a friendly relationship.

rivalry: (noun) If there is *rivalry between* people, each is competing with the other in order to get something that both want or in order to be better than the other in some way.

set-to: (noun) If someone has a *set-to with* someone, they have a big argument or a fight with them.

showdown: (noun) A *showdown* is an occasion when people who disagree meet together in order to settle their dispute by arguing angrily.

squabble: (verb/noun) If people *squabble with* each other or have a *squabble*, they argue with each other noisily, often about unimportant matters.

strife: (noun) Often used with an adjective to form phrases such as *political strife*, this means angry and violent disagreement or conflict.

take issue with: (idiom) If you take *issue with someone*, you say that you disagree with them or you argue with them, rather than saying nothing.

wrangle: (noun) In phrases such as *legal wrangle*, this means long and complicated argument.

COOPERATION

accommodating: (adjective) If someone is *accommodating*, they try to help someone get what they want rather than prevent them from having it.

band together: (idiom) If people *band together*, they join together to do something as a group.

camaraderie: (noun) If there is *camaraderie* among a group of people who spend a lot of time together, they like each other and are very friendly with each other as a group.

collaborate: (verb) If people *collaborate with* each other, they work together in order to produce or create something.

concerted effort: (idiom) If people *make a concerted effort* to do something, they join with others and together they try to do it.

give-and-take: (idiom) If something involves *give and take*, it involves people making compromises with each other so that they can avoid having a bad relationship.

harmony: (noun) If people are *in harmony*, they agree with each other, share the same opinions and attitudes, etc and therefore have a good relationship with each other.

in accord: (idiom) If people are *in accord* (*with* each other), they agree with each other on a particular matter.

in concert: (idiom) If people do something *in concert*, they do it by working together.

join forces: (idiom) If people *join forces*, they work together in order to achieve a common aim.

pool: (verb) If people *pool something*, such as ideas, resources, etc, they put together what they each have so that together they can use the total of the two amounts.

AGREE

acknowledge: (verb) If you *acknowledge that* something is the case, you say that you accept that it is the case.

acquiesce: (verb) If you *acquiesce in something*, you accept it or agree to it without protest or expressing opposition.

allow: (verb) If you *allow that* something is true, you agree or accept that it is true.

concede: (verb) If you *concede that* something is the case, you admit that it is the case, even though you wish that it was not.

consensus: (noun) If there is *(a) consensus*, there is general agreement among people about a particular matter.

grant: (verb) If you say to someone *I grant you that* something is the case, you are telling them that you accept or admit that it is the case, even though there are other things which you do not accept or believe.

see eye to eye: (idiom) If you *see eye to eye with someone*, you are in complete agreement with them or have exactly the same opinions and attitudes.

unanimous: (adjective) If something is *unanimous*, it has the agreement of everyone involved in it. If people are *unanimous*, they all agree about something.

TRY TO CREATE AGREEMENT

appease: (verb) If you *appease someone*, you give them or allow them to have something that they want so that they stop being angry.

conciliatory: (adjective) If you do something *conciliatory*, you do something that is intended to stop someone from being angry, because it indicates that they can have something they want.

defuse: (verb) If you *defuse something*, you make a situation in which people strongly oppose each other less serious, less severe or less likely to get worse or to result in violence.

intervene: (verb) If you *intervene in* a situation or *intervene between* people, you take action to resolve a disagreement or to prevent a dispute between people from getting worse or becoming violent.

mediate: (verb) If you *mediate between* people, you try to persuade people who are in disagreement with each other to reach agreement.

mollify: (verb) If you *mollify someone*, you make them less angry about something.

pacify: (verb) If you *pacify someone*, you cause them to stop being angry.

placate: (verb) If you *placate someone*, you make them less angry about something.

reconcile: (verb) If people are *reconciled* (*with* each other), they re-establish a friendly relationship with each other after a period of disliking each other or having no contact with each other as the result of a disagreement.

win over: (phrasal verb) If you *win someone over*, you persuade them to agree with your point of view.

TEST 3

p74 PAPER 1, PART 1

Note: all explanations in this part refer to the meaning or use of each option most closely related to the question, not necessarily to the only meaning or use of each option.

1 mark per question (Total: 8)

Horses

1 D: If something **is a matter of** something else, it results from it or depends on it. The writer is saying that the human desire to tame animals is not the only factor in whether or not they can be tamed, there are other factors too.

A: If something *is concerned* with something else, it is on the subject of it or connected with it. (*Her work is concerned with the investigation of serious diseases.*)

B: A *business* is a situation or something that is happening or has happened. (*I found the whole business very depressing so I tried not to get involved.*)

C: A *point* is a particular item or detail among others. (*Let's decide on the main points that we need to discuss.*)

All the options can mean 'thing related to a particular subject or situation', but only D correctly completes the required fixed phrase.

2 B: If you **take something/someone for granted**, their presence or value to you has been continuing for so long that you no longer appreciate them or show that you appreciate them. If you take it for granted that something is the case, you believe that it is the case and that there is no need to check to make sure that it really is the case. The writer is describing the various characteristics of horses that people assume them to have.

A: If you *assume something*, you automatically believe it to be true or expect it to happen, even though there is no proof of this. (*I assume that you've already heard the news about George.*)

C: *Given something* means 'Taking into consideration something which is known to be true'. (*Given her lack of ambition, it's amazing that she became so successful.*) *Given that ...* means 'Since it is known to be true that ...'. (*Given that you've never done this kind of work before, I think you're doing quite well.*)

D: If you *take it as read* that something is the case, you believe or assume that something is the case and therefore feel that there is no need to check that it really is the case. (*I'm taking it as read that you know all the background to this situation.*)

All the options are connected with the idea of believing that something is the case, but only B correctly completes the required idiom.

3 **B:** If someone/something **undergoes something**, they experience something unpleasant or go through a process which results in change. The writer is saying that horses have changed as a result of changes in their diet.

A: If someone/something is *subjected to* something, they are made to experience something undesirable or forced to suffer it. (*We were subjected to a long speech from the boss about what we were doing wrong.*)

C: If someone *submits to something* or *submits themselves to something*, they accept the control or authority of something more powerful than them, rather than fighting against it. (*We had to submit (ourselves) to the wishes of the people in charge.*)

D: If someone *commits something*, they do something illegal or morally wrong (*commit a crime/a sin*). If someone *commits suicide*, they kill themselves.

All the options are connected with the idea of experiencing something or taking action, but only B both fits the meaning in the context and fits grammatically. A could fit the meaning but the verb would have to be in the passive form.

4 **A:** If something **dies away**, it disappears over a period of time and ceases to exist. The writer is talking about the period of time when forests disappeared during the Ice Age.

B: If a person or creature *passes away*, they die. (*His grandmother passed away last year.*)

C: If something *dwindles*, it becomes weaker or smaller over a period of time. (*His influence in the world of politics dwindled after he lost that election.*)

D: If someone or something *vanishes*, it disappears. (*One day he vanished and we never saw him again.*)

All the options are connected with the idea of something disappearing or no longer existing, but only A both completes a phrase with 'away' and fits the meaning in the context.

5 **C:** If someone is **compelled to do something**, they are forced to do it because of circumstances beyond their control or because someone makes them do it. The writer is saying that environmental changes forced animals to change their diets.

A: If you are *coerced into doing something*, you are forced to do it by someone who puts you under pressure or threatens you. (*He was coerced into signing the agreement because he was told he would lose his job if he didn't do so.*)

B: If someone *enforces something*, they make sure that it is obeyed because they are in authority. (*It is the responsibility of the police to enforce the law.*)

D: If something *necessitates something*, it makes it necessary. (*His plans for restructuring the company will necessitate a certain number of job losses.*)

All the options are connected with the idea of things happening because of force or because they cannot be avoided, but only C both fits the meaning in the context and fits grammatically. D fits the meaning, but the sentence would have to be changed so that the verb was active and followed by an object.

6 **C:** If something **grows + comparative adjective** (**longer**, **older**, etc), it becomes longer, older, etc. The writer is talking about physical changes to the horse.

A: If *something expands*, it becomes bigger or wider. (*metals which expand when hot/The company has expanded and now has offices in several countries.*)

B: If *something increases*, it becomes bigger in number or size. (*The population of this city is increasing rapidly./I increased the speed at which I was working.*)

D: If something *enlarges* or someone *enlarges* something, it becomes larger or someone makes it larger (*enlarge a building/photograph*).

All the options mean 'get bigger in some way', but only C can be followed by a comparative adjective.

7 **D:** If something is **at a/some distance from** something, it is not close to it, it is apart from it. The writer is saying that the ur-horse developed a longer head, meaning that its eye was quite far from its mouth.

A: If there is *a space between* two things, they are separated from each other and there is an area between them. (*There was a big space between the two tables.*)

B: The *extent of* something refers to how much of something there is. (*After the accident, we discovered the extent of the damage to our car.*)

C: A *stretch* of land or water is an area (*a huge stretch of land with no trees in it*).

All the options are connected with areas and amounts, but only D both fits the meaning in the context and correctly completes a phrase with the prepositions given.

8 **A:** If you **keep a lookout for something** or if you **are on the lookout for something**, you look for it and make sure that you will notice it if it appears, either because it is dangerous and you want to avoid it or because it is something that you want. The writer is saying that the horse's eyes were positioned so that they could see whether they were in danger from other animals that might attack them.

B: If you *take heed of something* or *pay heed to something*, you take notice of it or pay attention to it, so that it has some influence on what you do or think. (*She took no heed of/paid no heed to my advice.*)

C: *Vigilance* is concentration or awareness involving looking out for possible danger, problems, etc. (*The police informed the residents that constant vigilance was required because a gang of burglars was operating in the area.*)

D: If you are *on the alert for something*, you are aware of possible danger and ready to react if it happens. (*Be on the alert for thieves if you go to that part of the city.*)

All the options are connected with the idea of being aware of the possibility of something or paying attention, but only A correctly completes the required idiom.

p75 PAPER 1, PART 2

1 mark per question (Total: 8)

Celebrity Crossover

9 **Somewhere:** In the context, this means 'in a place (that is)'. The writer has said that actors want to be pop stars *and vice versa*, which means 'and the other opposite way round', in other words 'and pop stars want to be actors'. He goes on to say that there is a place deep inside our brains in which we all have the desire to be both pop stars and actors.

10 **under:** If you *keep something under control*, you are able to control or deal with it so that others are not aware of it or it does not cause problems. The writer is saying that most people manage to control their desire to be pop stars and actors.

11 **one/former/first:** This refers back to *pop stars and actors* at the end of the first paragraph. The phrase *the one/former/first profession* means 'one of the two professions mentioned' or 'the first of the two professions mentioned'.

12 **sets:** If someone/something *sets an example for* someone, they do something which other people should copy or be influenced by. If someone *sets a bad example for* someone, they do something which it is considered others should not copy or be influenced by. The writer is saying that people who succeed in both professions are not a good example for others to follow because they are exceptions and most people who try to follow them will not succeed in both professions as they have done.

13 **For:** The structure *for every ... , there is/are ...* is used for comparing two things in terms of the relative numbers of them or the proportion of each. The writer is saying that if you analyse all the pop stars and actors who try to succeed in both professions, every time you find one who succeeds you also find *two dozen* (24) who fail – in other words, far more fail than succeed.

14 **how:** The adverb *how* is used before an adjective or adverb to talk about the extent of something. The writer is saying that the people who fail are not aware of the fact that they are not just bad but very bad at the other profession.

15 **Just:** The linking phrase *just as* is used with the meaning 'in exactly the same way as'. The writer is saying that power corrupts people and it is equally true that being famous destroys people's ability to judge what they are doing.

16 **yourself:** If you *make a fool of yourself*, you do something that makes you look foolish or ridiculous to others. The writer is saying that famous people tend not to realise that they are doing this.

p76–78 PAPER 1, PART 3

FURTHER PRACTICE AND GUIDANCE (p77–78)

For explanations, see the explanations to the questions in the test, which follow.

17 C	19 D	21 C	23 A
18 D	20 C	22 C	24 D

p76 PAPER 1, PART 3 (TEST)

Note: the letters in brackets refer to the relevant options in the Further Practice and Guidance pages.

1 mark per question (Total: 8)

King of the Watchmakers

17 **synonymous:** If a word is *synonymous* with another, it has the same meaning as it. More figuratively, if something is said to be *synonymous with* something else, it automatically involves it. In this context, the writer is saying that clocks and watches made in Coventry at that time were assumed to be excellent because they had a high reputation. **(C)**

The other words in the list do not exist.

18 reliability: If something such as a machine or piece of equipment possesses *reliability*, it always performs well without breaking down. The writer is saying that clocks and watches made in Coventry at that time were known to be both of high quality and reliable. **(D)**

Reliance on something is the situation of relying or depending on something in order to function, exist, succeed, etc (*the team's total reliance on one or two good players*). **(C)**

Reliably means 'in a way that can be relied on' (*a car that performs reliably over many years*). **(A)**

If you are *reliant on somebody/something*, you depend on them (*children who are totally reliant on their parents*). **(B)**

The word *reliableness* does not exist.

19 single-handedly: If someone does something *single-handedly*, they do it on their own and not together with others or the help of others. The writer is saying that Samuel Watson was almost alone in getting Coventry involved in the clock and watch business, he was almost the only person who *paved the way* for the city's involvement in it (created the situation which allowed the city to become involved in it). **(D)**

If something is *handily* placed, situated, etc, its place or position is convenient. (*The hotel is handily placed for all the city's main attractions.*) **(C)**

If someone is *high-handed*, they are in a position of power and authority and act towards others in a rude manner, without considering their wishes or consulting them (*a boss with a high-handed manner*). **(B)**

If something happens *beforehand*, it happens earlier, in advance of or before another event. (*I knew what I was doing because I'd checked beforehand.*) **(A)**

The word *handfully* does not exist.

20 positional: This means 'connected with position'. The phrase *positional changes* means 'changes in position'. **(C)**

An *imposition* is either an occasion when something is forced on others by authority (*the imposition of new regulations by the government*) or an action that causes inconvenience. (*I hope it's not an imposition but could you give me a lift?*) **(D)**

The other words do not exist.

21 ownership: If something is *in the ownership of someone*, they own it. The writer is saying that the Royal Family still own the astronomical clock made by Watson. **(C)**

Owning can be used in a noun phrase, with the meaning 'the fact or situation of owning'. (*The owning of vast numbers of houses and cars did not bring him happiness.*) It can therefore have the same

meaning as *ownership*, but it cannot be used in the phrase *in the ... of*. **(C)**

The other words do not exist.

22 residence: If you *take up residence* somewhere, you go to live there. Someone's *residence* is a formal word for the place where they live or their address. We are told that Watson moved from Coventry and began to live in London. **(C)**

A *resident* of a place is someone who lives there, as opposed to a visitor. (*Residents of the area objected to plans for a rock music festival.*) In a hotel, a *resident* is a guest who is staying there. **(B)**

Residential means 'involving people living there rather than working there or living elsewhere' (*a residential area/a residential course*). **(A)**

Residency is a formal, legal word, meaning 'permission to live in a country that is not your own' (*be granted permanent residency*) **(C)**; A *residency* is a situation in which a performer is employed to work at a particular place over a period of time. (*The band got a residency at a local club, appearing every Tuesday night.*) **(D)**

The word *residentity* does not exist.

23 standing: A person's *standing* is their reputation or status in a profession or among a group of people. The writer is saying that the fact that Watson became *Master of the London Clockmakers' Company* (presumably a very important position for which only someone highly respected is chosen) *is testament to* (is proof of) how high his reputation was in that industry. **(A)**

A person's *standpoint* is their point of view, the position they are in from which they regard a certain matter or issue. (*From the standpoint of the employees, the management's decision is a bad one.*) **(D)**

If someone/something *withstands something*, they endure it and continue despite it (*materials which can withstand heavy impacts; a politician who could withstand enormous criticism*). **(C)**

If someone/something is *outstanding*, they are remarkable in a positive way, or unusual in being better than others (*an outstanding performer/an award for outstanding achievement*). **(B)**

The word *standence* does not exist.

24 likelihood: The *likelihood of something happening* is the chance of it happening. If *the likelihood is that* something is the case, it is probably the case. The writer is saying that because there are no records of Watson's name after 1712, it is reasonable to think that he probably died that year. **(D)**

The other words do not exist.

p79 PAPER 1, PART 4

2 marks per question (Total: 12)

25 interference (1 mark)

everything would have gone smoothly (1 mark)

The first part of the third conditional *If + subject + verb* has been transformed into *Without + possessive* and therefore must be completed by a noun to go with the possessive. The noun from *interfere* is *interference*. If something happens without any problems, it goes smoothly.

26 himself to (1 mark)

the possibility of losing (1 mark)

If you *expose yourself to something*, you put yourself in a situation in which you may suffer in some way because you are not protected from something unpleasant or undesirable. *Possibility* is followed by of + *-ing*. It must be preceded by the definite article because the nature of the possibility is defined.

27 was/were deluged with calls (1 mark)

in (1 mark)

If someone is *deluged with something*, they receive so much/many of something that it is hard for them to deal with it all. The verb phrase *responding to* has to be transformed into the noun phrase *in response to*.

28 taken note of my complaints (1 mark)

and would act (1 mark)

If you *take note of something*, you pay attention to it or take notice of it. If you do something that is appropriate in the circumstances you *act accordingly*.

29 he conducted himself at the conference (1 mark)

(has) resulted (1 mark)

The way that you *conduct yourself* is how you behave. If something *results in something*, it causes it or has it as its result.

30 didn't/did not conform to (1 mark)

what were considered (1 mark)

If something *conforms to something*, it follows or accords with what is expected or demanded. The phrase *the standards that were considered acceptable* has to be transformed into the phrase *what were considered acceptable standards*, with 'what' as the subject.

p80–81 PAPER 1, PART 5

2 marks per question (Total: 12)

The Chess Player

31 A: The writer says that David R. Norwood *will be the first to admit* that he is *one of the hottest properties* (one of the most popular people, one of the people who is in the greatest demand) *on the international chess circuit* (the chess tournaments around the world featuring the best players). Normally, the phrase 'the first to admit something' is followed by faults or mistakes that someone is willing to admit to, but here the writer is being ironic, because it is followed by a claim to be important. The writer is therefore implying that David R. Norwood likes to say how good and important he is and to praise himself.

B: The writer knows David R. Norwood's name because he gives him a business card with his name on it. The writer tells us what the card says but he does not comment on that and it could be that many chess players have business cards. He describes him as a *boy wonder* (an exceptionally successful and talented young man) and uses the phrase *all of 19*, to emphasise how young he is to be a top chess player, so he does emphasise how young he is, but he does not make a particular point about the business card.

C: The writer describes the pub champion as looking like a *bum* (a very untidy, lazy or dirty person who has no particular home and moves from place to place), with untidy hair, a big beard and his possessions in a *white polythene bag* (this suggests they were in a shopping bag). He contrasts him with the *kid genius*, who seems to be a fresh and probably smart young man. However, he does not imply at this point that the pub champion is one of the best players or that he is in any way typical of the best chess players.

D: The game is being played on a container for beer that has been turned upside down so that it can be used as a table and the game is clearly taking place in a pub. However, although these are informal surroundings, the writer does not imply that he thinks it is good to see chess being played in such a place rather than in formal surroundings – his description of the surroundings is merely factual.

32 D: In the games, David R. Norwood is *not merely losing*, he is being *taken apart* (defeated easily and completely). The writer says that in the *argot* (words and phrases used only by a particular group of people) of chess players, he is being '*busted*' (this must logically mean 'totally defeated' in the language of chess players). After each game, Speelman sets up the pieces for *the next act of slaughter* (in this context, the next total defeat of his opponent). Speelman is therefore clearly a far better player than Norwood.

A: The writer says that something *funny* (in this context, this means 'strange') happens in the games. This is that Norwood keeps losing heavily. The reason why this is 'funny' is that Norwood usually wins games (we already know that he is a *kid genius* and a *boy wonder*). But he is not losing because they are playing in a pub rather than in formal surroundings or because they are not playing in a real tournament – he is losing because Speelman is much better than him. Therefore the writer believes that Norwood would lose wherever they played.

B: Norwood sometimes says to Speelman that he is *not such a bad player* and the writer says that of course this is a *joke* because Speelman is not simply *not a bad player, he is possibly the best player in the Western world*. Speelman *laughs* whenever Norwood makes the joke and simply prepares for the next game without saying anything further. Speelman therefore seems to appreciate that Norwood is joking and he certainly does not get offended by the comment. It seems that the games are played in a friendly way and Speelman's reaction is a good-humoured one. There is therefore nothing to suggest that Speelman has a low opinion of Norwood and he says nothing to indicate that he thinks Norwood is a poor player.

C: Norwood does joke occasionally that Speelman is *not such a bad player* but he also *does not seem too worried by this denouement* (the way in which something ends or is resolved, in this case the fact that each game ends with him being heavily defeated). He therefore does not seem embarrassed at losing and the implication is that he expects to lose because he knows Speelman is a much better player than him.

33 B: The writer says that he got the impression that although Speelman told him that he *liked to play with the pieces*, in fact *the pieces enjoyed playing with him*. By this he means that, because of Speelman's approach to the game, the pieces were moved around in ways that they normally weren't by other players. The writer talks as if chess pieces have feelings. He says that when Speelman is playing, he *gives them the time of their life* (he enables them to enjoy themselves thoroughly). Being in a pub, he says, they have probably never experienced *more than the intellectual equivalent of being cooped up in a shed* (because players in the pub are not very clever at chess, the pieces experience only restricted movement, like birds or animals confined in a small building in which they cannot move around much). But when Speelman is playing, he says, they are *roaming free across vast expanses* (they are wandering around freely across large areas, in this case of the board). His point, therefore, is that other people play in a restricted, narrow way, only moving the pieces small distances, whereas Speelman plays in an unrestricted, open way, moving the pieces all over the place.

A: When the writer asked Speelman why he *put up with* (tolerated) *chess jerks* (a slang word meaning 'stupid people') like him, his reply was *instant* (immediate) *and unanswerable* (it could not be argued against because it was clearly true). Speelman seems to have answered his question in a friendly way and the writer does not say anything to indicate that Speelman did not want to talk to him while they were playing.

C: Speelman seems to have enjoyed playing against the writer as much as he enjoyed any other game. The writer says that he got *more bored by losing*

than Speelman *did by winning*, which indicates that Speelman continued to enjoy winning each game against the writer and did not start to get bored by this. There is no indication that it was hard for Speelman not to get bored or that he made an effort to keep himself interested.

D: The writer's description of Speelman's style of play seems to be a general one concerning how he always plays. There is nothing to indicate that he normally played in a more restricted way if he was playing a serious game or that he was only playing in this way because he wasn't taking the games against the writer seriously.

34 B: His nickname, Spess, is a short form of 'Specimen', which was his original nickname, and the writer says that friends and other chess players called him that because they considered it *descriptively accurate* because of his *rather weird* (strange, not normal or common) *appearance*. A 'specimen' in this context means 'a creature used for scientific research because it is in some way unusual or interesting'. The nickname was therefore used because people thought he looked like a peculiar creature, which is not a very complimentary description of anyone.

A: The nickname is said to be related to his physical appearance, not to any aspect of his personality. Although the nickname refers to his peculiar appearance, it is not said that he was regarded as unfriendly.

C: The nickname originated in a report in a newspaper about a chess tournament he was playing in, but it is not related to the way he plays, it is related to his physical appearance.

D: His nickname was originally 'Specimen' and this was first used as a result of a mistake in a newspaper, when his surname Speelman was *inadvertently* (unintentionally, accidentally) printed as 'Specimen'. This happened not because it was a joke but because it was a mistake – when the writer says *Times sub-editors being Times sub-editors* he is implying that sub-editors working for that newspaper have a reputation for making mistakes.

35 C: The writer says that Speelman is *only too aware* (extremely aware) of how people might interpret things that he says. Because of that, he wanted to know what the writer was noting when he spoke to him and so while the writer was making notes, he would *stare at* (look keenly at) his pad and try to read his *scribble* (handwriting done very quickly and untidily). The result of this was that, *in an effort to* (trying to) *counter* (respond against) *this awkward* (causing difficulty) *turning of the tables* (reversing of situations, by which the person being investigated seems to be the person doing the investigating), the writer *deliberately* (consciously, intentionally) began to write in *messier and messier* (more and more untidy) *scrawl* (handwriting that is hard to read) so that Speelman would be unable to read what he was writing. As a result, after the interview the writer was unable to read many of the notes he had made. Later, he *surmised* (concluded) that Speelman had *calculated that his scrutiny* (close study) of the writer's notepad *would have this effect* (cause the writer to make notes he would be unable to read later) and that it was a *deliberate attempt to reduce the number of personal details* about Speelman that he would be able to *decipher* (succeed with difficulty in reading and understanding). Speelman therefore succeeded in his aim of disturbing the writer while he was making notes, so that later he would be unable to read a lot of his notes and use the information in them in his article.

A: The writer says that Speelman's behaviour while he was making notes happened because of *the chess player in Speelman* (it was natural for someone who was a chess player) and that it was *quite in character with Speelman's way of playing chess* (entirely typical of his playing method), which was *convoluted* (extremely complicated) and involved producing *chaos* rather than taking an ordered, simple approach. He is therefore saying that what Speelman did was typical of his approach to playing chess, but he did it to cause the writer problems, not because he thought the writer was expecting him to do such things.

B: Speelman was not trying to understand the personality of the writer when he looked at his notes, nor was he doing it in order to analyse his style of handwriting. He did it in order to limit the amount of information he could note down that he would be able to read clearly later.

D: Speelman was concerned about how the things he said to people might be interpreted but he didn't stare at the writer's notes while he was making them in order to make sure that he would represent what he said accurately, he did it in order to make sure that not many of the writer's notes would be of use to him when he came to write his article.

36 C: When the writer says *Now you get the picture*, he means 'Now you understand the situation, now you appreciate what I mean'. This follows his invitation to the reader to try to do what Speelman does throughout a game of chess, which is to predict the next 25 moves he will make in conjunction with the next 25 moves his opponent will make, making a total of 50 moves ahead that he is constantly predicting while he plays. The writer is implying that the reader will be totally unable to do such a thing because it is far too difficult and he is therefore emphasising that it is amazing that Speelman can do such a thing in his head.

A: It may be that other chess players can do what Speelman does, but the writer does not say this. The point he is making is that what Speelman keeps in his mind throughout a game is incredible and he is

not making a point about chess games in general. Furthermore, he is not emphasising how complex the games Speelman plays are, he is emphasising the extent of the mental effort that he personally makes during them.

B: It is true that the writer seems to regard Speelman's style of play as extraordinary – we have learnt previously that he moves the pieces around differently from other people and that his style is based on chaos rather than the simplicity of other players' styles. The writer does say in this paragraph that Speelman's style *makes enormous demands on the exponent's* (the person carrying it out's – Speelman's) *nervous system*, which again suggests that he finds it extraordinary. However, Speelman does not seem to find what he does extraordinary, because he says that it is *not too difficult to imagine a position in which one could calculate 25 moves ahead*. In this quote, *one* means 'you' or 'anyone' and so he is saying he thinks it is not something only he can do but something that is fairly easy for anyone to do. So although the phrase *Now you get the picture* is used to emphasise how extraordinary the writer thinks Speelman's way of playing is, it does not refer to Speelman's own view of this.

D: The writer describes Speelman when he plays as *all nervous, twitchy* (with sudden, involuntary movements) *movement*, says that he constantly touches his beard, his glasses and anything else he can reach and says that he will *stand over* (stand next to them while they are sitting, in a way that could make them nervous) his opponent, *nodding his head* (moving it up and down) *as if checking the variations* (in this context, possible future moves made by both him and his opponent). This behaviour may well appear peculiar to others but it is not what *Now you get the picture* refers to and his behaviour is not what the writer is emphasising here – what is going on in his head is what is emphasised.

p82–83 PAPER 1, PART 6

2 marks per question (Total: 14)

The Hammond Organ

37 G: In the opening paragraph, the writer has bought a Hammond organ *sight unseen* (without seeing it first) and arranged to have it delivered to his home in Texas.

In G, he talks about how a smell can *trigger a memory* (cause a memory to return suddenly) which *unravels years in an instant* (takes you back in time immediately), and gives an example of such a smell. Then he talks about when they (the people delivering the organ) *unbolt the container* (the one in which the organ has been transported to him), and before he sees *the instrument* (the organ he has bought) – these are all references back to what he mentions in the opening paragraph. At this point, a smell *wafts* (floats) up his nose and gives him a flash-back (a sudden image of a previous time) to 1964, when he first smelt it.

In the paragraph after the gap, he goes on to talk further about his first acquaintance with Hammond organs.

38 E: In the paragraph after gap 37, the writer talks about his desire when he was younger to own a Hammond organ. He says that he did some research into them but that, although he discovered that some models were better than others, he couldn't buy any of them because he didn't have any money.

In E, the writer says that not having any money didn't matter because he then discovered that he could have one without having to pay for it. While he was *thumbing through* (looking casually through) a magazine, he saw an advert offering a Hammond organ *on two weeks' free approval* (an arrangement by which customers can try out goods free of charge for a given period, after which they either buy it or return it). He wondered if this offer was genuine – *Pull the other one* (an informal expression meaning 'I don't believe it'), he thought, and he wondered what *the catch* (the hidden disadvantage of an apparently attractive offer) was.

In the paragraph after gap 38, he says that he responded to this advert and phoned the company who had placed it, when he discovered that the offer was genuine (the *drawback* in the second sentence refers back to *the catch* mentioned in E), as long as the organ wasn't moved once it had been delivered and *set up* (installed).

39 A: In the paragraph after gap 38, the writer talks about arranging for the organ to be delivered and the organ arriving the next morning. When it arrived, he and the men who brought it moved furniture in the house in order to create space for the organ.

In the first sentence of A, *This* refers to the action of moving tables and chairs back against the wall and the sentence means that as a result of doing that, enough space had been created for what the men had brought. The writer then lists what this consisted of and describes his excited reaction on seeing it all – when he says *My face must have been a picture*, he means 'I must have had an extraordinary expression on my face' and *This was the gear!* means 'This was exactly the equipment I wanted, this was the very best equipment'.

In the paragraph after gap 39, the first word *It* refers to *the gear* mentioned at the end of A, and he says that because it looked *polished and shiny*, it made the *dining-room suite* (set of table and chairs) in his house look quite *tatty* (in poor condition as a result of being used for a long time).

40 H: In the paragraph after gap 39, the writer says that he was shown how to get the organ working. After that, he went to get the record that had first made him want to have a Hammond organ, *plonked* (an informal word meaning 'put') the record on the record player and *cranked it up* (an informal expression, here meaning 'played it at loud volume'). Then he describes the intense feeling he experienced now that he had the organ and could try to copy the record.

At the beginning of H, he says that at this point he had to work out how to play *the beast* (this literally means 'big animal' and here refers to the organ, which we already know is big) and how to get *the same sound as that* (*that* refers back to the record 'Green Onions', which he is playing and wants to copy at the end of the paragraph before gap 40). He then describes how he successfully attempted to make the same sounds with his organ as were on the record.

In the paragraph after gap 40, he goes on to talk about the next stage, the next thing he had to do after he had succeeded in working out how to get the right sound out of the organ. This was to *master* (become fully skilled in using) the piece of equipment that the sound came out of.

41 B: In the paragraph before gap 41, the writer describes how the Leslie cabinet works.

At the beginning of B, he says that he *found all that out* (*that* refers to 'how the Leslie cabinet worked', which he has just described in the preceding paragraph) by *fiddling around with it* (trying various different things, moving, turning, pressing, etc different parts; *it* refers back to the Leslie cabinet previously mentioned). He goes on to say that, unlike some other instruments, a Hammond organ can be made to produce a good sound without much effort.

In the paragraph after gap 41, he moves on to talk about what happened next, after he had found out how to get the equipment to work well – his father came home.

42 D: In the paragraph before gap 42, he describes his conversation with his father when he arrived home. He went to the door to *head him off* (to stand in his way so that he could not go in a certain direction, in this case into the room that now contained the organ) and told him about the organ.

The first question in D is asked by his father, in response to the writer telling him that he has got a Hammond organ, which he tells him at the end of the preceding paragraph. The writer doesn't answer this question, but tells his father that the organ is free for two weeks. His father asks him where it is, and he tells him, adding that it is *fantastic* (marvellous, great) and repeating that it does not have to be paid for.

In the paragraph after gap 42, his father's reaction to learning all this is to go down the hall to the room where the writer has told him the organ is (which he does at the end of D). He describes his father as *peering* (looking with narrowed eyes) *round the door* to look at the organ.

43 F: In the paragraph before gap 43, the writer describes his father's reaction to seeing the organ. He is astonished – *Blimey* and *I'm blowed* are slang expressions expressing surprise. His father comments on how big the organ is and asks the writer why he didn't ask him and the writer's mother before getting the organ. The writer apologises and plays the organ to demonstrate how good it is. His father then says *Let me break it to your mum* (if you 'break something to someone', you tell them something that you think will upset them in a gentle way to try to minimise the effect the news has on them).

At the beginning of F, the writer says that he believed *that meant it was going to be all right* (*that* here refers back to what his father said at the end of the preceding paragraph and *it* means the situation regarding the organ – clearly, he thinks that his father will persuade his mother to let him keep it and that he will also persuade her not to be angry with him). The writer then says that the organ was removed two weeks later and a new one brought for him the following week.

In the final paragraph, the writer explains how this – the fact that he got a new organ, as mentioned in F – was possible. It was possible because he bought it *on the 'never never'* (this and *hire purchase* are old-fashioned terms describing a system of credit by which you buy goods by making regular payments over a period of time). He was able to do this because, although he was too young to get credit, his father also signed the form, guaranteeing that he would make the payments if the writer did not.

The paragraph which does not fit into any of the gaps is C.

p84–87 PAPER 1, PART 7

1 mark per question (Total: 10)

FURTHER PRACTICE AND GUIDANCE (p86–87)

For explanations, see the explanations to the questions in the test, which follow.

Section A 1, 4

Section B 2

Section C 4

Section D 2

Section E 1, 3, 4

Section F 2, 4

p84–85 PAPER 1, PART 7 (TEST)

John McCarthy – Computer Pioneer

44 E: He was immediately appointed to a *Chair* (the position of head of a university department) in Mathematics after receiving his *doctorate* (postgraduate qualification) in the subject. So he very quickly rose from being a postgraduate student to becoming the head of the department at Princeton University.

45 F: The writer says that McCarthy's work on time-sharing systems *led him to underestimate the potential of personal computers* – he failed to see their real potential and regarded them as only *toys*. His opinion on personal computers was later shown to be wrong.

46 B: He thought that if *computer time-sharing*, which he developed, *were adopted*, the result would be that *computing may some day be organised as a public utility*. He believed that his concept of computer time-sharing might lead to computing being of widespread public use (rather than having only academic purposes).

47 D: He *applied himself to* (focused his efforts on) both *theoretical* issues involving robots and *the ethics of creating artificial beings* (the moral issues connected with creating them).

48 E: A *symposium* (a discussion meeting involving experts) that he attended, *sparked his interest in developing machines that can think like people* (caused him to suddenly acquire this interest).

49 A: The problem described was how to get computers to *simulate* (perform in the same way as) *many of the higher functions of the human brain*. He felt that the *major obstacle* to solving this problem was the *inability to write programs taking full advantage of what we have*. The fact that computer speeds and memory capacities were insufficient was not what was stopping people from getting computers to perform these brain functions, in his opinion. What was needed was for people to write computer programs that took full advantage of the computers that already existed.

50 E: When he was at Princeton, he *proposed the programming language Lisp as a way to process more sophisticated mathematical concepts than Fortran, which had been the dominant programming medium until then*. We learn in A and B that he invented Lisp. So he tried to make his own language compete with the most widely used one.

51 F: Although he became disappointed in AI, because of the difficulty of developing computer programs that could function like the human brain, he *remained confident of the power of mathematics*.

52 A: He was *often described as the father of 'artificial intelligence'* – it was commonly believed that he was the first person to work in that area, the originator of the whole area of research.

53 C: He worked on a chess-playing program but *came to believe that computer chess was a distraction* (an unimportant issue that took attention away from more important things). He compared it to the idea of geneticists focusing all their efforts only on a kind of fly rather than on wider issues.

PAPER 1

PART 1	8 marks
PART 2	8 marks
PART 3	8 marks
PART 4	12 marks
PART 5	12 marks
PART 6	14 marks
PART 7	10 marks
TOTAL	**72 marks**

To be converted into a score out of 50 marks.

p88 PAPER 2, PART 1

Each answer is given marks out of 20

FURTHER PRACTICE AND GUIDANCE (p89–90)

1 B, E   **2** A, E

MARK SCHEME

Content

The essay should include a summary of these **four key points**:

Text 1 (a) experts say that adolescence is a terrible time

(b) in fact adolescence can be both a bad and a good time

Text 2 (a) it is normal for teenagers to be a problem for their parents

(b) action by parents can make the problems of adolescence even worse

Communicative achievement

This is an essay and so the register should be neutral or formal. The reader should be clear both as to what the key points in each text are and the candidate's own opinions and responses to those points.

Organisation

The essay should be coherently organised in paragraphs, with clear linking between the summaries of the key points and the candidate's own views. An introduction and conclusion are not essential.

Language

The essay should contain an appropriate level of accurate grammar and vocabulary. Vocabulary connected with the topics of youth and behaviour should be correctly used, as should grammatical structures for describing and comparing points of view/information, presenting and supporting opinions, and linking points in complex sentences.

ASSESSMENT OF SAMPLE ANSWER (p90)

Content

The two key points for the first text are included in the first paragraph, and the first key point for the second text is included in the second paragraph. However, the second key point for the second text is not included in the summary of the texts, though the issue is discussed in the last paragraph. Nothing irrelevant is included and the whole of the last paragraph consists of the writer's opinions on the subject.

Communicative achievement

The essay is appropriately neutral/formal in register. The texts are generally well-summarised, with key points paraphrased rather than copied in large chunks from the texts. The opinions given in response to the key points are very clearly and powerfully expressed.

Organisation

The essay is well-organised and appropriately divided into paragraphs, the first two summarising the points made in the texts and the third presenting opinions on the issues raised. Points are clearly and logically linked so that the essay flows well as a whole. The first and last sentences provide a clear and effective opening and ending.

Language

Generally a good level of both grammatical structures and vocabulary is displayed in the essay. Good grammatical structures used accurately include *how ... it can be* and *As ... as* in the first paragraph, and *are the people who should* and *such influences* in the third paragraph. Sentences are complex rather than short and basic, and control of sentence structure is generally very good. A lot of sophisticated vocabulary appropriate for the topic is used, including *irritating* and *emotionally demanding*, *When the time comes, step into, discomfort, traumatic, vital, emotional roller-coaster, side effects, reveal themselves in, mood swings, set an example to, soak up.* The only real error is in the first paragraph, where the sentence beginning *The time of growing* is not a proper sentence. It is a list of verb phrases with no subject or main verb. It could be turned into a grammatically correct full sentence by beginning it with *It is* or *Adolescence is.* Or it could be joined to the previous sentence with a dash to create one long but grammatically correct sentence (*... teenager – the time of ...*).

Mark

Band 4 (13–16 marks out of 20). This is a good essay, with no errors that seriously affect understanding. The grammar used is mostly accurate and competent. One of the key points is missing. However, this is balanced by the very impressive use of vocabulary, both single words and phrases, which demonstrates a high level of fluency in that area.

p91 PAPER 2, PART 2

Each answer is given marks out of 20

MARK SCHEMES

Question 2
Content

The article should describe a memorable day, including what led to it, what happened during it and the consequences – good, bad or both – of it.

Communicative achievement

The register could be formal, informal or neutral but should be consistent throughout. Article format – clearly divided paragraphs, perhaps short ones for impact on the reader. The arrticle could have sub-headings. The reader would be interested in following the description of what happened and would understand fully and clearly why it was memorable for the writer and what impact it had.

Organisation

Clear development of narration, description and comment, starting with the background, moving on to the events and then going on to the writer's views on the consequences of what happened. Appropriate linking within and between paragraphs.

Language

Language of narrating, describing and evaluating, and perhaps of analysing and hypothesising.

Question 3

Content

The review should inform the reader about the subject the writer has chosen and compare the writer's views on it with those of critics.

Communicative achievement

The register could be formal, informal or neutral but must be consistent throughout. The format should be appropriate for a review – description followed by comment and comparison in each paragraph or paragraphs of description, followed by paragraphs of comment and comparison. The reader would be informed about the subject chosen for the review and would have a clear idea of how critics' comments compare with those of the writer.

Organisation

Clear development with appropriate paragraphing and linking between description, comment and comparison.

Language

Language of narrating, describing and comparing, as well as language for expressing and supporting views.

Question 4
Content

The letter should describe the candidate's experiences at the hotel and how they reacted at the time, together with suggestions as to how the hotel could be improved.

Communicative achievement

Formal register, as appropriate for letter of complaint to someone in charge. Formal letter format. The reader would have a clear picture of what happened, how the writer feels about that, and what the writer is advising them to do.

Organisation

Brief introduction stating reason for writing, clear paragraphing for presenting account of what happened, opinions on these events and suggestions for avoiding repetition of them, with appropriate linking between these elements.

Language

Language of describing and narrating, together with language appropriate for expressing opinions, making suggestions and hypothesising.

ASSESSMENT OF SAMPLE ANSWER (p93)
Content

Most of the main points mentioned in the question are covered in the letter, since it describes what happened to the writer in the hotel and the results of this for the writer, and it also includes suggestions to the manager. There is no mention of complaints made to the staff at the time, but this is not a major disadvantage and does not reduce the effectiveness of the letter.

Communicative achievement

The letter is appropriately formal and appropriately laid out. The tone is entirely suitable, being forceful in the points made and the annoyance expressed but remaining polite throughout. The reader would be absolutely clear as to what happened, the writer's feelings about it and what the writer expects to happen as a result of the letter. At the beginning, the writer says that three problems will be detailed and each of them is explained very clearly. The fact that the writer does not want money in return, but to be informed that action on service has been taken is very clear at the end.

Organisation

The letter is extremely well-organised. The opening paragraph gives the appropriate background and explains precisely what the writer's purpose is. The next three paragraphs detail concisely and clearly what happened and why it caused problems for the writer. The final paragraph is excellent, presenting a forceful and very clear view as to what the writer thinks should happen and expects to happen. There is a great deal of excellent linking throughout, for example *Although* (first paragraph), *For some reason* and *Considering* (second paragraph), *Therefore* (third paragraph), *which meant* (fourth paragraph) and *as well as, especially for* and *although* (final paragraph). The only mistake with linking is in the fourth paragraph, where the last two sentences should be linked by *not to mention* rather than beginning another sentence with *Not mentioning*, which is incorrect.

Language

There is some very good use of vocabulary and structure, for example *made my stay rather complicated and unnecessarily unpleasant* and of *high standard* (first paragraph), *most* (meaning 'extremely') *unpleasant* (second paragraph), *knew nothing about* and *starving* (third paragraph), *omitted* (fourth paragraph), and *I strongly advise you to … , appalling, endure, steps that have been taken, to avoid such a situation* and *awaited* in the final paragraph, which is excellent. The language used is certainly not too simple, with excellent linking producing some longer sentences that make complex points very well, particularly in the final paragraph. The shorter sentences are used for brief, clear descriptions of what went wrong and are therefore entirely appropriate. There are a few mistakes. In the first paragraph, *Despite of* is incorrect (*of* should not be there). In the third paragraph *will be delivered* should be *would be delivered* as it refers to a past hope not a future one and the word order of the final sentence is wrong – it should be *wait for another 45 minutes for my dinner to be ready*.

Mark

Band 5 (17–20 marks out of 20). A very well-organised letter with some sophisticated language and a very high level of fluency. The few errors are balanced by the natural use of high-level grammar and vocabulary and by the fact that the letter flows very well and is entirely appropriate to the situation.

PAPER 2

PART 1	20 marks
PART 2	20 marks
TOTAL	40 marks

To be converted into a score out of 50 marks.

p94 PAPER 3, PART 1

1 mark per question (Total: 6)

1 **A:** The speaker says that British people *never expect their holiday plans to run to schedule* (to happen in the way and according to the timetable that has been planned) and that when things go wrong they *sigh* and say *I knew this would happen* (they are resigned to it rather than angry about it because it doesn't surprise them) and they react *with stoicism* (the ability to experience something unpleasant without reacting strongly or complaining). The problems mentioned are ones which affect people personally rather than only affecting someone else.

B: The speaker says that *administrators are for ever being pressed to disclose their contingency plans* (people are always asking them to reveal what plans they have if their original plans do not happen or work). British people don't expect administrators' plans to succeed and constantly ask them what they're going to do when their plans fail. This is an example of British pessimism but not an example of people believing what they are told.

C: The problems mentioned are presented as real ones that actually happen, rather than potential problems that might happen. They are not examples of things that people pessimistically think may go wrong, they are things that do go wrong and there is no suggestion that the speaker thinks people exaggerate these problems.

2 **B:** The speaker says that British pessimism is a *national trait* (characteristic) that *starts in childhood* and that the character of Eeyore in stories for children appeals to British children because he is pessimistic. Children relate to him because they, like him, have a *melancholy* (very sad), *phlegmatic* (not reacting strongly or getting angry) *side* (aspect of personality). The speaker is therefore saying British children are pessimistic by nature and that is why they like this character.

A: The speaker says that *irony* (saying the opposite of what you mean with a tone of voice that indicates what you really mean in order to be amusing, or situations which are contrary to expectation and therefore found amusing) is the basis of British humour and that the *prime ingredient* (most important, main element) of irony is pessimism. He is therefore saying that British people like irony but he does not say that this is something that they come to like later in life – in fact, he strongly implies that children also like irony.

C: The speaker says that British humour is *distinctive* (clearly different from other people's humour) and so he implies that some people might think it strange, but he doesn't say that children themselves think that their own sense of humour is strange.

3 C: The speaker says that the brain waits before focusing on the present and collects *information from the future of an event*. In other words, before thinking about what is happening now, we wait until the next thing has happened and then think about it. This is similar to what happens with live TV broadcasts – they are not genuinely live, what viewers see actually happened a few seconds earlier. The speaker says that the brain has a similar process of delay – it does not focus on what happens until a short time after it has happened, by which time something else has happened. He says that the brain develops *conscious awareness in an 'after-the-fact fashion'*, which means that it focuses on what happens after an event before *committing to a decision about what happened* (before making a firm decision about what happened in the actual event).

A: The speaker is not saying that people change their minds about something that happens. They don't have one perception and then later change it, they have no perception at all until after it has happened.

B: The speaker is not saying that the brain decides on what is important and what is not important when something happens. He is saying that it delays focusing on it until a short time after it has happened.

4 B: The speaker says that scientists have now measured the extent to which the brain delays before processing visual information and that in doing this they have provided *new insights into how we use vision to make sense of the world*. By saying that these are *new insights,* he is saying that their research has produced new information which helps us to understand something, and clearly this information adds to what is already known.

A: The speaker says that the brain's delay before focusing on an event is similar to the *slightly delayed broadcast of live TV shows*. The brain delays for *a minimum of 80 thousandths of a second* and he compares this with the delay in live TV broadcasts, which is *about three seconds*. He therefore compares the two delays but he does not say that the methods used in order to measure the length of the brain's delay was in any way based on the techniques used for live TV broadcasts. The scientists used a technique *called 'the flash-lag phenomenon'* but he does not say that this was based in any way on the techniques used in TV.

C: The speaker says that the research has provided *new insights* and he refers to the scientists' report, but he does not say or imply that what they have discovered is probably going to be shown not to be correct or true. In fact, he seems to believe that the information is reliable, because it adds to what we know about the brain.

5 C: The speaker says that Edison's *rueful observation* (comment expressing sadness and regret) expresses something that inventors today know to be a fact – that creativity is a *precious commodity* (something that is valuable because it is rare) and that therefore if you have a good idea you will have the experience that someone else will *lay claim to it* (claim that it was their idea). The difference today is that, although the same thing happens that Edison described, because of the existence of patents, you can do something about it when it happens.

A: The speaker says that in the past inventors were *ripped off* (cheated financially) by *the unscrupulous* (people with no moral principles) and that the situation is *not a whole lot* (not much) *better now*, but he does not say or imply that he considers inventors to be naive people. He is critical of the people who cheat them but he does not say that the inventors are themselves partly to blame because they lack experience or trust people too much.

B: The speaker implies that what happens to inventors is totally predictable – if they have a good idea, other people say it was their idea and other people cheat them financially. The change has been that inventors can now take action to make sure that they get *the credit* (that it is recognised that they invented the thing in question) and the money for their inventions.

6 B: The speaker says that *the philosophy behind the modern patent* is the same one that existed when patents began – that inventors can *exploit the fruits of* (take advantage of the products of) their *ingenuity* (ability to have clever and original ideas) for a fixed period of time and that in exchange for this they have to teach other people how to produce the thing they invented. The speaker clearly doesn't like this – he says that it has caused a lot of trouble. Because inventors have to *disclose* (reveal) details of their inventions, they have to give other people their *intellectual jewels* (most valuable ideas) and tell them what their *marketing strategy* (way of selling products) will be. He therefore believes that the rules concerning patents have always been to the disadvantage of inventors and to the advantage of those to whom they have to give details of their inventions.

A: The speaker does say that the rules are still the same but he clearly opposes the rules governing patents and he is explaining why he objects to them, not explaining why they are still the same as when patents first came into existence.

C: The speaker says that the rules are bad for inventors and so it is likely that some inventors may not wish to obey them, but he doesn't say that any inventors actually break the rules.

p95 PAPER 3, PART 2

1 mark per question (Total: 9)

7 **lead; limestone:** The area which contains the National Stone Centre used to be part of an *upland* (a piece of higher ground) and consist of *tropical lagoons* (a kind of lake) and *small islands*, and *fossils* (the remains of animals and plants) have been found in the *rock face* (surface of rock) there. From *medieval times* (the Middle Ages, approximately AD 1100–1400), *lead* (a metal) and *limestone* (a type of white rock used in building) have been mined there.

8 **consume/eat:** One *fascinating fact* that visitors to the centre learn is that every person 'consumes' (this can mean 'uses' or 'eats') six or seven tonnes of stone each year (a tonne = 1,000 kilos). The implication is that this seems like a very large and therefore surprising amount. James asks whether this means that we eat stone, and the speaker says that as well as using it in the various ways listed, we also eat it in the sense that it is used in certain products that people eat.

9 **tunnels; tennis courts:** The speaker gives many examples of the use of stone and we are told that it is used in *paint*, *computers* and *ceiling tiles*, in *plastics* and therefore in *cars*, *ships* and *planes* and in *sugar*, *flour*, *pharmaceuticals* and *poultry feed* (food given to birds that people eat or whose eggs people eat). The examples given of its use in construction, which accounts for 90% of the stone we use, are tunnels and tennis courts.

10 **teaching resource:** The headmaster said that the centre is a *splendid* (excellent, marvellous) *teaching resource* (thing that is useful for teaching with) because the place enabled teachers to teach children *all sorts of skills*, helped children to appreciate how much the world changes, and fitted into the *National Curriculum* (programme of what has to be taught in all schools in the country).

11 **Launch Pad:** The speaker says that all of Britain's interactive science and technology centres were *built on the foundation of* (in some way based on the example of) *Launch Pad*, which is part of the Science Museum in London and was the first place in the country of this kind.

12 **roll uphill:** The speaker says that Techniquest has *liquids you can cut* and *bubbles* (balls of liquid that contain air and float in the air) *you can walk in* and *structures that roll uphill* (move up sloping surfaces by turning over and over in the way that balls do).

13 **dentist's chair:** The speaker says that at Techniquest you might see a *granny* (grandmother) or an *eight-year-old* (child) *swivelling around* (turning sharply around, revolving), *under discreet supervision* (while being watched in a way that is not very noticeable by a member of staff, so that they do not come to any

harm) *in a specially adapted dentist's chair* (one that has been modified or made suitable for this purpose), in order to experience *the pull of centrifugal force* (the power of a force pulling an object away from the centre around which it is turning).

14 **sound waves:** The speaker says that visitors to Techniquest can observe *how sound waves can clash* (act in opposition to each other) *and distort one another* (cause each other to change from their natural sound and have a different sound).

15 **control systems:** The speaker says the *dragon* (a mythical, aggressive animal with wings and claws that breathes out fire and is used as a symbol of Wales, which is where Techniquest is) *responds instantly to the fingertip controls* that visitors use and that they can see clearly the parts of it that make it respond. This, the speaker says, *may not be a formal lesson in control systems, but you cannot fail to learn* – in other words, it certainly does teach visitors about control systems, even though this is done in an informal way.

p96–98 PAPER 3, PART 3

FURTHER PRACTICE AND GUIDANCE (p97–98)

For explanations, see the explanations to the questions in the test, which follow.

Question 16 A, B, E, G, H
Question 17 B, D, E, F
Question 18 B, C, E, F, H
Question 19 A, B. F, G, H
Question 20 A, C, E, G

p96 PAPER 3, PART 3 (TEST)

Note: the letters in brackets refer to the relevant options in the questions in the Further Practice and Guidance pages.

1 mark per question (Total: 5)

16 **D:** Paddy says that readers who enjoy her column *invariably* (always) say that it is *particularly the bad ones* (the reviews that are unfavourable towards the hotels in question) that they like. One reader said that *every other week* (once every two weeks), she used to give a *hotelier* (hotel owner or manager) *a bashing* (a verbal attack or verbal criticism) but that now *it's a rare treat* (something pleasurable that does not happen often) when she writes a review like that. That reader says that *I love it when you lay into* (are fiercely critical of) *a pretentious* (trying to be something better or more sophisticated than it really is) *but bad one* and that although it is helpful when she recommends a good hotel, she should find some *awful ones for entertainment's sake* (in the interests of providing entertainment for the readers). Paddy

uses the reader who wrote this letter as an example of readers who like reading her critical reviews and would rather be entertained by them than be told about hotels she recommends, which by implication they may wish to stay in one day. (E, G, H)

A: Paddy says that the readers she refers to like reading her criticisms of hotels but she does not say that they tell her that they believe she gets pleasure from criticising. It is the readers who she says get pleasure from it. (C)

B: Paddy says that she always has *high hopes* (is always very optimistic) when she goes into a hotel and thinks [I] *bet this one's going to be good* (I'm certain this hotel will be a good one). However, she says that *you never can tell* (it's impossible to be certain), because appearance and reality may be different from each other and that hotels that look *idyllic* (beautiful and peaceful and in beautiful surroundings) in a guidebook can be *a terrible letdown* (a very big disappointment). However, she does not say that her attitude has changed because of such disappointments. Moreover, she talks about the response of readers to her reviews, but she does not say that she has become more critical of hotels because readers like reading her reviews which are critical. She presents this as a fact, but does not say that her attitude to hotels has changed so that she can meet their demand for critical reviews. (A, B, D)

C: She says that they like reading her comments but she does not say that they have or refer to their own experiences of the hotels she reviews. If she recommends a good hotel, this may be helpful but she does not say that readers contact her to say that they liked a hotel she recommended or disliked one she was critical of. (F)

17 B: Paddy says that *hotel-keeping* (running a hotel) has been described as being *akin* to (similar to) *show business* (the entertainment industry that involves artists performing for the public) and that in her favourite hotels, there is always *a leading man or woman* (a hotelier who is like the actor playing the main role in a play). She says that these people are often so good that she believes they have *missed their true vocation* (followed the wrong career, because there is another profession that would be ideal for them and which they are naturally suited to – performing). This is what she thinks, she doesn't say that the hotel-keepers she is talking about think this too. (C, D)

A: She says that *Such hoteliers* (those who would be good actors) *usually have a sense of humour* and that they respond to what she says about them in her reviews *in a good-humoured way* (in a cheerful, friendly way), even if they don't like what she says. However, she does not say or imply that they have to try hard to behave in this way – indeed, she implies that it comes naturally to them. (E, G)

C: She says that she is happy to *slam into* (criticise harshly) pretentious hotels that don't *come up to scratch* (aren't satisfactory or of the standard they should be) but that it is a different matter *when the people are nice* (she is unhappy when she criticises a hotel whose owner or manager is a nice person). She says that she still has to write about that hotel but that sometimes doing so *hurts* (she finds it painful because she likes the people). However, she does not say that these hoteliers expect her to be critical of their hotels. What she says is that they react well when she does so. (A, B, F)

D: She talks about hoteliers who have responded well to bad reviews she has written about their hotels and says that they are *professionals* (in this context, people who can separate their professional lives from their personal lives) and that many of them have become friends. It may be surprising that she and people she has criticised have become friends, but she does not say that the hoteliers in question find it so, nor that she is surprised by it. (F, H)

18 C: Paddy says that when she speaks on the phone to people whose hotels she reviewed about including their hotels in her book, some of them refer to the fact they she didn't give their hotel a good review. She agrees and then suggests that perhaps they have improved their hotels since she reviewed them and *would like people to know* about the improvements they have made – the implication is that people will know about this if the hoteliers allow their hotels to be included in her book. She says that *Thus encouraged* (encouraged in this way), most of them have allowed their hotels to be included in the book and have also *entered into the spirit* of the book (adopted the same attitude to the book as Paddy has) by telling her interesting stories about things that go on *behind the scenes* (in the background, unknown to the public). In other words, these hotel-keepers have agreed to be included in her book and have given her interesting things to include in it, even though her reviews of them were critical. (F, H)

A: She says that if she thinks hotel-keepers might shout at her when she phones them – because her reviews of their hotels were critical – she invents someone called Emily, who is supposed to be her assistant, and Paddy pretends to be that person. She says that these hotel-keepers refer to the bad reviews *she* gave them when they think they are talking to someone called Emily, *she* meaning Paddy. This indicates that they do not realise they are actually talking to Paddy and that they believe they are talking to Emily. Therefore, they do believe that she has an assistant called Emily. (C, D, E)

B: She asks them to tell her about changes they have made to improve their hotels since she reviewed them and she implies that they do so. However, she does not say that anything she said about their hotels was not true at the time that she wrote the reviews of them and so she does not refer to any inaccuracies that they could correct. (**A**)

D: She says that she likes their attitude with regard to telling her interesting things she can put into the book but she does not say that she starts to feel that what she originally said about their hotels in her reviews was unfair. She also says that she has a penchant for hotels run by the people who own them and that she likes the owners of small hotels and that is why she has enjoyed contacting them concerning her book. However, she does not say that the fact that she likes them and enjoys talking to them has caused her to question whether what she said about their hotels was fair or not. (**B, G, H**)

19 **A**: The hotel-keeper, who presumably thought that he was talking to her non-existent assistant, said that people who have read Paddy's reviews *go to hotels where she's been fawned over* (treated as somebody special and important – the phrase is used to express disapproval of such treatment) but that *they* – the readers – *probably won't be fawned over*. He added that Paddy often goes to hotels that are *almost empty* and so in those hotels *they* (presumably the staff and managers) *have time to fawn over her* – he implied here that other people go to busier hotels where staff don't have time to treat each guest as someone special and important. Paddy comments that being fawned over is in fact *the last thing I want* (she really doesn't want it). (**G, H**)

B: He did discuss what she had said in her review. She says that *To specify the lies* (to give a specific description of the lies he claimed she had told about his hotel in her review), *he pounced on* (he enthusiastically and aggressively reacted to) something she had said about the food at his hotel. (**B, C**)

C: He said that because of what she says in her reviews, a lot of people *cross hotels off their potential list* (decide not to go to hotels they might otherwise have chosen to stay at and in some sense remove them from the list of hotels they would perhaps stay in) – he therefore said that her reviews do influence a lot of people. He did not, however, refer to the amount of influence he thought she believed her articles have, or imply that it is not as great as she thinks. He also did not suggest that people had told him that they had disagreed with what she had written in her reviews and now took no notice of what she said. (**E, F**)

D: He said that, because she had insulted his hotel and lied about it in her article, *there is no way we would help her perpetuate her grievances against the world in a publication* (we – he and others connected with his hotel – would certainly not help her to continue her feeling of bitterness towards the world in general). He therefore refused to allow his hotel to be included in her book because he felt that her review

of it was an example of her generally negative attitude and he did not want that attitude to be given further expression in a book. However, there is no reference to his having previously decided or agreed to have his hotel included in her book. Paddy says that she had wanted to include it because she had been *enthusiastic about* the food there and *would have liked to include his hotel in the book* but because he was *so disagreeable* (so unpleasant), his hotel could not be included. She does not, however, say that he had once agreed but had now changed his mind. (**A, D**)

20 **D**: The owner told her that he could not give a description of her to other hotels *because she is fairly nondescript* (if someone or something is 'nondescript', they have no remarkable or interesting features or characteristics to distinguish them). (**B, C**)

A: He said that other hotels asked him for various details about her (presumably so that they would know if she was staying at their hotels and going to write reviews of them) but that *Unfortunately* he couldn't describe her to them. He implied that, since there was nothing remarkable about her when she stayed at his hotel, he hadn't noted what car she drove or what credit card she used. (**A, B, D**)

B: She thinks that one reason why he might have agreed to have his hotel included in the book was that he had remembered that in her review she had said that he resembled a very popular comedian, who was now dead. She implies that he might have been flattered by being compared with a popular person, not that he would have been annoyed by this description. (**G, H**)

C: She says that *when it finally clicked* (when he suddenly realised or understood after some time) that he would not have to pay for his hotel to be included in the book, he decided that he did want it to be included after all. What he had not understood was that being included in the book was free, not why she wanted to include his hotel. (**E, F**)

p99 PAPER 3, PART 4

1 mark per question (Total: 10)

21 **E**: The speaker says that he is a member of a *committee* and all the members of it *get together every week, not just off and on* (occasionally). At their meetings, they *have serious discussions* and have to make *important decisions*.

22 **H**: The speaker says that this interest has replaced the *range of hobbies she used to have*. It began to *take over* (occupy all her time spent on interests) and she spends so much time doing it that friends say she has become *obsessed* (it occupies too much of her time and attention).

23 B: The speaker says that he helps to get *contributions* that are needed for the organisation to *function* and *to keep it going*. He says that it is *a worthwhile cause* (an important issue that deserves to be supported). He contacts people by email, asking them for contributions, and he is clearly talking about his role in raising money for a charity.

24 D: The speaker says that the activity involves *getting up in public* – doing something in front of an audience. She does *regular practice* and has *got really good at it*.

25 A: The speaker says that he finds a *venue* (a place where an event is held) and refers to *Putting on* (organising, presenting) *events*. The events he organises have *a small audience*. He does *a bit of publicity* to attract people to attend them and they are *just about viable financially* (they make a small profit or don't lose much money).

26 C: The speaker says that *the social side* and *spending time with that bunch of people* is what *matters* (is important) to him. He says that this group of people are among his best friends and being with them is what he enjoys most about his involvement.

27 E: The speaker says that the activity enables her to *switch off totally* (relax completely for a period of time). It is an *antidote to* (something that functions in the opposite way to) her work, which is *very demanding and exhausting*. It enables her to *go into another world* that is completely different from what she does *to earn a living*.

28 D: The speaker says that he *gets a nice feeling* because he is making his *own contribution to something that needs doing* – he is involved in something valuable, something that is required.

29 F: The speaker says that it is a *tremendous joy* to become good at *something you haven't done before*. She wanted to learn how to do it and finally *got round to* (found time to do) it. She had to *start from scratch* (start from the beginning because she knew nothing at first). Learning this new skill *wasn't all that hard*.

30 G: The speaker says that the *great thing* (the best aspect) is that people tell him afterwards that they really enjoyed the event, and these comments are what *makes it all* – makes all his efforts to organise the events – *worthwhile*.

PAPER 3

PART 1   6 marks
PART 2   9 marks
PART 3   5 marks
PART 4   10 marks
TOTAL   30 marks
To be converted into a score out of 50 marks.

p100–105 PAPER 4

Marks out of 25 are given for performance in the speaking paper.
To be converted into a score out of 50 marks.

FURTHER PRACTICE AND GUIDANCE (p102–105)

DESCRIBING MOVEMENT

WALK/RUN

amble: walk slowly because you are not in a hurry
dash: walk or run fast because of being in a hurry
hobble: walk with difficulty because of injury to a foot or feet
hop: move by jumping on one foot
limp: walk with difficulty because one leg is injured or stiff. Also used as a noun (*walk with a limp*).
shuffle: walk slowly, without lifting the feet from the ground completely
sprint: run as fast as possible. Used also for competitors in races over short distances.
stagger: walk in a way that suggests you are going to fall, because of being tired, ill, injured, etc.
stroll: walk slowly and in a relaxed way, especially when walking for pleasure. Also used as a noun (*go for a stroll*).
tear: walk or run fast because of being in a hurry
totter: walk in an unsteady way
trot: run slowly
wander: walk around in an area, going from place to place, with no particular purpose or simply to see what is there

SHAKE

quiver: shake slightly because of feeling nervous, excited, etc.
rock: move slowly and regularly from side to side or backwards and forwards while in a sitting or standing position
shiver: shake because of being cold, ill, etc.
shudder: shake suddenly, especially down your back, because of fear, cold, etc.
tremble: shake because of fear, illness, etc.

HIT

dig: push someone strongly in the chest with the elbow to attract their attention, used especially in the phrase *dig someone in the ribs*
nudge: push or touch someone with your elbow, in order to attract their attention
poke: push someone sharply with one finger to attract their attention or in order to hurt them
prod: push someone strongly with one finger, especially as an aggressive act
punch: hit someone hard with your fist (closed hand) as an act of aggression
shove: push someone violently
slap: hit someone hard with an open hand as an act of aggression

thump: hit someone hard in order to hurt them

whack: hit someone very hard

THROW

chuck: throw (this is an informal word)

fling: throw something violently or angrily

hurl: throw something violently in a particular direction or throw something a long distance

sling: throw something to a place with force or carelessly

toss: throw something in a fairly gentle way or carelessly

DESCRIBING VOCAL SOUNDS

SHOUT

bellow: shout very loudly

holler: shout (used especially in American English)

howl: let out a long, loud sound of laughter or pain

jeer: shout insults at someone in order to express disapproval or make them look ridiculous

shriek: shout suddenly in a loud high voice

whoop: make a loud noise that sounds like *ooh, ooh* repeatedly with a high-pitched voice, as a reaction of excitement or great happiness about something that has happened

yell: shout loudly

SPEAK/TALK

babble: talk too quickly to be understood

chatter: talk quickly and for a long period about unimportant things

drone: speak continuously in a low voice that is boring to listen to. Often used in the phrase *drone on + for + period of time.*

gibber: talk quickly, saying things that don't make sense

jabber: speak quickly and in an excited way

mumble: speak quietly and indistinctly in a low voice, making it hard to be heard or understood

murmur: speak quietly in a low voice

mutter: speak quietly in a low voice, making it hard for what you say to be heard

natter: talk for a long time with someone about social matters, such as gossip, etc. Also often used as a noun in the phrase *have a natter.*

whisper: speak quietly using only breath rather than the full voice, so that what you say is secret and only someone whom you want to hear it can hear it

LAUGH

cackle: laugh with a harsh sound that is considered unpleasant

chuckle: laugh quietly or to yourself

giggle: laugh in a high-pitched voice, as children do

roar: laugh loudly. Often used in the phrase *roar with laughter.*

snigger: laugh in a low voice in a way that is rude to someone or because you find them or something they have said ridiculous

titter: laugh with high-pitched, short, repeated sounds

SOUND UNHAPPY/COMPLAIN

groan: make an unhappy sound caused by pain, disappointment, disapproval, etc.

grumble: complain fairly quietly

moan: make a long, low sound caused by unhappiness or pain, or complain

sob: cry continuously with the shoulders moving up and down

wail: cry loudly in a high-pitched voice

weep: cry as a result of unhappiness

whimper: make a number of low, weak noises, caused by unhappiness, pain or fear

whine: make a complaining sound in a high-pitched voice which annoys

whinge: complain constantly and unnecessarily in a voice which has a sound that annoys

TOPIC VOCABULARY

OBEYING RULES

abide by: (phrasal verb) If someone *abides by* something, they obey or accept a rule or they stick to an agreement they have made.

adhere to: (phrasal verb) If someone *adheres to* something that they are supposed to do, they obey it and act in accordance with it.

binding: (adjective) If something that has been agreed between people, such as a contract, is *binding*, they are legally obliged to stick to it and cannot decide not to obey the terms of it.

comply: (verb) If someone *complies with* a rule, they obey it.

conform: (verb) If someone *conforms (with/to something)*, they do what is considered acceptable according to rules or expected standards of behaviour.

enforce: (verb) If someone in authority *enforces a rule/law*, they take action to make sure that it is obeyed.

etiquette: (noun) *Etiquette* is a set of unofficial rules concerning what is considered correct and polite formal social behaviour or behaviour among a certain group of people.

observe: (verb) If someone *observes* a rule/law, they obey it.

petty: (adjective) If someone behaves in a *petty way*, they have some authority and insist that other people obey rules which the other people regard as unimportant and unnecessary. If rules are *petty*, they are considered unimportant, unnecessary and annoying.

protocol: (noun) *Protocol* is a system of rules concerning what happens regarding official procedures and occasions.

toe the line: (idiom) If someone *toes the line*, they obey the orders of or express the opinions of those who have authority over them, rather than rebelling.

NOT OBEYING RULES

breach: (noun) If an action is a *breach of* a rule, an agreement, etc, it breaks it.

cheeky: (adjective) If someone is *cheeky*, they say something which does not show respect for the person in authority that they are talking to, perhaps because they are trying to be amusing.

contravene: (verb) If someone *contravenes* a rule/law, they do something which breaks or is against it.

defy: (verb) If someone *defies* someone or something, they refuse to obey them or to do what they are told by someone in authority.

dissent: (verb/noun) If someone *dissents* or *shows dissent*, they speak or act in disagreement with rules or what they have been told to do.

infringe: (verb) If someone *infringes* a rule/law, they break it.

insubordinate: (adjective) If someone is *insubordinate*, they do or say something that disobeys or does not show respect for someone who has authority over them in an organisation.

naughty: (adjective) If someone does something *naughty*, they do something considered fairly bad or unacceptable by someone in authority. This word is often used of children.

rebel: (verb/noun) If someone *rebels* or *rebels against* someone or something, they refuse to accept or continue to accept the control of authority or something that they are being forced to do by someone in authority. A *rebel* is someone who behaves in this way.

sin: (verb/noun) If someone *sins* or does something that is a *sin*, they break a religious or moral rule.

unruly: (adjective) If people behave in an *unruly way*, they refuse to be controlled by someone in authority and behave badly.

CONVENTIONAL

conservative: (adjective) If someone is *conservative*, they have traditional beliefs and cautious attitudes, and do not like great change.

middle-of-the-road: (adjective) If someone or something is described as being *middle-of-the-road*, they are considered to be conservative and moderate rather than extreme.

reactionary: (adjective) If someone is described as being *reactionary*, they are being criticised for being opposed to change.

stick-in-the-mud: (noun) If someone calls someone *a stick-in-the-mud*, they are criticising that person for being opposed to change.

UNCONVENTIONAL

eccentric: (adjective) If someone is *eccentric*, they behave differently from most people and are therefore considered slightly strange.

idiosyncratic: (adjective) If someone is *idiosyncratic*, they have attitudes and do things which are individual to them and different from what is considered normal.

offbeat: (adjective) If something is *offbeat*, it is unconventional and strikingly different from what is common or usual.

unorthodox: (adjective) If something someone does is *unorthodox*, it is different from what is usual or acceptable.

Verb	Adjective	Noun	Adverb	Opposites
1 behave	–	behaviour	–	misbehave (verb) misbehaviour (noun)
2 conform	–	conformity (noun) conformist (person)	–	nonconformist (person)
3 –	cheeky	cheek	cheekily	–
4 defy	defiant	defiance	defiantly	–
5 obey	obedient	obedience	obediently	disobey (verb) disobedient (adj) disobedience (noun) disobediently (adv)
6 rebel	rebellious	rebellion (noun) rebel (person)	rebelliously	–

TEST 4

p106 PAPER 1, PART 1

Note: all explanations in this part refer to the meaning or use of each option most closely related to the question, not necessarily to the only meaning or use of each option.

1 mark per question (Total: 8)
The Rejected Novel

1 **B: Thus far** means 'until now/then', 'so far'. The narrator is saying that at this point in time, his novel had been rejected by four publishers.

   A: *As yet* means 'until now/then', 'so far'. (*I applied three weeks ago but as yet I haven't heard anything.*)

   C: *Hence* means 'from/after this time' (*The contract expires three weeks hence.*) or 'for this/that reason', 'therefore'. (*Jane and Alan had a big argument some time ago, hence their dislike of each other.*)

   D: *By far* means 'by a great amount', 'a great deal' and is used with a comparative or superlative adjective. (*This shop is cheaper by far./It was by far the most embarrassing moment in my life.*)

   All the options can complete phrases connected with time or phrases with 'far', but only B correctly completes the linking phrase that fits the meaning in the context.

2 **A:** If something is **done behind someone's back**, it is done secretly so that they do not know about it because they would not like it or approve of it. The narrator says that he thinks his family were secretly laughing about his failure to get his novel published.

   B: If something is done *over someone's head*, it is done to someone who is in a higher position of authority than they are. (*He was only a junior manager so I went over his head and complained to a senior manager.*)

   C: If something is said *out of earshot*, it cannot be heard by the person mentioned. (*I called to him but he had gone so far away that he was out of earshot and didn't hear me.*)

   D: If you say something *to someone's face*, you say it directly to them rather than only saying it to someone else. (*I told him to his face exactly what I thought of him.*)

   All the options can complete idioms that include parts of the body, but only A correctly completes the required idiom.

3 **D:** If someone or something is **the exception**, they are the only case of something not being true. The narrator is saying that Rhona was the only member of the family who did not secretly make fun of him because of the rejection of his novel.

A: An *omission* is something that is left out of or not included in something, either intentionally or by mistake. (*There were several important omissions in his statement to the police.*)

B: The *exclusion* of something or someone is the act of not including them or of keeping them out. (*Her exclusion from the list of invited guests was the result of an argument.*)

C: The *difference* is the way in which something is different. (*I had been there many times before. The difference this time was that I was on my own.*)

All the options are connected with the idea of not being the same as or part of something, but only D fits the precise meaning in the context.

4 **A:** If you **can/can't bear something**, you are able/unable to accept, deal with or stand something that is very unpleasant and affects you personally without losing your self-control. The narrator is saying that he found Rhona's sympathetic looks when his novel was returned in poor condition more difficult to deal with than her sister's direct, rude comments.

   B: If you *defy someone/something*, you react to them by refusing to do what you have been told to do by someone in authority. (*She defied her parents and went to the night club anyway.*)

   C: If you *can/can't cope with something*, you are able/unable to deal with something that is causing you problems or putting you under pressure. (*Fiona simply can't cope with her enormous workload at the moment.*)

   D: If you *resist something/doing something*, you keep your self-control so that you do not do something which you are very tempted to do. (*I couldn't resist making a joke at that moment, even though I knew it wasn't the right thing to do in the circumstances.*)

   All the options are connected with the idea of reacting to things you are faced with, but only A both fits the meaning in the context and fits grammatically – C also fits the meaning but it would have to be followed by 'with' after the gap.

5 **D:** If you **pack in something** or **pack something in**, you give it up or stop doing it. The narrator is saying that Jack thought that he had given up his job in order to become a full-time artist.

   A: If you *break off*, you stop talking in the middle of doing so. (*He broke off when the phone rang.*) If you *break something off*, you suddenly end a relationship. (*They had a row and broke off their engagement.*)

   B: If you *wind something up*, you bring it to an end. (*Let's wind up this meeting now, it's gone on for too long.*) If you *wind up somewhere/doing something*, you are in that place or you do that thing at the end of a series of developments. (*I got lost and wound up on the other side of the city./After a number of temporary jobs, she wound up working in a bookshop.*)

C: If you *pull out of something*, you withdraw from or stop taking part in something. (*We pulled out of the negotiations when it became clear that none of our demands would be met.*)

All the options are phrasal verbs connected with the idea of stopping something or the end of something, but only D correctly completes the phrasal verb that fits the meaning in the context.

6 **C**: If something is physically **buried in** something, it is at or near the bottom of it. The narrator is saying that his novel had spent a long time in a big pile of other novels sent to publishers by hopeful writers.

A: If someone is *stationed* somewhere, they are sent to a particular place in order to perform an official duty. (*Armed guards were stationed outside the building.*)

B: If something is *encased in* something, it is inside a container and surrounded on all sides. (*Because of the injury, his arm was encased in plaster.*)

D: If something is *consigned to* a place, it is put there, usually because it is not wanted or because someone does not want to deal with it. (*His application was consigned to the list of those unlikely to be accepted.*)

All the options are connected with the idea of being placed somewhere, but only C both fits the meaning in the context and fits grammatically – D would fit the meaning, but it is followed by 'to' not 'in'.

7 **C**: If something is **thin on the ground**, there is not much of it or there is less of it than would be desirable. The narrator is saying that not many critical comments had been made about his novel, presumably because publishers hadn't actually read it.

A: If a comment or conversation is *light*, it is meant to be amusing or entertaining rather than serious. (*Keep the conversation light!*)

B: If someone is *shallow*, they show a lack of serious thought or sincerity. (*William is only pretending to have strong emotions about this because in fact he's rather shallow.*)

D: *Scant* means 'very little' or 'not enough'. (*He acted with scant regard for anyone else's feelings.*)

All the options are connected with the idea of 'not much of something' or 'not serious', but only C completes the required idiom.

8 **C**: If something **lies in something**, it can be found there or exists there. The narrator is saying that the people who had made comments about his novel all agreed that the main thing wrong with it was that it didn't have much of a story.

A: How something *stands* is its situation or the circumstances surrounding it. (*How do the negotiations stand at the moment – are you getting near to an agreement?*)

B: If something *revolves around something*, it has it as its main concern or most important aspect. (*Everything he does revolves around his job.*)

D: If something *centres on something*, it has it as its main point or most important aspect. (*The story centres on the experiences of its two main characters.*)

All the options are connected with the aspects of something, but only C both fits the meaning in the context and fits grammatically – B and D would fit the meaning, but only C is followed by 'in' to express the correct meaning.

p107 PAPER 1, PART 2

1 mark per question (Total: 8)

The Slow Arrival of the Wheel

9 **everything:** The writer has said that it is nearly impossible to imagine a world without wheels and lists things that have them as examples of the fact that *everything* has some form of wheel. In this context, by *everything*, he means every kind of machine or device that people use.

10 **without:** In this context *without* means 'not having'. The writer is saying that some civilisations became quite sophisticated even though they did not have the wheel because it had not been invented.

11 **that:** The conjunction *that* is required here to link the subject *explanation* and verb *is* with the clause that follows. The writer is saying that the wheel probably wasn't invented earlier because conditions did not suit it.

12 **in:** If someone/something is *in the grip of something*, they are suffering as a result of something powerful which they cannot resist or do anything about. The writer is saying that the last parts of the Ice Age were dominating most of the world.

13 **What:** In this sentence *What* is used as the subject, meaning 'the thing(s) that'. The writer is saying that places that were not affected by the Ice Age were affected by other conditions that were unsuitable for the wheel.

14 **from:** If something *evolves from something*, it develops naturally and gradually from it. The writer is saying that the wheel developed from things that Neolithic man did.

15 **by:** The preposition *by* is used here with the meaning 'through the means of' to explain how something is done. The writer is explaining how Neolithic man moved heavy objects.

16 **Such/These/Those:** This refers back to the technique of putting a roller under a heavy load to move it. *Such/These/Those techniques* means 'techniques such as the technique previously mentioned'.

p108 PAPER 1, PART 3

1 mark per question (Total: 8)
The Word 'Bogus'

17 forgeries: A *forgery* is something that has been created as a copy of something in order to deceive people or as an illegal act. The writer is saying that a 'bogus' was originally a machine for making false coins.

18 undergone: If someone/something *undergoes something*, they go through a process which has an effect on them. The writer is saying that the word became an adjective rather than a noun.

19 misleading: If something is *misleading*, it creates a false impression or gives people the wrong idea, either intentionally or unintentionally. The writer is saying that the word was used to describe anything that was intended to deceive people.

20 linguistic: *Linguistic* is an adjective meaning 'connected with language' and *linguistic innovation* means the introduction or creation of something new in a language. The writer is saying that computer scientists in America in the 1960s were responsible for the invention of a number of new words.

21 emergence: The *emergence of something* is its first appearance in a particular context or its development into something that is known, noticeable or important. The writer is saying that the word started to be used by people in a certain part of America who had attended certain universities.

22 adoption: The *adoption of something* is the act of it being used or taken over by someone or a group of people for a purpose. The writer is saying that American teenagers then started using the word with a different meaning.

23 Interestingly: An adverb can be used at the beginning of a sentence, followed by a comma, with the meaning *It is/was, etc + adjective + that ...* . In this case, it means 'It is interesting that ...' . The writer is saying it is interesting that there have been no acceptable explanations for the origins of a great many English words.

24 corruption: A *corruption of* a word is a word that has come into existence as a result of another word being changed from its original form. The writer is saying that one American theory is that the word is an inaccurate version of someone's name.

p109–111 PAPER 1, PART 4

FURTHER PRACTICE AND GUIDANCE (p110–111)

For explanations, see the explanations to the questions in the test, which follow.

Question 25	Question 28
1 C	1 D
2 B	2 A/E
Question 26	**Question 29**
1 B/E	1 A/E
2 A/E	2 C
Question 27	**Question 30**
1 A/E	1 C
2 A/E	2 E

p109 PAPER 1, PART 4 (TEST)

2 marks per question (Total: 12)

25 the controversy (1 mark)

(that was) caused by (1 mark)

The grammatical structure *Such + to be + noun + that + result = Noun + to be + so + adjective + that + result*. The adjective *controversial* therefore has to be changed into the noun *controversy*, preceded by the definite article *the*, as it is a specific controversy. The second part is passive because *the film* is the subject of the verb *caused*. The part of the relative clause before the verb can be omitted.

26 did he know/realise (1 mark)

what lay/was in store for (1 mark)

Little did he know means 'he had no idea'. The sentence starts with *Little* and so the verb must be inverted in the question form, even though it is not a question. *What lies/is in store for someone* is what is going to happen to them in the future.

The phrase *set store by* in the exercise (2C) does exist and means 'attach importance to'. (*My boss sets great store by punctuality.*)

27 prey on you/your mind (1 mark)

to such an/to such a great/to so great an/to that extent (1 mark)

If something worries you, especially if it worries you over a period of time so that you cannot forget it, it *preys on you* or *preys on your mind*. The preposition that goes with *extent* is *to*. The phrases *to such an extent, to such a great extent* and, more formally, *to so great an extent* all mean 'so much'. *To that extent* means to an extent as great as the one mentioned.

The phrases *be prey to something* and *fall prey to something* in the exercise (1B and 1D) do exist, and they can both be used with the meaning 'be a victim of' (*He was naive in business and so he was/fell prey to all sorts of cheats and fraudsters*).

28 to fame (1 mark)

was/came at the expense (1 mark)

If you *rise to something*, you make upward progress and achieve it. The adjective *famous* has to be changed to the noun *fame*. If something *is/comes at the expense of something*, the fact that it happens results in damage or loss to something else or it is to the disadvantage of something else.

The phrases *meant the expense* (2C) and *led to expense* (2D) could be used in contexts in which *expense* means 'money spent' or 'a lot of money spent'.

29 did Ray a favour/did a favour for Ray (1 mark)

as a result of/because of/due to (1 mark)

If you *do somebody a favour* or *do a favour for somebody*, you do something that helps them, usually because they ask you to do it, and in this way you are kind to them. The word *which* after the gap refers to 'the fact that I did Ray a favour' and is therefore a substitute for a noun clause. It has to be preceded by a phrase referring to the fact that the favour was the cause of his success or that it resulted in his success. When completed, the second part of the sentence therefore means 'the result of the fact that I did him a favour was that his business became successful' or 'the fact that I did him a favour caused his business to be successful'.

The phrase *in somebody's favour* in the exercise (1b) does exist, meaning 'to somebody's advantage' (*The decision went in his favour, which pleased him*). The phrase *find favour with somebody* in the exercise (1c) also exists, and it means 'be approved of or liked by somebody' (*My proposal found favour with the others at the meeting*).

30 me waiting (1 mark)

for the best part of (1 mark)

If you *keep somebody/something doing something*, you make them continue to do it, although they may not wish to continue doing it. The phrase *the best part of* means 'almost all of', 'most of', and is often followed by a period of time.

The phrase *to the best of* in the exercise (2A) can be used in the phrase *to the best of my ability*, meaning 'as well as I can/could' (*I did the work to the best of my ability.*) and in the phrase *to the best of my knowledge*, meaning 'as far as I know, although I am not completely sure'. (*To the best of my knowledge, George still lives at the same address he had two years ago.*) The phrase *at best* in the exercise (2B) means 'taking the most optimistic or tolerant view'. (*At best, this will prove to have been only a small mistake.*) The phrase *at the best of times* in the exercise (2C) means 'even when the best circumstances exist'. (*Michael is bad-tempered at the best of times.*) The phrase *with the best of* in the exercise (2D) can be used in the phrase *with the best of intentions*, meaning 'intending only to do good things or to help'. (*I went there with the best of intentions but I only made the situation worse.*)

p112–113 PAPER 1, PART 5

2 marks per question (Total: 12)

Progressives in the US

31 B: The writer says that the word *progressive*, which had previously been widely used in ordinary conversation, began to be used also at this time to describe *a political party*, a *movement* (a group of people with the same political beliefs and aims) and *an era* (a period in history). He says that it *remains a curiously empty word* (it is still a word which, strangely, has little or no meaning) but that *historians will never be able to do without it*. His point is that, although he doesn't think that the word adequately describes what it is meant to describe, historians have always used it to describe the period and continue to use it now.

A: The writer says that this was *an epoch* (a period) *very much to the American taste* (that appealed very much to Americans), in that it proved to them something they wanted to feel – that their belief in progress and in the idea that America was capable of it was *justified*. It is clear, therefore, that Americans at this time liked the idea that was signified by the word *progressive*, but the writer is not saying that it can be applied only to this period. He is simply saying that it was widely used and popular during this period.

C: The writer says that the word was widely used but he does not mention inappropriate use of it. In fact, he says that *after all due reservations have been made* (after all justified doubts have been expressed) *it would be churlish* (unfair and narrow-minded) to deny that the US did make progress during this period – his point here is therefore that the word is appropriate now and was appropriate then to some extent.

D: The writer does say that all kinds of different people were united during this period – he lists types of people all over America who *acknowledged* (accepted) *the necessity* (this refers to the necessity for *radical improvements* previously mentioned). He says that all these people *had a hand in* (played a part in) shaping these improvements. However, he does not say that the fact that the word *progressive* came into use caused these people to unite – his point is that they became united in their common aims and that the word began to be applied to what they were doing.

32 D: The writer says that big business *made itself felt* (was a big factor that people were aware of) throughout this 'progressive' period but that this was *not, by any means as a purely reactionary force* (it was certainly not a force that was completely against change). His point here is that big business was to a certain extent, as might be expected, opposed to change but it was not entirely so, which means that its influence to a certain extent helped to bring about change. He then says that *All the same* (Despite this, in spite of the fact that big business to a certain extent encouraged change), it would be wrong to think that big business *was the key to* (the most important factor in) *progressivism*. His point, therefore, is that big business had a major influence on the way in which progressivism developed but that it was not the most significant contributor to it.

A: The writer says that the industrial working class, even though it was very active, could not *muster* (gather together, accumulate) *the power* that was necessary *to dominate the epoch* (to be the most powerful force of the period). However, he does not say that this was because big business prevented it from doing so.

B: The writer says that *That privilege* (the fortunate position of being the major force of the period) *belonged to the new middle class*. He is therefore saying that the new middle class became the dominant force, but he does not say that big business failed to pay enough attention to the rise of that class.

C: The writer says that big business *had shaped* (determined the nature of, greatly influenced) and *now coloured* (affected) everyday life in America. He is therefore saying that it had already had a great influence on daily life in America before this period.

33 C: The writer says that the new middle class had *emerged* (come out) *as the chief beneficiary of* (the people to benefit most from) the enormous change in American society because this change, which involved *industrialism and urbanisation, implied* (in this context, this means 'had as its logical consequence') a need for professional services and that this in turn *implied* the need to recruit and train new people to supply these services. As a result, there was a *mushroom growth* (a sudden, rapid increase) *among the professions*. His point, therefore, is that the number of people working in the professions (he lists examples of these) grew suddenly and enormously because the great changes in American society had created a need for them.

A: The writer says that this was *the age* (historical period) *of the expert* and that these experts, the people working in the professions that he lists, were *given a free hand* (allowed to act without restrictions) of a kind that they have *seldom enjoyed since*. He is therefore saying that the way in which people in the professions worked was mostly only possible during that period, but he is not saying that people thought the rise in the numbers of them would not last for long.

B: The writer does say that the people in the professions enjoyed a freedom that they have hardly ever had since that period, but he does not say that the rise in their numbers was caused by a wish for fewer restrictions in the way they operated. Their numbers increased because of the demand for them, not because of their own desires.

D: The writer talks about the enormous changes in American society but he does not say that the American people were worried about these or that people in the professions helped the American people to come to terms with these changes. In fact, he says that the changes resulted in greater wealth in American society and that American society *was now rich enough* to pay for the professional services that the changes had created a need for.

34 A: The writer says that people had faith in experts and believed that *there was a sound* (sensible, functional) *technical answer to every problem, even to the problem of government*. In Galveston it was decided that politicians were not capable of solving the problems caused by the hurricane and flood and instead *a commission* (a group of people officially chosen to carry out a public task) *of experts* (people with specialist knowledge) was appointed to do that. This pattern – the appointment of experts rather than politicians to solve problems – was *widely followed* later. Therefore, the writer uses what happened in Galveston to illustrate the faith that people had in experts at the time.

B: It is clear that the people in Galveston did not think that politicians would be able to deal with the problems caused by the hurricane and flood as well as experts could, but the writer does not say or imply that problems caused by natural disasters were different from other problems, in the sense that authorities had always failed to solve problems of that particular kind.

C: The writer does not refer to how quickly the problems of Galveston were solved – his point is not that experts solved problems more quickly than *the regular authorities* (politicians), it is that experts and not politicians were given the responsibility for solving them.

D: The writer does not say that the fact that people wanted to be provided with technical solutions to problems resulted in disagreements, he is saying that it resulted in different people (experts, not politicians) being given the task of solving problems of the kind found in Galveston, with the expectation that they would be able to solve them.

35 B: The writer says that the new class wanted to change society and thought that it knew how to solve social problems. This new class, which consisted of experts, had themselves benefited from being in a society that was *open to the rise of the talented* (one in which talented people had the opportunity to do well) and they wanted people less fortunate than themselves to *rise* (improve their position) just as they had done. This *democratic individualistic ideology* (their political theory that society should be based on fair and equal treatment for everyone and the freedom of the individual) made people think that it was *legitimate* (reasonable) *to bid for* (to try to get) political power and that *to go down into that arena* (to enter the field of politics) *was simply to carry out one's civic duty* (to do what was expected of you as a citizen). When people did so (attempted to get elected to positions of political power), *Motives* (their reasons for doing so) *did not need to be examined too closely* because they were *self-evidently* (clearly, with no need for proof) *virtuous* (good, based on high moral standards). The writer's point here is therefore that people didn't wonder why members of the new class stood for election, because they believed they already knew why – it was assumed that they were doing so in order to improve the position of the disadvantaged people in society.

A: The writer says that there were social problems *All round* (in all places and parts of society) that had to be solved and he lists some of these problems. He says that the new class thought they knew how to solve these problems. However, he does not say that these problems were sometimes too great for them to solve or that some of them did not appreciate how great these problems were.

C: The writer says that their ideology was such that they believed that *their disadvantaged* (poor, lacking in the basic things considered essential to all members of society) *fellow-citizens* should *rise* and that they tried to get political power in order to make this happen. However, he does not say that these disadvantaged people were not capable of doing what the new class thought they could do or that the new class had an unrealistic image of the disadvantaged people.

D: The writer says that these people brought a new *tool-kit* (set of tools in a bag – this is used here to refer to the expertise these people had) to the task of solving social problems and that in a way, they had *improved spanners* (a spanner is a tool for turning screws, etc: here it is used to mean that they had technical knowledge that was greater than people had previously had), which they tried to use when dealing with *contraptions* (this literally means 'strange or complicated machines') such as the existing political parties and the new *urban wastelands* (cities or parts of cities that were in poor condition and not serving any useful function). His point is that their methods for achieving their aims were new and practical and it is possible that as a result people thought that they could achieve their aims. However, he does not say that he believes that expectations of what they could achieve were realistic, he merely describes their attitudes, aims and methods.

36 D: The writer says that *Behind the zeal of these technocrats lay an older tradition* (an older tradition was the real but hidden basis for the enormous enthusiasm of these technical experts). The fact that they were in fact part of an older tradition was *betrayed* (in this context, this means 'unintentionally revealed') by their use of the word *settlements* for

the *philanthropic* (created by rich people to help poor people) centres they established in *the slums* (crowded districts of cities in which people live in terrible conditions). This word had previously been used by *the settlers of old* (people in the past who had been the first to go and live in various parts of America) to describe places they had established. Their use of the word *settlements* showed that they had the same attitudes as *the settlers of old* because the word had the same implications to them as it had to these settlers. This, he says, reveals *limitations* (abilities that are limited and do not go beyond a certain extent) in the new class that were likely to *impede their quest* (make it difficult or impossible for them to achieve what they were trying to achieve). They were mostly from *old American stock* (descended from American families that had been in existence for a long time), they had been brought up according to the *old pieties* (traditional religious and moral beliefs) and their new expertise only *veneered* these (only covered the surface of these so that they were still present just under the surface). Their use of the word *settlements* therefore showed how much they had in common with previous generations, as a result of which they were too *conservative* (naturally reluctant to see major change) and too *parochial* (concerned with only local matters) to want to carry out major changes to American society.

A: The writer is not saying that the progressives were only pretending that they wanted to solve social problems because it would make them look good. He is saying that they had inherited an attitude towards cities which was part of a general attitude that prevented them from bringing about the enormous change they wanted to. He is not saying that they didn't genuinely care about disadvantaged people in cities, he is saying that their attitude towards them was the same as that of the old settlers towards the people in the places they settled in.

B: The writer is not saying that the word indicates that some of their beliefs were based on misunderstandings – he is not saying that their attitude towards cities indicated that they did not really understand them or that they had wrong ideas about the problems in them. He is saying that there was nothing new about their approach to solving the problems in them.

C: Their approach seems to have been clear and the writer does not say that they were not sure how to deal with the problems of cities – they believed they were bringing *superior* techniques and ideas to the problems. He says that their approach was *conservative* and *parochial* because of attitudes they inherited and that this prevented them from carrying out the changes they wanted, but he does not say that they were aware of this or that it meant that they were confused in their own minds.

p114–115 PAPER 1, PART 6

2 marks per question (Total: 14)

Rainmaker with his Head in the Clouds

37 H: In the opening paragraph, we learn that Dr Mather tried to make clouds rain and that almost everyone else in the *meteorological community* (people involved in the study of the earth's atmosphere and the weather) advised him not to. We also learn that a film has been made about him. The opening sentence is a play on words – if you 'have your head in the clouds', you have unrealistic aims or ideas, which some people thought was true of Dr Mather, who was also involved in the study of actual clouds.

In H, the phrase *to do so* refers back to the end of the opening paragraph and means 'to make clouds rain'. As a result of his desire to make clouds rain, he set up a project. A film has been made which shows that various experiments have proved that he was right to think it could be done.

The paragraph after the gap gives some information about what had happened regarding *weather modification* (causing the weather to change) before Dr Mather got involved in it.

38 G: In the paragraph before the gap, we learn that the science of weather modification had *claimed many reputations*, which means that many scientists had lost their good reputations as a result of getting involved in it. We also learn that the idea began in the 1940s and grew after the Second World War.

In G, *They* at the beginning refers back to the *efforts* made after the Second World War that are mentioned at the end of the paragraph before the gap. The paragraph then describes efforts to prevent clouds from producing *hail* (frozen rain that falls as little balls of ice) that would damage crops and make them produce rain instead.

In the paragraph after the gap, we are told that the *entire discipline* (the whole field of weather modification) then acquired a bad reputation.

39 A: In the paragraph before the gap, we learn that the science of weather modification got a bad reputation because commercial companies *hijacked the idea* (took it over for their own purposes) and *failed to deliver on their promises* (failed to do what they had promised to do – this must mean they they did not prove that cloud-seeding was possible, as they had promised to). As a result, the process *became the preserve* (an activity exclusively done by) *of crackpots* (crazy people) *and charlatans* (cheats who make false claims about being experts in something in order to make money).

In A, we are told that Dr Mather *refused to be daunted by this image*. *This image* refers back to the image that people had of weather modification, or cloud-seeding, which was that it was *the preserve of crackpots and charlatans*. Dr Mather was not discouraged by the fact that people had this image of weather modification because *the principle* (the basic idea on which a theory is based) *seemed perfectly plausible* (believable). The rest of the paragraph consists of a detailed explanation of what that principle is with regard to what happens in clouds.

In the paragraph after the gap, this explanation is continued, moving on from what happens in clouds to what scientists believed they could do to change what naturally happens in clouds.

40 C: In the paragraph before the gap, we learn that none of the experiments which were carried out to prove the theory that clouds could be affected by scientists worked. Dr Mather had no success himself in this, and so he was about to *admit defeat* (accept that success was impossible and give up), but then *serendipity* (the ability to make fortunate discoveries completely by chance) *intervened* (entered into the situation and changed it).

In C, we are told what happened when *serendipity intervened*. The *last batch of data* refers back to the *experiments* he made that are mentioned in the paragraph before the gap and means that he collected a last batch of data before giving up these experiments. When he was collecting this, there was an unexpected storm, which he discovered was directly above a *paper mill* (a factory for processing paper).

In the paragraph after the gap, *the place* and *from there* both refer back to the paper mill mentioned at the end of C. We learn in this paragraph that Dr Mather thought that the paper mill had caused the storm.

41 F: In the paragraph before the gap, we learn that Dr Mather decided that there was a direct link between the *hygroscopic salts* coming from the paper mill and the storm and that subsequent experiments he conducted proved that rain could be caused by certain substances being put into clouds.

In F, we learn that the scientific community did not believe this *apparent proof* – that clouds could be made to produce rain by putting certain substances into them, as described in the paragraph before the gap. The scientific community remained *sniffy* (contemptuous) and *Foremost among the sceptics* (one of the main people to be extremely doubtful) was Dr Cooper. He saw Dr Mather present *his astonishing claims* – this refers back to his claims concerning the effect of hygroscopic salts on clouds in the paragraph before the gap – at a conference.

At the beginning of the paragraph after the gap, *He* is Dr Cooper and the first sentence means that Dr Cooper was *wary* (cautious, suspicious) when he heard the claims referred to at the end of F. In this paragraph we learn that he was wary because Dr Mather was considered to be *a smooth-talking salesman* (someone who tried to convince others of something that is probably not true by means of speaking persuasively), because scientists don't trust other scientists who are *charming and charismatic* (having great personal charm that makes them have influence over other people because other people are impressed by them), because Dr Mather had been working *in the commercial sector* (this implies that Dr Mather's conclusions might have been influenced by commercial considerations) and because Dr Mather was considered to be a *maverick* (someone in a particular field of work with unconventional views and methods which are often disapproved of). The phrase *On that occasion* refers back to Dr Mather's appearance at the conference, mentioned at the end of F.

42 E: In the paragraph before the gap, we learn that Dr Cooper considered Dr Mather's results impossible but felt that the statistical evidence for them was *overwhelming* (enormous) and as a result was confused.

In E, Dr Cooper goes to South Africa to prove Dr Mather wrong but comes back believing that Dr Mather was *on to something* (had discovered something that could have important consequences). Dr Cooper is now conducting two experiments himself – in Arizona and in Mexico – to *verify* (to confirm, to make sure that they are what they seem) the results so far obtained in South Africa, using a kind of salt.

In the paragraph after the gap, Dr Cooper is speaking about the experiments referred to in E. In the first sentence, *those findings* refers back *to the South African results* in E and *there* refers back to Arizona and Mexico in E. He talks about how significant it would be if his experiments have the same results as those already conducted in South Africa, since this would prove that clouds can be made to produce rain if certain substances are put into them.

43 B: In the paragraph before the gap, we learn that, although it might have been proved that cloud-seeding is possible, scientists must *exercise* (use) *caution* on the matter because it is a subject that is still *mired in* (prevented from making progress because of) *controversy*. Another reason why caution is necessary is that because water is such a *precious resource*, the possibility that it can be produced from making clouds rain puts the subject into the *political arena* (the world of politics).

In B, *such matters* refers back to the controversy surrounding cloud-seeding and the fact that it could become a political issue, both of which are mentioned in the paragraph before the gap. Dr Mather won't be involved in discussing these issues because he died shortly before the film about him had been completed. However, we are told that the film will result in Dr Mather getting the recognition he deserves.

In the paragraph after the gap, we are told why Dr Mather deserves such recognition.

The paragraph which does not fit into any of the gaps is D.

p116–117 PAPER 1, PART 7

1 mark per question (Total: 10)

Parental Favouritism

44 B: The writer says that there is a report on the subject *every couple of years* (regularly) and that *Most often* (in the majority of cases), though not always, these reports show that *older siblings seem to come out on top* (are the most favourably treated).

45 F: The writer says that parents should *keep a watchful eye on their own behaviour* so that their children do not feel that they are showing favouritism towards a particular child. Even if they are not really doing so, they may appear to be doing so, resulting in *perceived unfairness*.

46 C: The writer describes the belief that firstborn children receive favouritism because when they are the only child, they are *given a huge amount of parental time and energy*. After parents have given them all this time and energy, it is logical that they keep doing this *to protect the investment* (so that the time and energy already spent is not wasted).

47 F: The writer says that children are *Scrupulous emotional accountants* who are *constantly totting up incidents of perceived unfairness* – they watch their parents' behaviour towards them extremely carefully and add up the number of occasions when they think they have been treated unfairly.

48 D: The writer says that because the research has *so many contradictory variables* (data that shows different patterns which are the opposite of each other), the subject of parental favouritism *hardly seems* (doesn't really seem) *like science at all*. Also, because all the experts say that favouritism is extremely common, the writer suggests that this means it is simply normal behaviour and therefore *does not merit* (does not deserve, is not worth) scientific study.

49 C: The writer says that that the survey which showed that parents favour younger children indicated that parents *let them have their own way* (allow younger children to do what they want rather than what parents want them to do).

50 E: The writer says that the way parents treat their children *is affected by any number of shifting, interlacing factors* (a lot of constantly changing but closely connected factors) and she lists these: *birth order, gender, changes in circumstances, our own childhood experiences.*

51 A: The writer says that *people behave less naturally when they are being watched* and this could affect how reliable results of any study into parents' treatment of children is. In the case of the Californian study, according to the writer, this factor means that the figures are *almost certainly under-representative* and that in fact higher percentages of mothers and fathers show preference for a particular child than the percentages found in the study.

52 A: According to Kluger, the 5% of people who say they do not have a favourite child *are lying* because in his opinion *parental favouritism is hard-wired into the human psyche* and every parent without exception does it.

53 F: The writer says that *it's a big deal to admit to such parental malpractice, if only to yourself* (it is very difficult for parents to admit to favouritism, even to themselves and not to other people). She is saying that parents don't want to accept that they show favouritism and find it hard to do so.

PAPER 1

PART 1	8 marks
PART 2	8 marks
PART 3	8 marks
PART 4	12 marks
PART 5	12 marks
PART 6	14 marks
PART 7	10 marks
TOTAL	72 marks

To be converted into a score out of 50 marks.

p118 PAPER 2, PART 1

Each answer is given marks out of 20

MARK SCHEME

Content

The essay should include a summary of these **four key points**:

Text 1 (a) popular culture is for the commercial profit of companies

(b) popular culture is dictated by the people, not by companies

Text 2 (a) popular culture cannot be forced on the people, it is created by the people

(b) the people are individuals, not a single group, and may accept or reject what is offered to them

Communicative achievement

This is an essay and so the register should be neutral or formal. The reader should be clear both as to what the key points in each text are and the candidate's own opinions and responses to those points.

Organisation

The essay should be coherently organised in paragraphs, with clear linking between the summaries of the key points and the candidate's own views. An introduction and conclusion are not essential.

Language

The essay should contain an appropriate level of accurate grammar and vocabulary. Vocabulary connected with the topics of culture and commerce should be correctly used, as should grammatical structures for describing and comparing points of view/information, presenting and supporting opinions, and linking points in complex sentences.

p119–121 PAPER 2, PART 2

Question 2

MARK SCHEME

Content

The report should include a brief summary of how the survey was conducted, the findings of the survey regarding different specific ideas and possibilities for the content of a weekly magazine supplement and a conclusion summarising local people's views and preferences regarding a possible weekly magazine supplement.

Communicative achievement

Register appropriate to employee/employer relationship – fairly formal. Report format, probably with section headings and perhaps with headings for each possible section of the magazine covered by the survey. The reader would understand the findings of the survey and the writer's summary of them fully and clearly.

Organisation

The report should be well-structured, with each aspect of the possible magazine dealt with clearly and the results of the findings clearly presented. Clear introduction and conclusion, and clear linking of areas of the report throughout.

Language

Language of analysing, describing and perhaps hypothesising.

ASSESSMENT OF SAMPLE ANSWER (p121)

Content

The report covers all the aspects mentioned in the question. It includes a description of what the survey involved, the information that was gathered from the survey and conclusions as to what has been discovered with regard to the supplement.

Communicative achievement

The register is appropriately neutral, since the writer is reporting objectively on factual information. The format is entirely appropriate, with a heading for the report as a whole and clear sections, each with clear section headings.

The reader would be perfectly clear as to what has been done, what has been discovered and how this should be interpreted. The report totally fulfils the requirements in the question.

Organisation

The report is extremely well-organised in a coherent order, starting with the research that was carried out, moving on to the information gained from it and concluding with a summary of the position, which states briefly and clearly the outcome. The Research section describes clearly what the survey consisted of and how it was carried out, the Findings section explains clearly what ideas proved popular and unpopular and the Conclusions section indicates clearly and briefly how the findings should be interpreted. The linking is appropriate and accurate throughout, and enables the whole report to flow well.

Language

There is some very good use of vocabulary and structure, for example *in which* and *if so* (Research section), *see the point* (Findings section) and *It would appear that, make it worth doing* and the *prefer ... rather than* structure in the Conclusions section. Most of the vocabulary and structures are relatively straightforward, but this is entirely appropriate for a report of this kind. There are no mistakes in the report.

Mark

Band 5 (17–20 marks out of 20) An excellent report with no errors that covers everything it should. Language entirely appropriate for the task is used throughout and a very high level of fluency is demonstrated.

Question 3

Content

The article should cover the points mentioned and, as instructed, consist of a list of what the writer considers to be the good things in life, together with reasons why they are good.

Communicative achievement

The register should be appropriate for an article of a light-hearted nature – informal – or neutral if the subject is treated as a more serious one. Article format, in this case a series of probably short paragraphs forming a list, perhaps with sub-headings. The reader would understand fully the things chosen for inclusion in the list and why they have been chosen and may be entertained by the article.

Organisation

A list of things considered good in life, accompanied by clear and coherent reasons for choosing them. The article could have a brief introduction and/or conclusion intended to have an impact on the reader. Appropriate linking between items in the list and between each item and the reason(s) for choosing it.

Language

Language of describing, evaluating, expressing and supporting views and perhaps recommending and hypothesising.

Question 4

Content

The letter should describe the visit and present a list of aspects of the visit and the place, together with personal experiences and comments relating to those aspects. It should also include recommendations arising from the personal experiences and comments on the visit and the place. Candidates may be enthusiastic about the place or critical of it, or they may combine enthusiasm with criticism.

Communicative achievement

Formal letter, as appropriate for a member of the public writing to an official they have not met or spoken to, concerning something the official has authority over. Formal letter format. The reader would be completely clear as to what the writer's experiences were, the writer's opinions arising from them and what the writer is recommending.

Organisation

Brief introduction, giving a clear reason for writing. Clear paragraphing, each paragraph dealing with separate aspects of the trip and the place, followed by comments and, if appropriate, recommendations for action on the part of the recipient. Appropriate linking so that comments and recommendations logically follow descriptions and narration and so that paragraphs together form a coherent whole.

Language

Language of narrating (for the visit and personal experiences), describing (the place), and recommending, including language for expressing opinions (praise, complaint, etc.).

PAPER 2

PART 1   20 marks

PART 2   20 marks

TOTAL   40 marks

To be converted into a score out of 50 marks.

p122 PAPER 3, PART 1

1 mark per question (Total: 6)

1 **C:** The speaker says that confidence is an *elusive* (difficult to be precise about) *thing* and that everyone has an idea what they mean when they talk about it. The implication is that different people have different ideas about what it is because it is hard to define it precisely.

A: The speaker mentions one dictionary definition she regards as not *quite right* (not completely accurate) but she does not say that the majority of dictionary definitions of confidence are wrong.

B: The speaker says that *self-assurance* is *more like it* (closer to being an accurate definition of confidence), not that it involves a lot more than just self-assurance.

2 **A:** The speaker uses *We* to mean 'everyone' or 'people in general'. She says that nobody wants to feel inferior to others or be *bullied* by someone else (treated badly by someone who threatens or frightens them) and that we all want to feel that we are equal to others. She says that *of course we all want these things* and since these are signs of confidence, she is saying that everyone wants to have confidence.

B: She says that people don't want to feel inferior and that they want to feel that they are *just as good as* (exactly equal to) other people but she doesn't say that people who lack confidence can gain so much of it that they start to feel superior.

C: She says that wanting confidence and having it are *very different*, which means that for some people it may be very hard to get confidence. However, she says that if we don't have confidence or don't have

an abundance (a very large amount) of it, we *must set about obtaining more* (we must begin the task of getting more, we must start making an effort to get more). She is therefore saying that people who lack confidence have to start gaining it, and this may be difficult, but she is not saying that it is impossible for some people.

3 **C:** The speaker says that Goldman's *insincerity detector* (his ability to notice that someone is insincere) is working *perhaps too industriously* (too hard). By this he means that Goldman finds insincerity where it does not really exist and criticises people for insincerity when in fact they are sincere. He says that, in the book, actors *come in for stick* (receive severe criticism) because of their *egos* (because they are selfish and arrogant) and that even when they are being *modest* (not saying how wonderful they are), Goldman thinks they are being insincere. The speaker is saying that this may not be fair.

A: The speaker says that Goldman's previous book contained *splenetic* (very angry) *observations* and this book clearly does too. In this book, Goldman's *principal grouch* (main complaint) is the same as in his previous book (that in the film industry, writers get blame, directors get credit and actors get awards – in other words, writers are unfairly treated). The speaker therefore does not say that the two books differ in terms of Goldman's opinions – both seem to have the same opinions.

B: The speaker says that Goldman heavily criticises actors and his references to directors in the index indicate that he heavily criticises them too, but he does not say that Goldman's comments are confusing, they seem to be very clear. He lists the index references to illustrate how critical Goldman is of directors, not because those references are confusing.

4 **B:** The speaker says that Goldman allows the reader *glimpses* of (only short looks at) his own life and that through these he seems to be a *desk-bound adult in awe of men of action* (someone who spends his life sitting at a desk and feels enormous respect for people who do active things). The implication here is that Goldman feels his work is not admirable in comparison with what these *men of action do*.

A: The speaker doesn't indicate that Goldman finds his job difficult. For example, when he has to write about *pain* (suffering, unhappiness), he approaches that with confidence because it is relatively easy for him. The speaker also says that Goldman may like the pain that is involved in his business. He therefore does not say that Goldman describes his job as more difficult than it really is.

C: The speaker says that an example of the pain of Goldman's business is the *dismaying* (upsetting, discouraging) fact that nobody knows the name of the person who wrote a film, but he thinks that Goldman may like this and that he may enjoy suffering in his job without anyone knowing anything about him. The speaker is therefore saying that Goldman is, like all film writers, unknown to the general public, and he is not saying that he is more widely recognised than he thinks he is.

5 **A:** The speaker says that when he listened to the two records he mentions, he was *enthralled* (enormously interested and entertained) because they did not contain what were simply *arbitrary lists of places* (lists of places chosen for no particular reason), they were *celebrations of America* (expressions of what a wonderful place America was). They therefore communicated the idea that America was a marvellous place.

B: The first record – 'Night Train' – was so successful that James Brown made another similar one, which also listed places in America – 'Mashed Potatoes'. He describes him as *repeating the trick* (producing the same kind of success) with the second record. He is therefore saying that both records were successful but he does not say or imply that this was surprising.

C: The two records were similar to each other, in that they contained lists of the names of places, but the speaker does not say that they were completely different from other records James Brown made.

6 **B:** The speaker says that people growing up in Britain in the 1960s thought that America was *an object of romance* (a romantic place, in the sense that it appealed to the imagination and seemed wonderful) *forged in song* (this image was created by songs). It seemed like a place that should be celebrated. He says that even Americans themselves had this view of it, because for them their own country was *exotic* (attractive and special) and they were excited about living there. He says that they found it an exciting place and so did he when he was growing up in Britain in the 1960s.

A: He says that American songs *hinted at* (suggested) *a vastness* (an enormous place), *a variegated* (very varied) *landscape and a range of experiences* but he does not say that this impression they created was a false one or that it was inaccurate because it was not a complete picture of what America was really like. He does not compare the impression that people got of America through songs with the reality of the place.

C: He says that American songs *described a vista* (in this context, this means 'range') *of possibilities that found no equivalent in British music*, by which he means that the songs suggested that life had much more to offer than British songs did. He lists some of these things (*prettier girls, bluer skies*, etc), which American songs seemed to create images of and his point is that British songs did not communicate such images of happy lives. He is therefore saying that

American songs suggested more images of life than British songs, but he is not saying that British music was more limited than American music – he is not comparing them in terms of the music itself, but in terms of the images suggested by the music.

p123 PAPER 3, PART 2

1 mark per question (Total: 9)

7 **meat importer:** We are told that his father was a *provision dealer* (someone who traded in food and drink) and that he was a *book-keeper* (a kind of accountant) *and cashier* (person who deals with money received and money paid out) *for a meat importer* (someone who imported meat into the country employed him in these roles).

8 **Self(-)Help:** The book was about the problems inventors had to deal with before they became successful and was written by someone called Samuel Smiles. These days, *self-help books* are a category of book, in which people are told how to make their lives better, or how to do things themselves so that they do not need other people to do these things for them.

9 **submarine:** He read about someone who invented a *white glaze for earthenware* (surface for pottery) and who failed many times before succeeding with it. Hornby himself wanted to invent something that would *solve the problem of perpetual motion* (continuous movement of something unless it is stopped by an outside force), but he gave that up and started trying to invent a *submarine* (ship that can operate under the surface of water). The submarine he invented did go under the surface of the water on its own, as intended, and travel some distance under the water, also as intended, but *alas* (unfortunately), it did not *re-emerge* (come back up to the surface of the water), as was intended.

10 **interchangeable:** We are told that as Hornby obtained more and more tools, *his ideas turned to interchangeable parts* (he began to think about producing parts which could be exchanged with each other in something) and which would have a *variety of purposes*. This was the *germ* (the beginning of something, from which it develops) *of the Meccano system*. His idea was that, if the parts were interchangeable, a number of different things could be built using them.

11 **series of holes:** To achieve his aim with the parts, he realised that there would have to be *a standard method of fitting one part to any other part* (something common to all the parts that would make each one fit together with another). What *came to* him (the idea he had) was the *conception* (idea) of parts all *perforated with a series of holes* (with holes made in them) *of the same size and the same distance apart*.

12 piece of copper: The first parts he made were *strips* (long, narrow pieces) that he made from *a large piece of copper* (a reddish brown metal). He chose copper because it was soft and easy to work with.

13 crane: He worked out the measurements for the strips of metal and made all the other parts required for making different things with (*nuts, bolts, angle brackets, axles and wheels*) and then eventually he and his sons succeeded in making a model of a *crane* (a machine with a long arm used for lifting and moving large, heavy objects), which was the first model made with the parts he had invented.

14 Mechanics Made Easy: His invention was *originally called Mechanics Made Easy* and marketed by Hornby and his employer operating under the name *Elliott and Hornby*. Later, in 1907, it was given the *trademark* (the registered name of a product) Meccano and made by a firm called *Meccano Ltd* (Limited – a word used after the names of private companies in Britain).

15 E(e)xtension P(p)ack: Different Meccano sets were produced and each set could be converted into the *next larger-sized set* (the set that was one size bigger in the series) *by means of* (by using) an *Extension Pack*.

p124 PAPER 3, PART 3

1 mark per question (Total: 5)

16 C: David says that visual planning usually involves putting a designer and a manufacturer together in order to create *an appropriate image for a product*. However, now that it is *the age* (period in history of something being widespread or popular) *of the focus group*, which involves *garnering* (collecting) opinions from small groups of people, *the process has been short-circuited* (a quicker and simpler process has replaced a longer and more complicated one). The process now involves members of the public designing products themselves, rather than designers and manufacturers doing it. During David's session, women were asked to do that and so the session was an example of this new kind of visual planning.

A: He says that the session lasted for three hours and that it was a *brainstorming session* (one in which the people taking part produce and discuss ideas), but he does not say that the sessions he conducts do not normally go on for as long as three hours.

B: He talks about what focus groups are and what they do and says that the use of them is *almost an industry in itself* (they are used so widely that the use of them has almost grown into a distinct and separate area of business), but he does not express his own views about them or compare his personal views on them with other people's views. What he says about them simply describes their function and he does not say that the session shows that he is right about them with regard to any beliefs he has.

D: He says that in the session, the women were asked to *unleash* (release, freely express) *their cleaning foibles* (personal weaknesses or unusual habits), *hates and woes* (things that cause unhappiness). These are all negative aspects and no positive aspects are mentioned.

17 A: David says that they filmed shoppers *dithering* (hesitating because of being unsure what to do or what to decide) in supermarkets over washing powders and then the focus group met. He had therefore seen that shoppers were unsure which washing powder to buy when they went shopping before the session took place.

B: He says that the *congested market* (a market in which there are a great many different goods available) *is failing to bloom* (prosper, flourish) *as healthily as manufacturers might wish* – it is not growing as much or being as profitable as they would like. His firm was employed to *arrest* (stop) *this crisis* (serious, problematic situation that requires action). What he is saying, therefore, is that manufacturers were very worried that sales were not increasing as much and that the market was not as profitable as they would like, but he does not say that sales were actually falling.

C: The problem for shoppers is that cleaning products are *a confusing mass* like a *many-headed monster* because they are *cluttered with scientific jargon* (full of technical terms) *and swathed in* (wrapped or enclosed in) *lurid* (brightly coloured but unattractive) *packaging*. As a result, they are often *unintelligible* (impossible to understand). What he knew from research before the session, therefore, was that people were confused by cleaning products, not that they found them dull or uninteresting to look at.

D: He says that people were confused by the *jargon* (technical terms) on cleaning products and couldn't understand it, not that they felt that what was stated on cleaning products was untrue.

18 D: David says that one woman told him that she spent *quite some time down that aisle* (quite a long time in the row in a shop in which cleaning products were displayed) and that then *I just grab what I know* (I simply pick up quickly a product I know). This means that after hesitating for a while, she then always buys a product she is familiar with, rather than one she has never bought before.

A: All of the comments he quotes are about difficulties experienced when deciding which product to buy or about aspects of cleaning products the women dislike, but none of the comments expresses the view that the speaker doesn't care which product she buys.

B: One woman says that she doesn't understand the difference between different types of cleaning products (*concentrated and non-concentrated* ones and *biological and non-biological* ones), but this is connected with what they contain and how they work, not with the appearance of the products.

C: One woman says that the products *don't say clearly what they do* and another says that she doesn't want *all this science* (all the scientific terms used on cleaning products). These comments are about not understanding what is stated on products, and do not express a view that what is stated on them is stated with the intention of giving shoppers false information.

19 A: What they produced was a visual representation of *how they would want a cleaning product to make them feel* and so it was meant to represent their preferred emotional response to a product rather than a representation of what it did. Their *collages* (pictures made from putting different pieces of paper, cloth, etc together and sticking them on a surface, in this case a board) presented images of *homely comfort* rather than of *germ-busting explosions* – they showed peaceful images of comfortable, peaceful, pleasant homes rather than of products violently attacking dirt that is harmful to people.

B: David is not saying that there were contrasting images in their collages – the images all seem to have been similar and to have been consistent with each other. The colours were *soft* rather than bright, and the *fruit and flowers* were part of the overall image of *homely comfort*.

C: David says that the images they produced were *a dramatic shift from* (were very noticeably different from) *the way these goods are normally presented* and this may well have surprised him but he does not say that it surprised the women themselves or that they had expected to produce different images beforehand.

D: He says that what they produced was different from how cleaning products are normally presented but he does not say that this meant that the images they produced were similar to those involved in the presentation of other types of product.

20 B: David says that *the accepted belief* is that people's emotions are not involved much and that they are *on automatic pilot* (doing things that are routine without thinking about them at all, like a plane that is being flown by a computer rather than a human being) when they buy cleaning products. He says that his company's research shows that this is not true and that he believes that shoppers' *emotional needs* need to be considered. He says that the session showed him that, *as I suspected* (as I previously thought was the case), there needs to be *emotion* in the marketing of cleaning goods. He is therefore saying that he thought the *accepted belief* was probably not true and that he concluded from the session that he had been proved right about that.

A: He is not saying that his firm's methods will need to change, but that the methods of those manufacturing and marketing cleaning goods will have to change so that products appeal to people on an emotional level. He also thinks that what his firm discovered through research was proved right in the session, and so he clearly thinks his firm's methods are right as they are.

C: He is saying that there is a general pattern to the buying of cleaning products – people currently do not enjoy buying them, 73% of decisions about which product to buy are made when the customer is actually in the shop rather than before they go there, and that people in general want to feel more involved emotionally when it comes to buying these products. In addition, he does not say that cleaning products differ from other kinds of product or are an exception to what happens with other products – in fact, he implies that people would like them to be more like other products.

D: He says that there is *an opportunity for genuine innovation* here, by which he means that in the work he is doing on cleaning products, it is possible that some truly original ideas will result, but he is not saying that these ideas will be required because his beliefs about cleaning products before the session were not absolutely right – he is saying that the method he is using might lead to changes in the way cleaning products are created and marketed. In addition, he says that he already knew from his company's research that the *accepted belief* was wrong, so he didn't learn that he was wrong to share that belief; he didn't share it before the session.

p125–127 PAPER 3, PART 4

FURTHER PRACTICE AND GUIDANCE (p126–127)

For explanations, see the explanations to the questions in the test, which follow.

Questions 21 and 26   F, G

Questions 22 and 27   C, H

Questions 23 and 28   A, D

Questions 24 and 29   C, G

Questions 25 and 30   A, F

p125 PAPER 3, PART 4 (TEST)

1 mark per question (Total: 10)

21 E: The speaker says that *the main thing* for him about the job is that he gets *very well-rewarded*, meaning that the most important and best aspect for him is that he gets a very high salary (**F**). He gets this high salary because he is very good at sorting out problems that customers have and he says *I get on with* (I work hard at, I focus on) doing that, but he doesn't say he enjoys the work, only that he is good at it and gets paid a lot of money.

22 F: The speaker says that she likes the fact that her *decisions matter* (that they are important and have an important effect). She says that being *in charge* is *a position that comes naturally to me* (responsibility is something that suits her very well)**(C)**. She likes to think that she is *good at running things*. So, having a position of responsibility is what she likes most about her job.

23 A: The speaker says that *what makes going to work enjoyable* is the fact that he and his colleagues *have a laugh* and *have fun* together, despite the problems they face at work. In the speaker's department, they *all get along very well* (have good relationships with each other)**(A)**. This stops them getting *fed up* (unhappy). So the atmosphere at work among the colleagues in the department is what the speaker most likes about the job.

24 B: The speaker says that *what makes me stay* in the job is that it gives her the chance to *realise my potential* and show what she is *capable of*. She likes *having to get to grips with things I haven't tackled before* (dealing with difficult things she hasn't done before) and that is what she does in this job. So what she likes most about the job is that it is challenging for her, unlike her previous job, where she *wasn't being stretched* (it was too easy for her and did not involve challenges)**(C)**.

25 G: The speaker says that what is *really good* about his job is that people are not *looking over your shoulder all the time* (checking on what you are doing, supervising you). People are *left to our own devices* (allowed to do their jobs independently without being given orders or constantly supervised). The place is not *obsessed with their systems and rules and regulations* (people are free to do their jobs in the way they think best rather than having to follow orders all the time)**(A)**.

26 E: The speaker says that the place is *very poorly run* (the people in charge do their jobs badly) and as a result of this, *all sorts of mistakes* happen (the work is not done well). The speaker describes this as *very irritating* (the lack of efficiency annoys him a lot). He does not refer to the management's attitude, only to the fact they are not efficient.

27 F: The speaker says that the *downside* of the job for her is that *I tend to take on too much* (she takes responsibility for more work than she should and so gives herself a workload that is too great for her). As a result, she has a very difficult time getting all these things done. **(H)**

28 C: The speaker criticises the *people at the top*, saying that their attitude is that they should *hand out orders* to people and *tell them off* (criticise them from a position of authority, tell them they have done badly). The speaker says that the managers treat people very badly because they have a bad attitude. **(D)**

29 B: The speaker says that what she isn't *so keen on* (what she doesn't like) is *the constant changes of personnel* (changes involving staff moving or leaving and being replaced by different staff). The group of people she works with often changes suddenly and she doesn't like that. **(G)**

30 A: The speaker complains that the building he works in is *shabby* (in poor condition) and this *really gets me down* (makes me very unhappy). He says that the company should spend money *doing it up* (improving the condition of the building). **(F)**

PAPER 3

PART 1   6 marks
PART 2   9 marks
PART 3   5 marks
PART 4   10 marks
TOTAL   30 marks
To be converted into a score out of 50 marks.

p128–131 PAPER 4

Marks out of 25 are given for performance in the speaking paper.
To be converted into a score out of 50 marks.

FURTHER PRACTICE AND GUIDANCE (p130–131)

DESCRIBING PERSONALITY

KIND/PLEASANT
affable: friendly, easy to talk to
compassionate: feeling sympathy for the suffering of others and wishing to help them
considerate: kind and thoughtful, taking care not to upset others and doing things that are helpful to others
courteous: polite, having good manners
decent: pleasant and honest
generous: kind in your treatment of others and happy to give them things
genial: friendly and cheerful, not at all frightening
indulgent: allowing someone to have whatever they want
lenient: tolerant towards someone who has done something wrong and not punishing them severely, when others might do so
mild-mannered: gentle and kind
tactful: careful in what you say or do so as not to upset someone
warm: friendly and pleasant

FEELING SUPERIOR

aloof: unfriendly towards others and not wishing to have a close relationship with them because of considering yourself superior to them

arrogant: too self-confident, in a way which others dislike

big-headed: having too high an opinion of yourself

conceited: too self-satisfied, happy in the belief that you are wonderful, in a way that others dislike

condescending: treating others in a way that indicates that you think you are superior to them and that you are doing them a favour by dealing with them at all

patronising: speaking in a way that indicates that you consider yourself superior to those you are talking to and that you consider them stupid

pompous: speaking or acting in a way that shows you feel you are very important and much more important than others

smug: too pleased with yourself and too happy in the belief that your own situation is better than other people's, in a way that is disliked

snobbish: considering yourself socially superior to others

stuck-up: behaving towards others as if you are superior in a way that annoys them

supercilious: showing the attitude that you think you are better than others by being rather rude to them

UNKIND/UNPLEASANT

ignorant: rude and bad-mannered

mean: unkind or unpleasant in what you say or in being unwilling to give things to or share things with people

moody: tending to change moods constantly, so that you suddenly become angry or unhappy when previously you were not, in a way that others find it difficult to deal with

narrow-minded: not tolerant of others or willing to listen to or consider their views, when these differ from yours

petulant: having a tendency to become angry suddenly because something is not the way that you want it to be, with the result that others suffer

ruthless: cruel and totally unsympathetic to others because you want to achieve something and do not care who suffers as long as you achieve it

spiteful: saying or doing things that are deliberately intended to cause suffering to someone you personally dislike intensely

surly: unfriendly, unpleasant and rude, especially in the way you deal with others

vindictive: doing things in order to get revenge on others or because you want to cause someone you personally dislike to suffer

DETERMINED

assertive: showing that you are determined to be listened to or taken seriously, rather than keeping quiet and allowing others to dominate

intransigent: completely certain that you are right and unwilling to listen to opposing views, even if these are reasonable

obstinate: refusing to change your mind or be influenced by other views, despite attempts to persuade you to do so, in a way that others disapprove of

persistent: refusing to give up, despite failure or opposition

pig-headed: refusing to change your opinion, even though it appears quite possible that you are wrong

pushy: openly determined to get what you want by persuading others to do things for you, in a way that is disliked

resolute: very determined, especially when this involves having courage

single-minded: determined to achieve something in particular and concentrating on that entirely, in a way that others admire

strong-willed: determined to get what you want and making every effort to get it

tenacious: not giving up an aim or changing a belief, despite difficulty or opposition

tireless: continuing in your efforts to achieve something you are determined to achieve, even though this requires an enormous amount of effort and energy

DISHONEST

calculating: clever at planning and doing things that are to your advantage, without other people realising what you are really doing

crafty: clever in using deceitful ways to get what you want, rather than doing things openly

cunning: clever at deceiving and tricking people, in a way that is disapproved of

devious: being deceitful and dishonest in order to get what you want by indirect means

hypocritical: criticising others for moral reasons while being guilty of the same things yourself

scheming: making secret plans to get what you want because other people would disapprove if they knew what you are doing

two-faced: deceiving others by pretending to like them when dealing with them but then saying bad things about them to others

TOPIC VOCABULARY

1

FASHIONS/FASHIONABLE	UNFASHIONABLE
a craze	antiquated
a fad	behind the times
all the rage	dated
contemporary	obsolete
in fashion	old hat
in vogue	out of fashion
trendsetting	outdated
trendy	outmoded

2

a hooligan
a kid
a lad
a lout
a yob
a youngster
a youth
adolescence
adolescent
childish
infantile
immature
immaturity
juvenile
the young/youth
youthful

grow up
grown up
a grown up
mature
maturity
getting on
middle aged
over the hill
past it
in your dotage
ancient
senile
senior citizen
old age
an old age pensioner
elderly
the elderly